Macromedia® Fireworks® MX

fast&easy® web development

Yesh Singhal
Priyanka

Premier Press

©2002 by Premier Press, Inc. All rights reserved. No part of this book may be reproduced or transmitted in any form or by any means, electronic or mechanical, including photocopying, recording, or by any information storage or retrieval system without written permission from Premier Press, except for the inclusion of brief quotations in a review.

The Premier Press logo, top edge printing, and related trade dress are trademarks of Premier Press, Inc. and may not be used without written permission. All other trademarks are the property of their respective owners.

Publisher: Stacy L. Hiquet
Marketing Manager: Heather Buzzingham
Managing Editor: Sandy Doell
Acquisitions Editor: Stacy L. Hiquet
Project Editor: Kezia Endsley
Editorial Assistant: Margaret Bauer
Marketing Coordinator: Kelly Poffenbarger
Technical Reviewer: NIIT
Copy Editor: Kezia Endsley
Interior Layout: Marian Hartsough
Cover Design: Mike Tanamachi
Indexer: Tom Dinse
Proofreader: Jennifer Davidson

Important: Premier Press cannot provide software support. Please contact the appropriate software manufacturer's technical support line or Web site for assistance.

Premier Press and the author have attempted throughout this book to distinguish proprietary trademarks from descriptive terms by following the capitalization style used by the manufacturer.

Information contained in this book has been obtained by Premier Press from sources believed to be reliable. However, because of the possibility of human or mechanical error by our sources, Premier Press, or others, the Publisher does not guarantee the accuracy, adequacy, or completeness of any information and is not responsible for any errors or omissions or the results obtained from use of such information. Readers should be particularly aware of the fact that the Internet is an ever-changing entity. Some facts may have changed since this book went to press.

ISBN: 1-59200-031-2
Library of Congress Catalog Card Number: 2002108329
Printed in the United States of America

02 03 04 05 06 RI 10 9 8 7 6 5 4 3 2 1

About NIIT

NIIT is a global IT solutions corporation with a presence in 38 countries. With its unique business model and technology-creation capabilities, NIIT delivers software and learning solutions to more than 1,000 clients across the world.

The success of NIIT's training solutions lies in its unique approach to education. NIIT's Knowledge Solutions Business conceives, researches, and develops all of its course material. A rigorous instructional design methodology is followed to create engaging and compelling course content.

NIIT trains over 200,000 executives and learners each year in information technology areas using stand-up training, video-aided instruction, computer-based training (CBT), and Internet-based training (IBT). NIIT has been featured in the Guinness Book of World Records for the largest number of learners trained in one year!

NIIT has developed over 10,000 hours of instructor-led training (ILT) and over 3,000 hours of Internet-based training and computer-based training. IDC ranked NIIT among the Top 15 IT training providers globally for the year 2000. Through the innovative use of training methods and its commitment to research and development, NIIT has been in the forefront of computer education and training for the past 20 years.

Quality has been the prime focus at NIIT. Most of the processes are ISO-9001 certified. It was the 12th company in the world to be assessed at Level 5 of SEI-CMM. NIIT's Content (Learning Material) Development facility is the first in the world to be assessed at this highest maturity level. NIIT has strategic partnerships with companies such as Computer Associates, IBM, Microsoft, Oracle, and Sun Microsystems.

About the Authors

YESH SINGHAL has a bachelor's degree in Physics (honors) from Delhi University, India. In addition, he has completed the three-year GNIIT course. Also, he is a Microsoft Certified Solution Developer (MCSD) and has a work experience of more than three years with NIIT Ltd. He spent his first year in Career Education Group (CEG) of NIIT. In the CEG group, he was involved in the training of NIIT students. He was also extensively involved in scheduling and managing resources. For the past two years, he has been working in Knowledge Solutions Business (KSB) of NIIT. In his two years of work experience at NIIT, he has authored several ILT's and books, which include *Crystal Reports 8.0*, *Access XP*, and *Visual Studio All In One Desk Reference for Dummies*, among others. At NIIT, Yesh has been an ITR (Independent Technical Reviewer) for books on the languages in the .NET Framework.

Yesh is very fond of partying and loves the game of Cricket. When Yesh is not working, you can catch him watching cricket or enjoying time out with friends.

PRIYANKA is an advanced diploma holder in Multimedia. She completed her bachelor's degree in Computer Science from Delhi University, and is also pursuing her master's degree in computer applications (MCA). She is currently employed as a Media Executive with NIIT. She has a wide spectrum of experience in multimedia technologies. She has created graphics and animations for an entire suite of interactive courseware for SmartSchools, a project of the Ministry of Education, Government of Malaysia. Currently her work involves creating and visualizing graphics and technical diagrams for computer-based books, such as Palm OS Programming, Java Security, and Cisco Security. Priyanka's wide variety of experience also includes extensive research and development of 2D and 3D ad films using 3D Studio MAX and Macromedia Flash, for some satellite channels in India.

Acknowledgments

Our families have been a strong support to us while we worked long hours to complete this book. They really helped us bring out the best in the book. Thank you, dear ones, for your support.

Our project manager, Anita Sastry, has worked meticulously reviewing and giving here valuable inputs to the book. Without her help, the book would not have been in its present form.

Thank you Kezia Endsley for editing the book so well. Your valuable inputs make it a wonderful book! We would also like to thank Stacy Hiquet for making this book happen at the first place! She has provided active support in all development stages of the book.

Our special thanks also go out to Sunil K. Pathak for helping us out with data files and graphics for some important chapters of the book.

Contents at a Glance

Introduction xv

PART I
GETTING STARTED 1

Chapter 1	Installing Fireworks MX 3
Chapter 2	Getting Started with Fireworks MX 9
Chapter 3	Customizing Fireworks MX 25

PART II
DESIGNING GRAPHICS 37

Chapter 4	Getting Started with Graphics 39
Chapter 5	Working with Vector Graphics 49
Chapter 6	Working with Bitmaps 69
Chapter 7	Working with Colors 91
Chapter 8	Using Text in Graphics 115
Chapter 9	Managing Images Using Layers 129
Chapter 10	Enhancing the Appearance of Objects 141
Chapter 11	Optimizing and Exporting Graphics 153

PART III
DESIGNING INTERACTIVE WEB GRAPHICS 173

Chapter 12	Creating Hotspots and Slices 175
Chapter 13	Adding Rollovers to Graphics 193
Chapter 14	Adding Buttons to a Graphic 209
Chapter 15	Displaying Options Using Pop-up Menus 227
Chapter 16	Adding Animations to Graphics 243
Chapter 17	Automating Tasks 259
Chapter 18	Integrating Fireworks MX with Macromedia Dreamweaver MX. 281

PART IV
APPENDIXES 299

| Appendix A | Keyboard Shortcuts in Fireworks MX .... 301 |
| Appendix B | Creating an XML Document .... 307 |

Index 311

Contents

Introduction xv

PART I
GETTING STARTED 1

Chapter 1   Installing Fireworks MX 3
Identifying System Requirements 4
    For Windows Users 4
    For Mac Users 4
Installing Fireworks MX on a Windows Computer 5

Chapter 2   Getting Started with Fireworks MX 9
Fireworks MX Basics 10
The Fireworks MX Workspace 11
    Working with Fireworks MX Documents 11
    The Tools Panel 16
    The Property Inspector 17
    Other Panels 18
    Working with Panels 20
Fireworks MX Help Resources 23

Chapter 3   Customizing Fireworks MX 25
Setting Preferences 26
    Setting General Preferences 26
    Setting Editing Preferences 29

CONTENTS

Setting Options for Bitmap Objects............................ 30
Setting Launch and Edit Preferences 30
Setting Folders Preferences 31
Setting Import Preferences...................................... 31
Setting Layer Options 32
Setting Text Options... 32
Setting Keyboard Shortcuts 33
Specifying a Shortcut Key Set................................... 33
Specifying a Keyboard Shortcut 34

PART II
DESIGNING GRAPHICS 37

Chapter 4 Getting Started with Graphics...................... 39
Selecting Images 40
Using the Pointer Tool 40
Using the Subselection Tool 41
Viewing Images 42
Using the Zoom Tool 43
Using the Hand Tool 46
Cropping Images.. 47

Chapter 5 Working with Vector Graphics..................... 49
Drawing Objects by Using Tools................................... 50
Drawing a Line 50
Drawing Rectangles and Polygons............................ 51
Drawing Curved Paths 56
Bezier Curves 57
Drawing Freeform Objects...................................... 59
Manipulating Objects 60
Adding Colors to Objects.. 64
Applying Strokes to an Object 64
Applying Fills to an Object..................................... 66

Chapter 6 Working with Bitmaps 69
Importing Bitmap Objects.. 70

Drawing, Painting, and Erasing Bitmap Objects 71
    Using the Pencil Tool 71
    Using the Brush Tool. 73
    Using the Eraser Tool 74
Selecting Parts of Bitmap Objects 76
    Using the Marquee Tool 76
    Using the Magic Wand Tool 78
    Working with Lasso Tools. 80
    Modifying the Selection Marquees. 82
Retouching Bitmap Objects 84
    Adjusting Focus of a Bitmap Object. 84
    Making a Bitmap Object Lighter or Darker 86
    Smudging a Bitmap Object. 88
    Cloning a Bitmap Object 89

Chapter 7   Working with Colors 91
Using the Tools Panel for Applying Colors 92
    Using the Colors Section 92
    Using the Eyedropper Tool. 93
    Using the Paint Bucket Tool 94
Using the Colors Panel Group. 96
    Exploring the Swatches Panel. 96
    Using the Color Mixer Panel. 101
Using Fill Options 104
    Applying Gradient Fills. 104
    Applying Pattern Fills 108
    Applying Web Dither Fills. 109
Using Stroke Options 110
    Using Advanced Stroke Options 110
    Placing Strokes 114

Chapter 8   Using Text in Graphics 115
Adding Text to a Graphic 116
    Using the Text Tool. 116
    Importing Text 118

CONTENTS

	Enhancing the Appearance of Text	119
	Formatting the Text	120
	Spacing the Text	122
	Applying Strokes and Fills to Text	124
	Attaching Text to a Path	125
	Spell-Checking the Text	127
Chapter 9	**Managing Images Using Layers**	**129**
	Using the Layers Panel	130
	Looking at the Layers Options Pop-up Menu	130
	Creating Layers	131
	Working with Layers	133
	Locking a Layer	134
	Arranging a Layer	134
	Compositing Images	135
	Hiding a Layer	136
	Duplicating a Layer	137
	Deleting a Layer	139
Chapter 10	**Enhancing the Appearance of Objects**	**141**
	Using Effects to Beautify Objects	142
	Applying Effects to an Object	142
	Editing Effects	144
	Removing Effects	145
	Saving Effects for Future Use	146
	Applying Styles	147
	Applying Third-party Filters	148
	Using Masks to Combine Objects	150
	Creating Bitmap Masks	150
	Creating Vector Masks	151
Chapter 11	**Optimizing and Exporting Graphics**	**153**
	Optimizing Graphics	154
	Choosing a File Format	154
	Specifying File Format Specific Settings	156
	Using Preset Optimization Settings	165
	Previewing the Document	167

Exporting Graphics 168
Using the Export Wizard 169

PART III
DESIGNING INTERACTIVE WEB GRAPHICS 173

Chapter 12 Creating Hotspots and Slices. 175
Creating Image Maps Using Hotspots 176
    Creating a Hotspot. 176
    Testing a Hotspot 180
    Creating an Image Map 182
Cutting and Optimizing Images Using Slices 184
    Creating a Slice 184
    Naming Slices 187

Chapter 13 Adding Rollovers to Graphics 193
Creating a Simple Rollover 194
    Creating the Source Object 194
    Creating the Target Object 195
    Adding a Frame 196
    Assigning a Behavior. 197
    Testing the Simple Rollover 198
    Seeing the JavaScript Code 199
Creating a Disjoint Rollover. 200
    Creating the Trigger and Target Areas 201
    Assigning a Behavior. 202
    Changing the Event of a Rollover. 206
    Testing a Rollover 207

Chapter 14 Adding Buttons to a Graphic. 209
Creating a Button 210
    Creating the Up State. 210
    Creating the Over State 212
    Creating the Down State 213
    Creating the Over While Down State. 214

CONTENTS

Creating the Active Area of a Button	215
Testing a Button	217
Creating a Navigation Bar	218
Creating Button Instances	219
Editing a Button	221
Editing Properties at Symbol-level	221
Testing a Navigation Bar	224

Chapter 15 Displaying Options Using Pop-up Menus 227

Creating a Pop-up Menu	228
Adding Content to a Pop-up Menu	229
Enhancing the Appearance of a Pop-up Menu	235
Specifying Advanced Pop-up Menu Settings	237
Specifying the Position of a Pop-up Menu	240
Modifying a Pop-up Menu	241
Testing a Pop-up Menu	242

Chapter 16 Adding Animations to Graphics 243

Getting Started with Animations	244
Looking at Frames	244
Creating an Animation	245
Placing Guides	251
Working with Animations	252
Modifying an Animation	254
Exporting an Animation	257

Chapter 17 Automating Tasks 259

Using the Find and Replace Panel	260
Using the Library Panel	264
Creating a Symbol	264
Creating an Instance	266
Exporting a Symbol	268
Importing a Symbol	270
Using the History Panel	271
Creating Commands	273
Using the Data-Driven Graphics Wizard	275

Chapter 18 Integrating Fireworks MX with Macromedia Dreamweaver MX **281**

Understanding the Roundtrip HTML Feature 282
    Making Fireworks MX the External Image Editor
        for Dreamweaver MX 282
    Setting Launch-and-Edit Preferences in Fireworks MX 284
Working with Fireworks MX Images in Dreamweaver MX. 285
    Creating Fireworks MX Images from
        Dreamweaver MX Placeholders. 285
    Editing Fireworks MX Images from Dreamweaver MX 288
Working with Fireworks MX HTML in Dreamweaver MX. 290
    Exporting Fireworks MX HTML to Dreamweaver MX 290
    Inserting Fireworks MX HTML in Dreamweaver MX 292
    Editing Fireworks MX HTML from Dreamweaver MX 293
    Updating Fireworks MX HTML Exported
        to Dreamweaver MX 294
Exporting Documents with the Quick Export Button. 296

PART IV
APPENDIXES **299**

Appendix A Keyboard Shortcuts in Fireworks MX **301**

Keyboard Shortcuts for the Document Window. 302
Keyboard Shortcuts for the Panels in the
    Fireworks MX Workspace. 303
Keyboard Shortcuts for the Tools Panel 304
Generating a List of Shortcut Keys 305

Appendix B Creating an XML Document **307**

Index **311**

Introduction

Fireworks MX has long been used as a Web graphic development package. A good number of Web sites on the Internet have been using Fireworks to create graphics. Fireworks MX is the next version of the Fireworks that simplifies the creation of Web graphics.

With the release of Fireworks MX, creation of graphics for the Web has never been simpler. The simple-to-use interface and power of Fireworks MX make creating Web graphics an easy and interesting exercise.

Fireworks MX Fast and Easy Web Development equips you with the necessary skills to create Web graphics. The characteristic visual emphasis of the book introduces concepts of Fireworks MX to novice developers. These concepts help get started on Fireworks MX. Thereafter, the book includes advanced features of Fireworks MX, which include creating simple and advanced rollovers, creating buttons and pop-up menus, and automating various tasks.

Who Should Read This Book

Readers who are proficient in using any graphics package will benefit most from this book. However, the book is built keeping in mind a novice. Readers without any experience with a graphics package will find it useful.

After reading this book, you will be proficient in Fireworks MX and you will be able to create smart Web graphics that are faster to download. After reading this book, you should create a similar, or even more sophisticated Web pages. This will give you adequate hands-on practice to create Fireworks MX applications. If this is your aim, the book is certainly for you!

PART I
Getting Started

Chapter 1
　　Installing Fireworks MX 3

Chapter 2
　　Getting Started with Fireworks MX 9

Chapter 3
　　Customizing Fireworks MX 25

1

Installing Fireworks MX

Before being able to use Fireworks MX, you need to install it. To install Fireworks MX, you need to purchase the Fireworks MX CD-ROM, or download the 30-day trial version from Macromedia's Web site (www.macromedia.com). Fireworks MX includes a thorough documentation that you can refer to, in addition to this book, to understand the various features. In this chapter, you'll learn how to:

- Identify the system requirements for Fireworks MX
- Install Fireworks MX on a Windows computer

Identifying System Requirements

Fireworks MX is designed to function on both Mac and Windows operating systems. However, in order to make Fireworks MX function, your computer should match the requirements listed in the following sections.

For Windows Users

A Windows computer should match the following requirements:

- 300MHz Intel Pentium II Processor
- Windows 98 SE, Windows Me, Windows NT 4 (Service Pack 6), Windows 2000, or Windows XP
- At least 64MB of available system RAM (128MB is recommended)
- 800 X 600, 8-bit (256 colors) color display or better
- CD-ROM drive

For Mac Users

A Mac computer should match the following requirements:

- Power Macintosh G3 processor
- Mac OS 9.1 or higher, or OS X 10.1 and higher
- At least 64MB of available system RAM (128MB is recommended)
- 800 x 600, 8-bit (256 colors) color display or better
- CD-ROM drive

INSTALLING FIREWORKS MX ON A WINDOWS COMPUTER

Installing Fireworks MX on a Windows Computer

To install Fireworks MX on a Windows-based computer, follow these steps:

1. Double-click on the FireworksMXInstaller icon. The welcome screen will open.

2. Click on Next. The License Agreement dialog box will open.

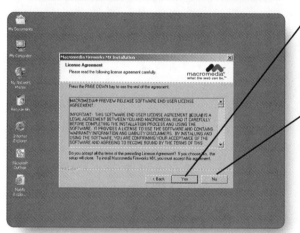

3a. Click on Yes if you agree with the agreement. The Choose Destination Location dialog box will open.

OR

3b. Click on No if you disagree and want to exit the installation process.

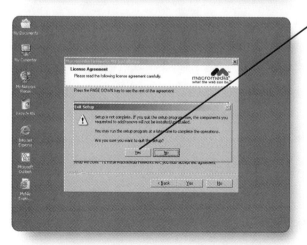

The Exit Setup dialog box will open. Click Yes to exit setup.

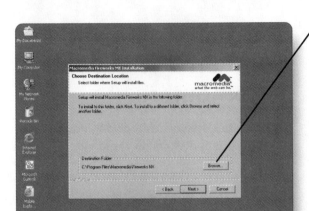

4a. Click on Browse to specify a different location.

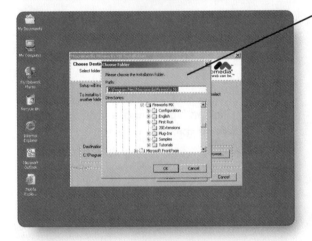

The Choose Folder dialog box will open.

OR

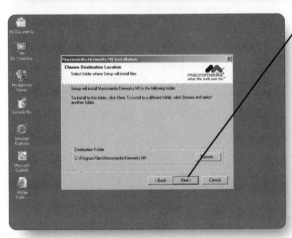

4b. Click on Next. The FrontPage Edit Options dialog box will open.

INSTALLING FIREWORKS MX ON A WINDOWS COMPUTER 7

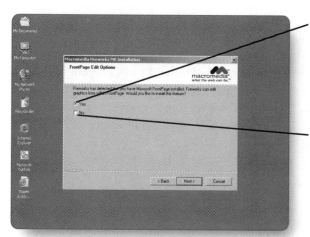

5a. Click on the Yes option. The Yes option will be selected and the feature that enables you to edit Fireworks images from FrontPage will be installed.

OR

5b. Click on the No option. The No option will be selected and the feature that allows you to edit Fireworks images from FrontPage will not be installed.

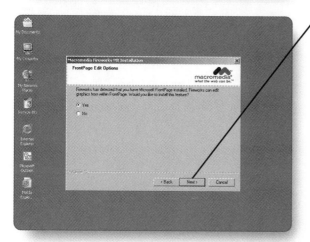

6. Click on Next. The Start Copying Files dialog box will open.

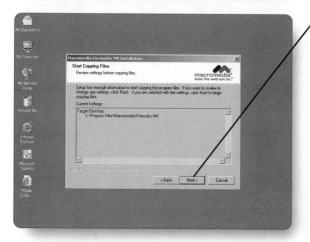

7. Click on Next. The InstallShield Wizard Complete dialog box will open.

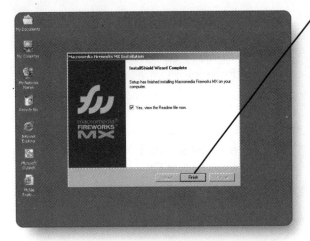

8. Click on Finish. The dialog box will be closed.

This installs Fireworks MX on your computer. You can now go ahead and use it to work with your graphics. The next chapter discusses the interface of Fireworks MX.

2

Getting Started with Fireworks MX

Fireworks MX is valuable software for developing Web sites. Whether you are a professional Web developer or a Web graphic designer, you'll find the features of Fireworks MX user-friendly and very handy.

In this chapter, you'll learn about these aspects of Fireworks MX:

- The basics
- The user interface
- Help resources

Fireworks MX Basics

Fireworks MX provides you with an integrated environment for working with all elements of a Web site, such as graphics, animations, and interactivity. You can either import graphics from other applications or create them directly in Fireworks MX. You can also optimize graphics for the Web and export them to commonly used file formats, such as GIF or JPEG. In addition to still graphics, you can create animations.

You can use Fireworks MX to add interactivity to your Web site by creating various HTML and JavaScript controls, such as:

- Buttons
- Navigation bars
- Rollovers
- Pop-up menus

Furthermore, Fireworks MX allows you to work in conjunction with other applications, such as Dreamweaver MX, Flash MX, and Microsoft FrontPage. As a result, you can easily import various file formats into Fireworks MX and also export them to other formats.

Before you start using Fireworks MX, you'll need to get familiar with its user interface. To explore the Fireworks MX interface, you need to first launch the application. To launch Fireworks MX, follow these steps:

1. Click on Start. The Start menu will appear.

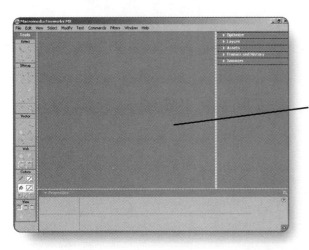

2. Move the mouse pointer to Programs. The Programs submenu will appear.

3. Click on Macromedia. The Macromedia submenu will appear.

4. Click on Macromedia Fireworks MX. The Macromedia Fireworks MX application will launch, and the Fireworks MX workspace will appear.

The following section discusses the various components of the Fireworks MX workspace.

The Fireworks MX Workspace

Fireworks MX presents a well-organized workspace that consists of the following components:

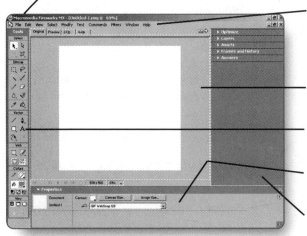

- **Title bar**. Displays the name and magnification setting of the currently active Fireworks MX document.
- **Menu bar**. Contains several pop-up menus, such as the File, Edit, and View menu. You'll learn to use these menus in relevant sections of this book.
- **Document window**. Contains the main work area.
- **Tools panel**. Contains the tools that you use to work with documents.
- **Property Inspector**. Controls properties of tools, objects, and documents.
- **Other panels**. Used for other purposes, such as managing colors and objects.

The following sections describe these components in detail.

Working with Fireworks MX Documents

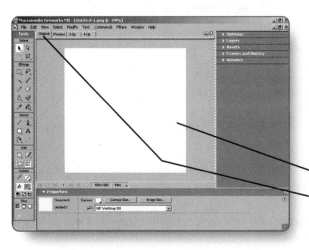

All work done in Fireworks MX, such as creating and editing graphics, is done in documents. You can create a new document or work with an existing one. In the Fireworks MX workspace, a document appears in the Document window. The following list explains the components of the Document window:

- **Canvas**. Area where you do all the work.
- **Original tab**. Shows the document as it appears while editing.

CHAPTER 2: GETTING STARTED WITH FIREWORKS MX

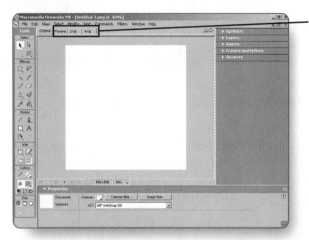

- **Preview tabs.** Comprises the Preview, 2-Up, and 4-Up tabs, which display the document based on the current optimization settings. The 2-Up and 4-Up preview tabs show split preview in two and four parts, respectively. Use these split previews to compare different optimization settings.

> **NOTE**
> See Chapter 11, "Optimizing and Exporting Graphics," to learn more about using the Preview tabs.

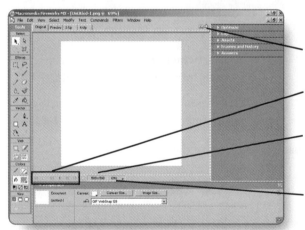

- **Quick Export button.** Exports your document to other applications.

- **Frame controls.** Used to navigate the frames present in the document.

- **Page Preview box.** Displays a preview of the dimensions and resolution of the document.

- **Magnification list.** Sets a magnification percentage for the document.

> **NOTE**
> Frames are used to create animations in Fireworks MX. See Chapter 16, "Adding Animations to Graphics," to learn about frames and animations.

Creating a New Document

To create a graphic, you need to first create a new document. Fireworks MX allows you to specify the height, width, resolution, and background color for the new document when you create it.

THE FIREWORKS MX WORKSPACE   13

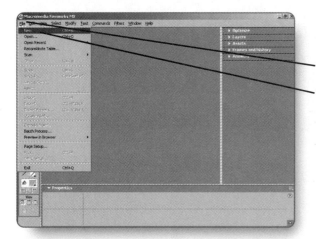

To create a new document, follow these steps:

1. Click on File. The File menu will appear.

2. Click on New. The New Document dialog box will open.

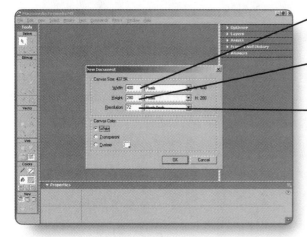

3. In the Width box, type the width of the canvas.

4. In the Height box, type the height of the canvas.

5. In the Resolution box, type the resolution of the canvas.

TIP

It's best to set the resolution at 72 pixels per inch for Web graphics to ensure an optimum and consistent image display across all platforms.

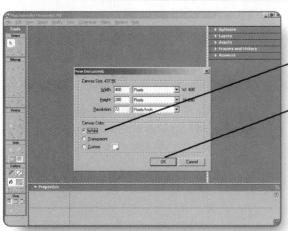

6. Select an appropriate background color for the canvas.

7. Click on OK.

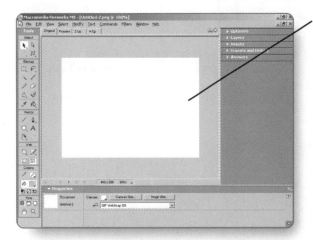

The new document will appear in the Document window.

Saving a Document

You might need to refer to a document that you created earlier. For this, you must save the document. You can either save the document at the default location or specify a location of your choice.

To save a document, follow these steps:

1. Click on File. The File menu will appear.

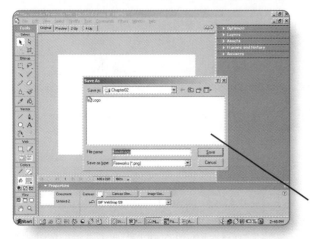

2. Click on Save. The Save As dialog box will open.

3. In the Save As dialog box, specify the location and the name of the document.

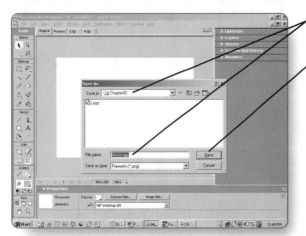

4. Click on Save. The document will be saved in the specified file.

The native file format that Fireworks MX uses for saving and creating documents is Portable Network Graphic (PNG).

THE FIREWORKS MX WORKSPACE   15

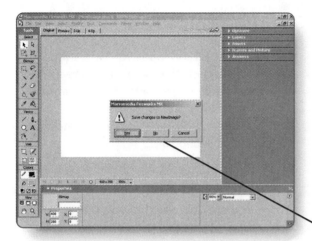

Closing a Document

After you have finished working with a document, you can close it. To close a document, follow these steps:

1. Click on File. The File menu will appear.

2. Click on Close. The document will be closed.

> **TIP**
> If any recent changes made to the document have not been saved, Fireworks MX prompts you to save the document before closing it.

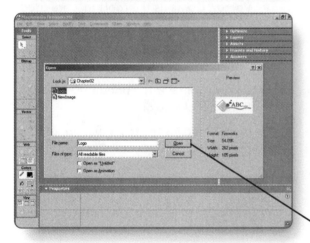

Opening an Existing Document

To open an existing document, follow these steps:

1. Click on File. The File menu will appear.

2. Click on Open. The Open dialog box will open.

3. Select the appropriate file and click on Open. The file will open.

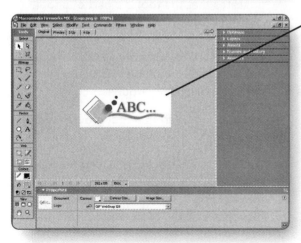

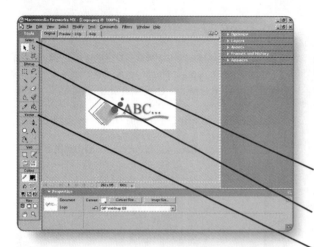

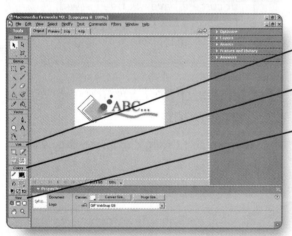

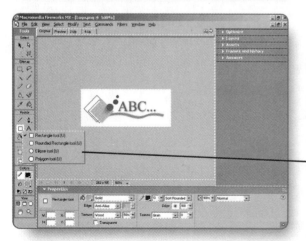

The Tools Panel

Fireworks MX provides you with a wide variety of tools that help you to create and modify various elements of your Web site. All these tools are contained in the Tools panel. The Tools panel is divided into the following sections:

- **Select**. Contains the tools that are used to select objects.
- **Bitmap**. Contains the tools that are used to select, create, and edit bitmap objects.
- **Vector**. Contains the tools that are used to select, create, and edit vector objects.
- **Web**. Contains the tools that are used to work with slices and hotspots.
- **Colors**. Contains the options to specify fill and stroke colors.
- **View**. Contains the tools that are used to control the view of your document.

Some of the tools in the Tools panel are grouped together to form a tool group. You'll notice that there is a small triangle at the lower-right corner of some tools. This indicates that the tool is a part of a tool group. A tool group is a group of tools that perform similar tasks. For example, the Marquee tool group contains Rectangular and Oval Marquee tools, which are used for creating selection marquees.

To select a tool from a tool group, follow these steps:

1. Click on the tool (containing a small triangle) in the Tools panel and hold the mouse button. A pop-up menu will appear that shows all the tools that constitute the tool group.

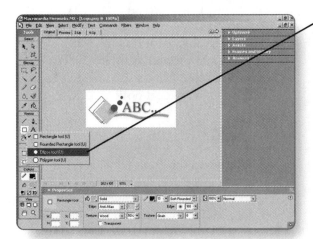

2. Drag the mouse pointer to the required tool and release the mouse button. The required tool will be selected.

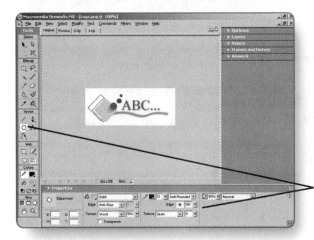

The Property Inspector

The Property Inspector, as the name suggests, allows you to control the properties of the currently active tool, the selected object, or the document. It is a dynamic panel because it displays options based on the current selection, as discussed in the following list:

- If you select a tool in the Tools panel, the Property Inspector displays the options that are available with the currently selected tool.

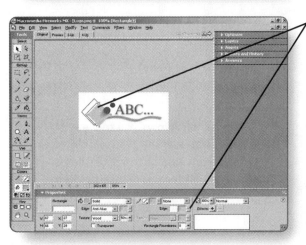

- If you select an object in the Document window, the Property Inspector displays the properties associated with the currently selected object. For example, if a vector object is selected, the Property Inspector displays properties, such as the object's stroke and fill color.

18 CHAPTER 2: GETTING STARTED WITH FIREWORKS MX

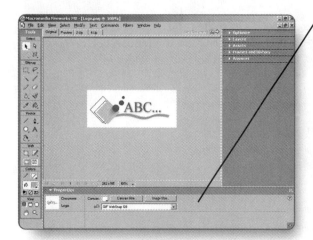

- If no object or tool is selected, the Property Inspector displays the document properties, which include canvas color, canvas size, image size, and default export options.

Other Panels

In addition to the Tools panel and the Property Inspector, there are several other panels available with Fireworks MX. Each of these panels serves a different purpose. You can open any of the available panels from the Window menu. The following list introduces these panels:

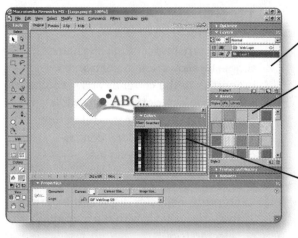

- **Layers panel**. Allows you to work with the layers of a document.

- **Styles panel**. Allows you to apply predefined combinations of various effects, known as styles, to the selected objects. You can also create your own styles.

- **Swatches panel**. Allows you to control the color of a selected object.

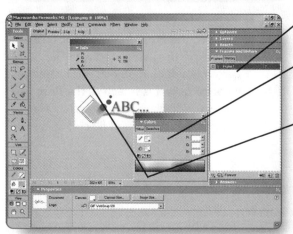

- **Frames panel**. Allows you to create animations.

- **Color Mixer panel**. Allows you to view and modify the values of the active color.

- **Info panel**. Allows you to view the coordinates of the mouse pointer and the color value of the pixel that is directly under the mouse pointer.

THE FIREWORKS MX WORKSPACE   19

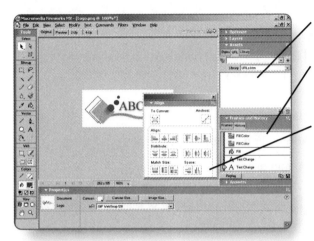

- **URL panel.** Allows you to access frequently used URLs in your document.
- **History panel.** Allows you to access a list of the recent tasks that you have performed in a document.
- **Align panel.** Allows you to arrange objects in the Document window.

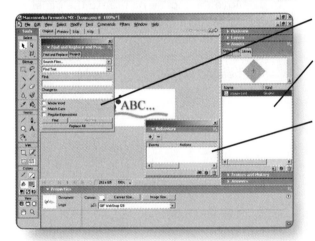

- **Find and Replace panel.** Allows you to find and replace elements.
- **Library panel.** Allows you to store frequently used elements as reusable symbols.
- **Behaviors panel.** Allows you to add interactivity.

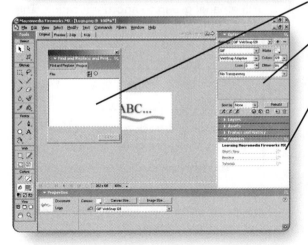

- **Project log.** Allows you to track multiple files.
- **Optimize panel.** Allows you to specify optimization settings for the object to be exported.
- **Answers panel.** Allows you to access various Fireworks MX learning resources.

> **NOTE**
> You'll learn more about the uses of these panels in subsequent chapters of this book.

Working with Panels

Panels in Fireworks MX are docked in groups (called panel groups) on the right side of the workspace. Based on your requirements, you can perform any of the following:

- Dock and undock panels and panel groups.
- Rearrange the panel groups by adding and removing panels.
- Expand and collapse panels and panel groups.

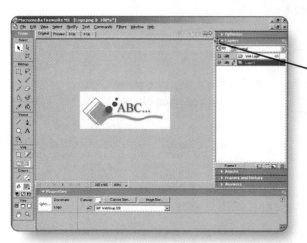

To undock a panel or a panel group, follow these steps:

1. Move the mouse pointer to the panel gripper in the upper-left corner of the panel or the panel group. The mouse pointer will change to the move pointer (a four-headed arrow).

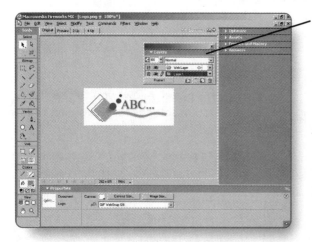

2. Click and hold the mouse button and drag the mouse pointer to move the panel or the panel group to another location. The panel or the panel group will be undocked to the new location.

TIP
To dock back a panel or a panel group, drag it back to the docking area by using the panel gripper.

You can rearrange the existing panel groups by using the panel or panel group Options pop-up menu.

THE FIREWORKS MX WORKSPACE 21

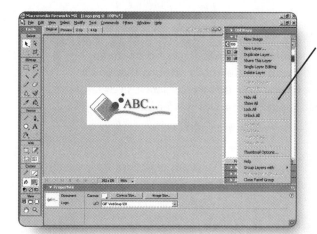

To regroup a panel, follow these steps:

1. Click on the Options menu icon in the upper-right corner of the panel or panel group. The panel or panel group Options pop-up menu will appear.

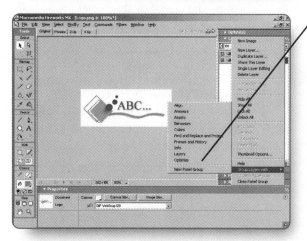

2. Move the mouse pointer to the Group *Panel* With menu option, where *Panel* refers to the name of the panel whose Options pop-up menu you are accessing. For example, if you are using the Layers panel, this option pop-up will be displayed as Group Layers With. A pop-up menu containing the list of panels will appear.

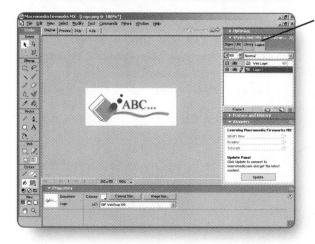

3a. Click on a panel name. The current panel will be grouped with the selected panel.

OR

3b. Click on New Panel Group from the pop-up menu. The current panel will be separated from the existing group.

> **NOTE**
> The panel or panel group Options pop-up menu provides you with several more options that you'll learn about when you study these panels in detail in the subsequent chapters of this book.

You might also need to expand or collapse a panel or a panel group. To expand or collapse a panel or a panel group, follow these steps:

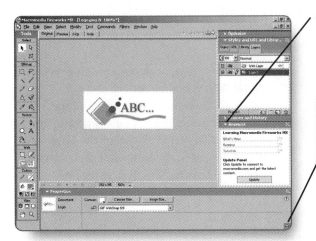

- Click on the expander arrow in the upper-left corner of the panel or panel group. The panel or the panel group will be expanded or collapsed accordingly.

> **TIP**
> You can collapse the Property Inspector to half of its original height by clicking the expander arrow in the lower-right corner.

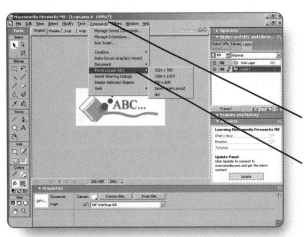

After you have reorganized the Fireworks MX workspace according to your convenience, you may also want to save this layout for further use. To save the current panel layout, follow these steps:

1. Click on Commands. The Commands menu will appear.

2. Click on Panel Layout Sets. A submenu with the list of the default layouts and any previously saved layouts will appear.

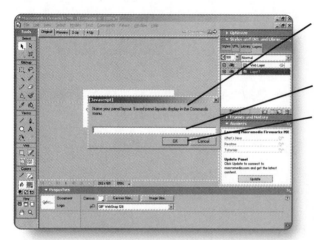

3. Click on Save Panel Layout. A dialog box will open for naming the current panel layout.

4. Type a name for the panel layout.

5. Click on OK. The panel layout will be saved.

NOTE
Try using relevant names for saving panel layout, so that you can identify them easily later.

TIP
You can revert to any of the default panel layout sets or choose another previously saved layout from the Panel Layout Sets submenu in the Commands menu.

Fireworks MX Help Resources

Fireworks MX is equipped with a variety of resources that allow you to learn and troubleshoot the software. While working in Fireworks MX, you can view tooltips by moving the mouse pointer over a user interface element. You can view an exhaustive Fireworks MX documentation by accessing the Help files that are packaged with the software. The Help files describe the use of every Fireworks MX element. The documentation also provides you with some simple tutorials that help you get started with some of the commonly used functions in Fireworks MX.

24 CHAPTER 2: GETTING STARTED WITH FIREWORKS MX

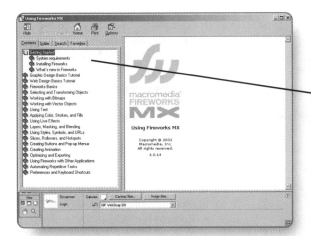

To access the Help files, follow these steps:

1. Click on Help. The Help menu will appear.

2. Click on Using Fireworks. The Fireworks MX help window will open.

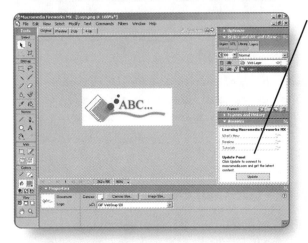

In addition to the Help files, Fireworks MX provides you with the Answers panel. This panel acts as a single reference point for all Fireworks MX resources, tutorials, and TechNotes. To access the Answers panel, select Answers from the Window menu.

In this chapter, you received an overview of the Fireworks MX interface. Fireworks MX also allows you to modify the interface as you see fit. You will learn about customizing Fireworks MX interface in the next chapter.

3

Customizing Fireworks MX

You can control the appearance of the Fireworks MX user interface and also make specific settings, such as specifying default colors. To do so, you need to set preferences for Fireworks MX. In addition, Fireworks MX provides you with a number of keyboard shortcuts to help you work faster. In this chapter, you'll learn how to:

- Set preferences
- Set keyboard shortcuts

26 CHAPTER 3: CUSTOMIZING FIREWORKS MX

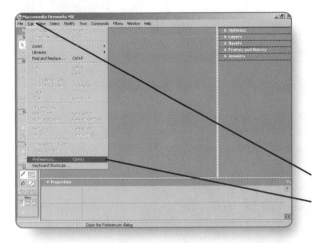

Setting Preferences

Fireworks MX allows you to control its appearance, specify editing options, and specify import options. You use the Preferences dialog box to set these preferences. To view the Preferences dialog box, follow these steps:

1. Click on Edit. The Edit menu will open.

2. Click on Preferences. The Preferences dialog box will open.

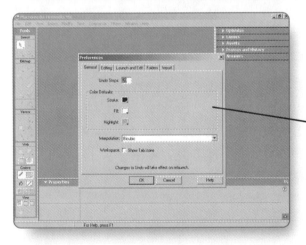

> **TIP**
> You can also press Ctrl+U to open the Preferences dialog box.

The Preferences dialog box contains various tabs, such as General, Editing, and Launch and Edit. These tabs contain a number of options for customizing Fireworks MX. In this section, you will learn to use these tabs to specify various preferences.

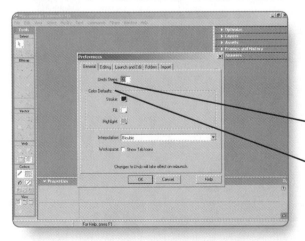

Setting General Preferences

You use the General preferences tab to set the following:

- **Undo steps.** Used to specify the number of steps that can be undone.

- **Color defaults.** Used to specify default colors for brush, fill, and highlight.

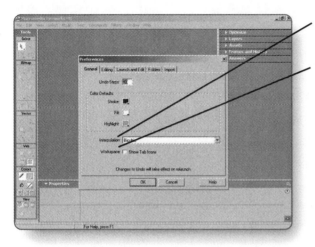

- **Interpolation.** Used to specify the scaling method for images.
- **Workspace.** Used to display icons with panel names. Also, displays the minilauncher bar.

In the following sections, you will learn to set these options.

Setting Undo Steps

Use the Undo Steps box to specify the number of undo steps. This number can be between 0 and 999. The value that you specify in this box is applicable to the Undo command in the Edit menu and the History panel. Keep in mind, though, that specifying a large value, such as 999, in the Undo Steps box requires more memory to store all the steps.

You need to restart Fireworks MX for the changes to take effect.

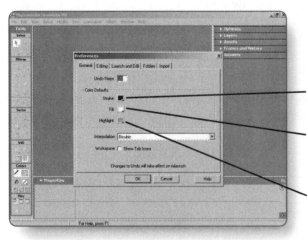

Setting Color Defaults

To specify color defaults, the General tab contains the following:

- **Stroke color box.** Use this color box to specify default color for brush strokes.
- **Fill color box.** Use this color box to specify default color to fill the insides of a path.
- **Highlight color box.** Use this color box to specify default color for highlighted paths. A path appears highlighted when you select it.

> **TIP**
> The default color that you specify for strokes and fills is applied when you click the Set Default Stroke/Fill Colors button in the Tools panel.

Setting Interpolation

Interpolation is used to estimate a missing color value by taking an average of known color values at neighboring points while scaling the images. Use the Interpolation list to specify the scaling method that is used by Fireworks MX to interpolate pixels. The list provides the following four options:

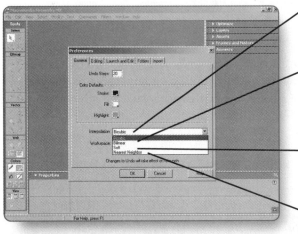

- **Bicubic**. Used to produce the sharpest and the best quality images. This option is selected by default.

- **Bilinear**. Used to add sharpness to an image. However, the sharpness is less than the bicubic interpolation but more than the soft interpolation.

- **Soft**. Used to provide a soft blur to an image. This option removes sharpness details.

- **Nearest Neighbor**. Used to produce jagged edges and sharp contrasts in an image. It does not include blurring details. The effect of this type of interpolation is similar to that of zooming in or out of an image.

Setting Workspace Options

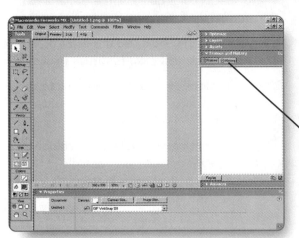

The Show Tab Icons option allows you to display icons in front of a panel name. Also, this option displays a mini-launcher bar to display various panels, such as Behaviors and Styles. To set the Workspace option, check Show Tab Icons and click on OK.

Setting Editing Preferences

The Editing preferences tab contains options to control the mouse pointer, bitmap objects, and the Pen tool.

Setting Options for the Mouse Pointer

The following list explains some options for the mouse pointer provided by the Editing preferences tab:

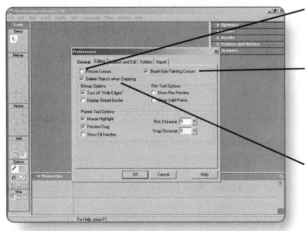

- **Precise Cursors.** Check this option to replace tool-specific icon pointers, such as the pen, with the crosshair pointer.

- **Brush-Size Painting Cursors.** Check this option to set the size and shape of various tool pointers, such as Brush, Eraser, Blur, and Sharpen, to depict the size of the tip.

- **Delete Objects when Cropping.** Check this option to delete the pixels or objects that lie outside the selection, when you choose the Crop Document command from the Edit menu. This option is also applicable to the Canvas Size command of the Modify, Canvas menu.

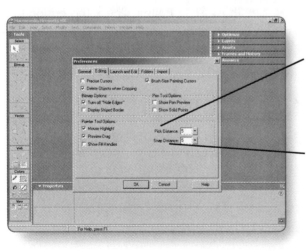

- **Pick Distance.** Use this box to specify the maximum distance between an object and a pointer at which the object can be selected. You can specify a value between 1 and 10 pixels.

- **Snap Distance.** Use this box to specify the maximum distance between an object and a grid at which the object can snap to the grid. You can specify a value between 1 and10 pixels.

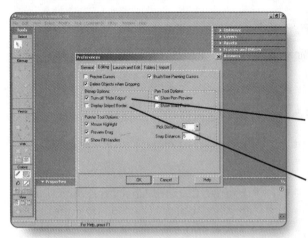

Setting Options for Bitmap Objects

The Editing preferences dialog box contains the following options for bitmap objects:

- **Turn off "Hide Edges"**. Check this option to disable the Hide Edges option when you select another object.

- **Display Striped Border**. Check this option to get a striped border around the canvas while working with bitmap objects.

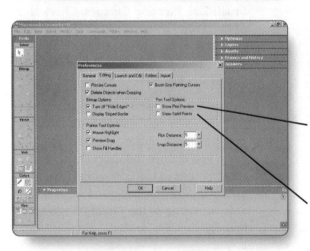

Setting Options for the Pen Tool

The Editing preferences dialog box contains the following options for the Pen tool:

- **Show Pen Preview**. Check this option to see a preview of the next path segment when you click at a point using the Pen tool.

- **Show Solid Points**. Check this option to make selected points appear hollow and deselected points appear solid.

Setting Launch and Edit Preferences

Use the Launch and Edit preferences tab to specify how external applications launch and edit graphics in Fireworks MX. Some of these external applications are Macromedia Flash, Macromedia Director, and Microsoft FrontPage.

SETTING PREFERENCES   31

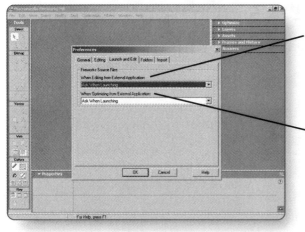

This tab contains the following two options:

- **When Editing from External Application.** Use this list to specify whether the original PNG file should open when you edit images by using Fireworks MX from other applications.

- **When Optimizing from External Application.** Use this list to specify whether the original PNG file should open when you optimize a graphic.

Setting Folders Preferences

Use the Folders preferences tab to refer to additional Photoshop plug-ins, textures, and patterns. This tab contains the following options:

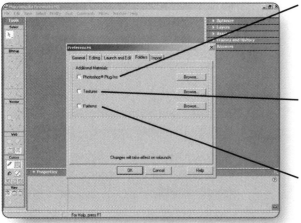

- **Photoshop Plug-Ins.** Check this option to use Photoshop plug-ins. Click on Browse to locate the folder containing these plug-ins. The plug-ins appear in the Filters menu and Effects pop-up menu.

- **Textures.** Check this option to use extra textures. The list of textures appears in the Texture pop-up menu in the Property Inspector.

- **Patterns.** Check this option to use extra patterns. The list of patterns appears in the Pattern pop-up menu in the Property Inspector.

Setting Import Preferences

Use the Import preferences tab to manage Photoshop file conversions. The tab contains various options for layers and text.

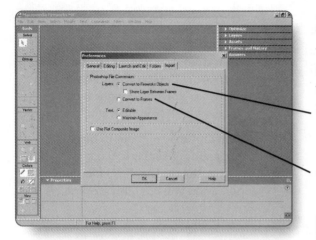

Setting Layer Options

To specify layer settings while importing Photoshop files in Fireworks, you can use the following options:

- **Convert to Fireworks Objects**. Select this option to convert layers to objects in Fireworks.
- **Convert to Frames**. Select this option to convert layers to frames.

> **TIP**
>
> See Chapter 9, "Managing Images Using Layers," for more information on layers and Chapter 16, "Adding Animation to Graphics," for more information on frames.

Setting Text Options

To specify text settings while importing Photoshop files in Fireworks, you can use the following options:

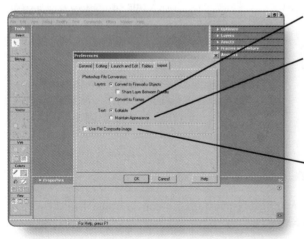

- **Editable**. Select this option to make the text editable after import.
- **Maintain Appearance**. Select this option to maintain the appearance of the imported text.

> **TIP**
>
> Check the Use Flat Composite Image option to import the complete Photoshop file as a flattened bitmap object.

RESTORING THE DEFAULT PREFERENCES

The preferences that you specify for Fireworks MX are stored in the Fireworks MX Preferences.txt file, which is stored on the hard disk of your computer. You may need to restore the default preferences. In such situations, delete the Fireworks MX Preferences.txt file. To delete this file, you need to quit Fireworks MX, delete the file, and relaunch Fireworks MX.

The location of Fireworks MX Preferences.txt file may vary from one computer to another. In a Windows 2000 computer, it is stored in the C:\Documents and Settings/<User Folder>/Application Data/Macromedia/Fireworks MX folder. In a computer running Mac OS X, preferences are found in the Library/Preferences folder within your user folder.

Setting Keyboard Shortcuts

Keyboard shortcuts help you work faster as you can access a menu item or a tool by pressing a key on the keyboard. Fireworks MX provides you with keyboard shortcuts to access most of the menus and tools. In addition, Fireworks MX allows you to use a shortcut key set of some other application, such as FreeHand or Illustrator. This is helpful in situations when you are proficient in other applications. In this section, you will learn to specify a shortcut key set and keyboard shortcuts to access tools.

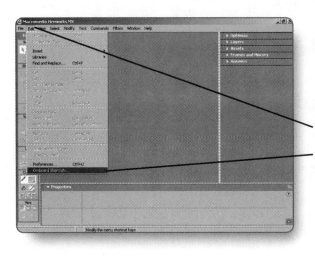

Specifying a Shortcut Key Set

To specify a shortcut key set, follow these steps:

1. Click on Edit. The Edit menu will open.

2. Click on Keyboard Shortcuts. The Keyboard Shortcuts dialog box will open.

CHAPTER 3: CUSTOMIZING FIREWORKS MX

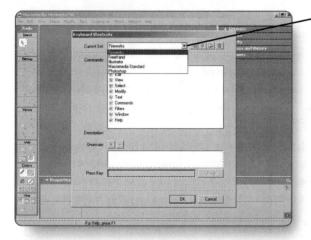

3. Click on the drop-down arrow in the Current Set list. The list of available shortcut key sets will open.

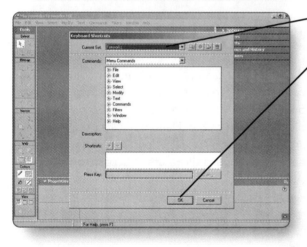

4. Click on the appropriate key set. The key set will be selected.

5. Click on OK. The new shortcut key set will be applied.

Specifying a Keyboard Shortcut

Fireworks MX allows you to create your own custom keyboard shortcuts for the menu commands or the tools. These shortcuts are based on a preinstalled key set. If a shortcut already exists for a command, the new shortcut that you create is called a secondary shortcut.

SETTING KEYBOARD SHORTCUTS   35

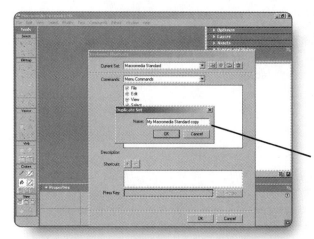

To specify a keyboard shortcut, follow these steps:

1. Open the Keyboard Shortcuts dialog box.

2. Select the required key set from the Current Set list.

3. Click on the Duplicate Set button in the Keyboard Shortcuts dialog box. The Duplicate Set dialog box will open.

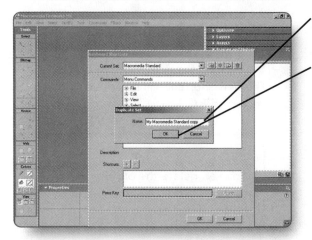

4. Type a name for the new key set in the Name box.

5. Click on OK.

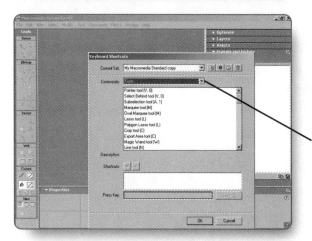

TIP
You create a duplicate set in order to prevent any changes to the original key set.

6. Select the appropriate command category from the Commands list. For example, I selected the Tools category.

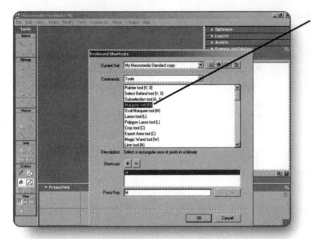

7. Select a tool for which you need to create a shortcut. The Add Shortcut (+) and Delete Shortcut (–) buttons will become active.

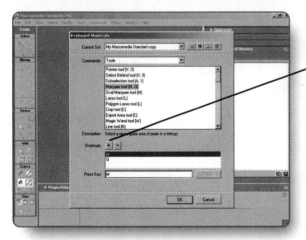

8. Type the new shortcut key in the Press Key box.

9. Click on the Add Shortcut button (+). The new shortcut will be added to the shortcuts list.

> **TIP**
> You can delete the old shortcut by clicking on the Delete Shortcut (–) button if you prefer.

You can now customize Fireworks MX as per your requirements. You will get started with creating graphics in the next chapter.

PART II
Designing Graphics

Chapter 4
Getting Started with Graphics **39**

Chapter 5
Working with Vector Graphics **49**

Chapter 6
Working with Bitmaps **69**

Chapter 7
Working with Colors. **91**

Chapter 8
Using Text in Graphics **115**

Chapter 9
Managing Images Using Layers **129**

Chapter 10
Enhancing the Appearance of Objects . . **141**

Chapter 11
Optimizing and Exporting Graphics **153**

4

Getting Started with Graphics

Fireworks MX allows you to work with vector and bitmap graphics. A vector graphic is made up of two components, points and paths. A bitmap graphic is made up of pixels. To work with any of these graphics, you need tools (for example, to draw a vector graphic or to add colors to a bitmap image). Fireworks MX provides you a separate set of tools for both vector and bitmap graphics. However, there are certain tools that you can use with both types of graphics.

Before going into the discussion on vector or bitmap graphics, I will discuss some of these common tools. In this chapter, you'll learn how to:

- Select images
- View images
- Crop images

CHAPTER 4: GETTING STARTED WITH GRAPHICS

Selecting Images

To work with images, you need to select them. For example, to move a line object from the top to the bottom of a document, you need to select it first as only then can you drag it to the appropriate location. Fireworks MX provides you with tools to select images. In this section, you will learn to use these selection tools.

Using the Pointer Tool

You use the Pointer tool to select and move an object. To select and move an object, follow these steps:

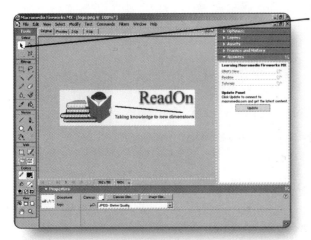

1. Click on the Pointer tool in the Tools panel. The color of the mouse pointer will change to black.

> **TIP**
> You can also press V or 0 to select the Pointer tool.

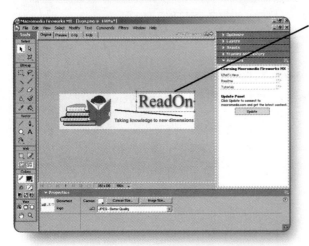

2. Point to the object that you need to select. A rectangle will appear on the sides of the object.

SELECTING IMAGES   41

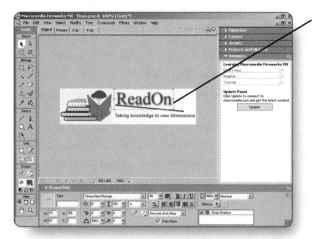

3. Press and hold the mouse button and drag the mouse pointer to move the selected object to the appropriate location. The object will move to the new location.

In addition to selecting an image, you may need to modify its path. To do so, you use the Subselection tool, which is discussed in the following section.

Using the Subselection Tool

Like the Pointer tool, the Subselection tool lets you select an image. So, how is it different from the Pointer tool? The difference between the two tools is in their use with vector images. When you select a vector image by using the Subselection tool, it displays the points that constitute the image. You can then move any point by using this tool to change the shape of the image. See Chapter 5, "Working with Vector Graphics," for more information on vector images.

To modify an image using the Subselection tool, follow these steps:

1. Click on the Subselection tool in the Tools panel. The Subselection tool will be selected.

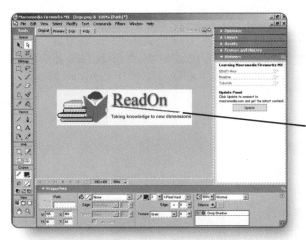

> **TIP**
> You can also press A or 1 to select the Subselection tool.

2. Click on the object that you need to modify. The object will be selected, and the points will appear.

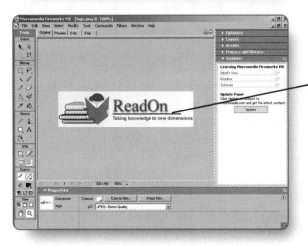

3. Press and hold the mouse button on the point that you need to move. The point will be selected.

4. Drag the mouse pointer to move the point to the appropriate position. The point will move to the new position.

Viewing Images

To make your graphics with precision, you need to view them correctly. For example, in a graphic displaying a number of books, you may need to modify the color of the book that is in the center. In such situations, you can zoom the image to a higher magnification and then make changes in it. Fireworks MX provides the Zoom tool, which helps you to magnify an image. When you magnify an image, its size may exceed the size of the Document window. To scroll such documents, Fireworks MX provides the Hand tool.

In this section, you'll learn to use the Zoom and Hand tools.

Using the Zoom Tool

You can use the Zoom tool to zoom in or zoom out of an object. To zoom in means to increase the magnification of the image, and to zoom out means to decrease the magnification. Fireworks MX allows you to zoom the image:

- At a point
- On a user-defined area

In this section, I will discuss both the aforementioned methods of zooming.

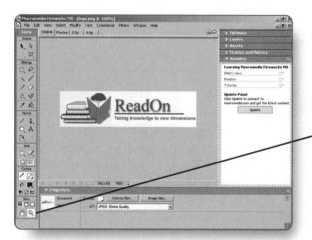

Zooming at a Point

Zooming at a point increases or decreases the magnification in preset values, such as 100%, 150%, or 200%. To zoom on a point, follow these steps:

1. Click on the Zoom tool in the Tools panel. The shape of the pointer will change to a magnifying glass with a plus sign.

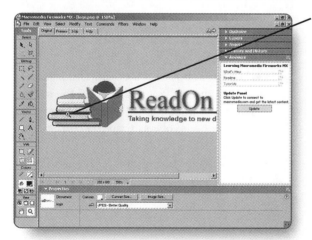

2. Click on any point in the Document window. This point will become the center point and the image will be magnified to the next preset magnification percentage.

CHAPTER 4: GETTING STARTED WITH GRAPHICS

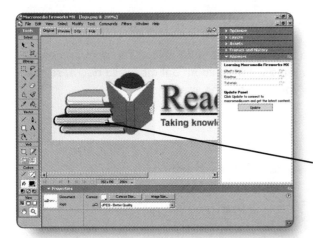

TIP

When you create a center point, it remains in view, even when the size of the image is greater than the size of the Document window.

3. Click on the same point again. The object will zoom to the next preset magnification level.

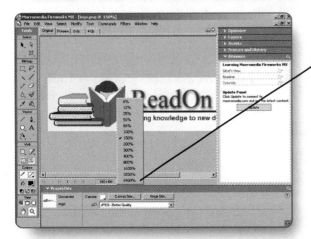

TIP

You can also set a zoom setting by selecting a value from the Set Magnification pop-up menu located at the bottom of the Document window. Otherwise, you can click on the Zoom In or Zoom Out menu item in the View menu.

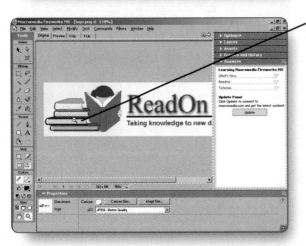

4. To zoom out of the document, press and hold the Alt key and click on the same point in the document. The zoom level will move to one level less than the current one.

TIP

While you are holding down the Alt key, the plus symbol present inside the magnifying glass changes to a minus symbol.

Zooming on a User-defined Area

Fireworks MX lets you zoom an area of an image and this increases or decreases the magnification in variable values depending on the size of the area. The smaller the area, the higher the magnification. To zoom the document on a user-defined area, follow these steps:

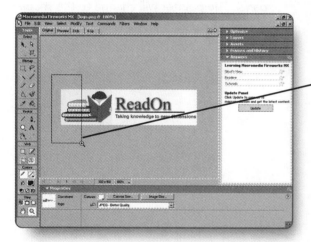

1. Click on the Zoom tool in the Tools panel. The shape of the pointer will change to a magnifying glass with a plus sign.

2. Press and hold the mouse button and drag the pointer over the part of the document that you need to magnify. The area of the image will be zoomed.

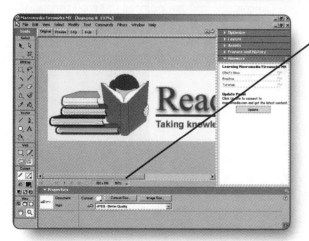

TIP

You can see the value of magnification in the box next to the Set Magnification pop-up menu.

TIP

You can zoom out by pressing and holding the Alt key while repeating Step 2. You can return to 100% magnification level by double-clicking on the Zoom tool in the Tools panel.

After you have zoomed in an image, its size may exceed that of the Document window. As a result, you may not be able to see the complete image. What will you do then? The next section introduces the Hand tool, which helps you to scroll a zoomed in image.

Using the Hand Tool

You use the Hand tool to scroll a zoomed in image. This process is also called panning. Remember that the Hand tool works only when you have magnified the image larger than the Document window. To scroll a zoomed in image, follow these steps:

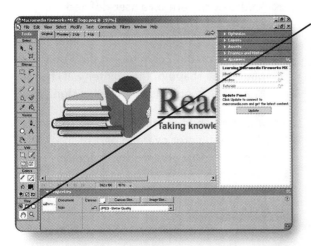

1. Click on the Hand tool in the Tools panel. The pointer will change to the shape of a hand.

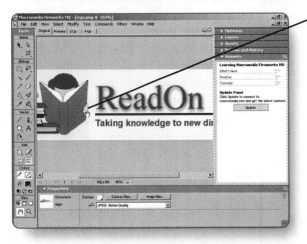

2. Press and hold the mouse button and move the mouse pointer to scroll through the image. The view will move to a different part of the image.

CROPPING IMAGES 47

Cropping Images

Cropping an image refers to cutting out a part of an image and discarding the remaining part. For example, in an image showing a number of books, you may need to cut out one book. In such situations, the Crop tool comes in handy. To cut out the part of an image, follow these steps:

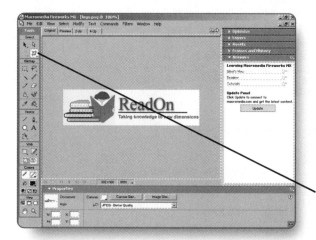

1. Click on the Crop tool in the Tools panel. The shape of the pointer will change.

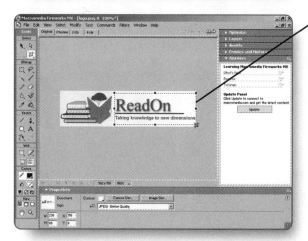

2. Press and hold the mouse button and move over the area that you want to keep. The required area will be surrounded by a dotted rectangle.

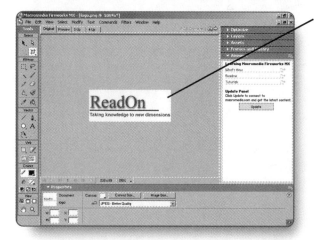

3. Double-click on the dotted rectangle. The left-out portion will be removed.

> **TIP**
>
> If you cropped an image incorrectly, you can undo it. To do so, click on Edit to display the Edit menu and select the Undo Crop Document command. The image will be restored.

In the next chapter, you will learn to work with vector graphics.

5

Working with Vector Graphics

A vector graphic is a series of mathematically defined points joined together by lines. A vector graphic is made up of two components, paths and points. A path is the outline of the shape that you want to draw, and it contains a number of points. For example, a line is the path between two points. In Fireworks terminology, anything that you create or import is called an object. Therefore, in this example, a line is an object. In all further discussions, I will use the word object.

Each vector graphic has two important characteristics, stroke and fill. A stroke represents the outline (or path) of the object, whereas a fill represents the area enclosed inside the outline (or path). The advantage of having vector graphics is that they are resolution-independent, which means you can resize, rotate, magnify, or transform them without compromising clarity. Moreover, these graphics require a small amount of storage space, are scalable, and easily portable.

Fireworks MX provides you with a variety of tools to ease your working with vector graphics. In this chapter, you'll learn how to:

- Draw objects by using tools
- Apply strokes and fills to objects

Drawing Objects by Using Tools

Your graphic may consist of a number of objects. For example, a graphic may contain lines, rectangles, polygons, and freeform images. Fireworks MX contains a Tools panel, which, in turn, contains a number of tools, such as Line and Rectangle, that help you create vector graphics. In this section, you'll learn to use some of these tools.

Drawing a Line

You use the Line tool to create a line. To create a line, follow these steps:

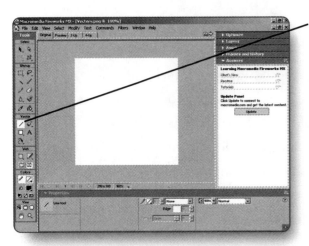

1. In the Tools panel, click on the Line tool. The shape of the mouse pointer will change to a crosshair pointer.

> **TIP**
> Alternatively, you can press N to select the Line tool.

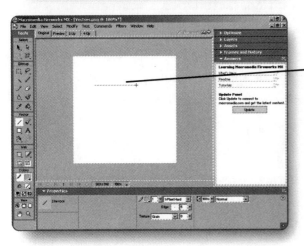

2. In the Document window, point to the starting position of the line.

3. Press and hold the mouse button and drag the mouse pointer to draw a line of an appropriate size. The line will appear in the Document window.

DRAWING OBJECTS BY USING TOOLS   51

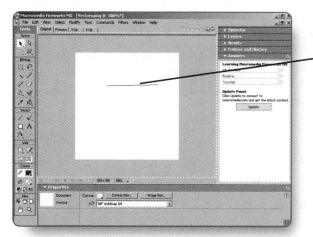

> **TIP**
>
> While drawing the line, the line may not appear to be straight. To avoid such situations, press and hold the Shift key while performing Step 3. This "locks" the line in place so that it remains straight.

After successfully creating a line, you'll now learn to create various other shapes, such as rectangles and polygons.

Drawing Rectangles and Polygons

To draw shapes such as a rectangle, ellipse, or polygon, you use the Rectangle, Ellipse, or Polygon tool, respectively. All these tools are a part of the basic shape tool and you can select any of them by using the Rectangle tool pop-up menu. In the subsequent sections, I discuss the use of these tools.

Drawing a Rectangle

To draw a rectangle, follow these steps:

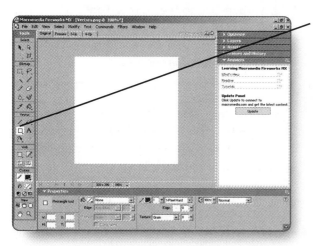

1. In the Tools panel, click on the Rectangle tool. The shape of the mouse pointer will change to a crosshair pointer.

52 CHAPTER 5: WORKING WITH VECTOR GRAPHICS

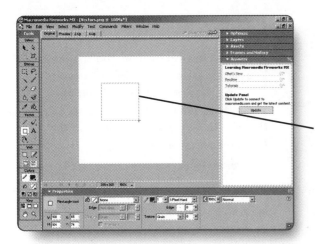

TIP

You can also press U to select the Rectangle tool.

2. In the Document window, press and hold the mouse button and drag the mouse pointer to draw a rectangle. The rectangle will appear in the Document window.

You may need to make changes to the rectangle that you created. For example, you may need to change the size of a rectangle or make the edges of a rectangle rounded. Or, you may need to create a square. The following sections provide details on solving these issues.

MODIFYING THE DIMENSIONS OF A RECTANGLE

To modify the dimensions of a rectangle, follow these steps:

1. In the Document window, click on the rectangle that you created by using the Pointer tool. The rectangle will appear selected.

TIP

See "Using the Pointer Tool" in Chapter 4, "Getting Started with Graphics," for more information on using the Pointer tool.

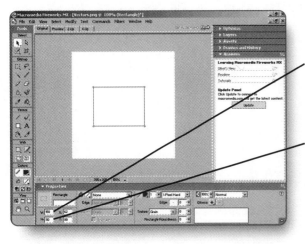

2. In the W box of the Property Inspector, type the new width of the rectangle and press Enter. The width of the rectangle will change to the specified value.

3. In the H box of the Property Inspector, type the new height of the rectangle and press Enter. The height of the rectangle will change to the specified value.

DRAWING OBJECTS BY USING TOOLS   53

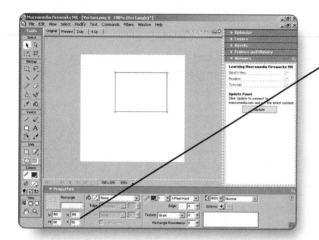

TIP

You can also change the position of the rectangle. One way to do so is to select the rectangle and drag it to a new position. The second way is to enter appropriate values in the X and Y boxes in the Property Inspector.

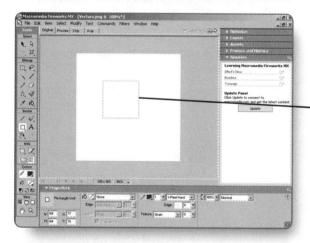

DRAWING A SQUARE

To draw a square, follow these steps:

1. Select the Rectangle tool.

2. Press and hold Shift along with the mouse button and drag the mouse pointer. A square will appear in the Document window.

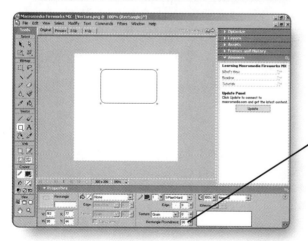

ROUNDING THE EDGES OF A RECTANGLE

To make the edges of a rectangle round:

1. Select the rectangle in the Document window. The rectangle will be selected.

2. In the Rectangle Roundness box in the Property Inspector, type an appropriate value and press Enter. The edges of the selected rectangle will be rounded.

CHAPTER 5: WORKING WITH VECTOR GRAPHICS

> **NOTE**
> The value that you enter in the Rectangle Roundness box specifies the curvature of the corners of the rectangle. The larger the value, the larger is the curvature of the corners.

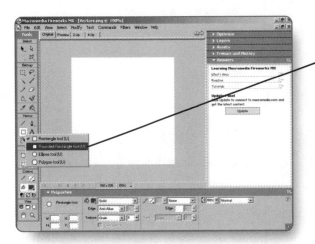

> **TIP**
> You can also use the Rounded Rectangle tool to create a rounded rectangle. All you need to do is select the Rounded Rectangle tool from the Rectangle tool pop-up menu. Next, press and hold the mouse button and drag the mouse pointer to draw a rounded rectangle.

Drawing an Ellipse

To draw an ellipse, follow these steps:

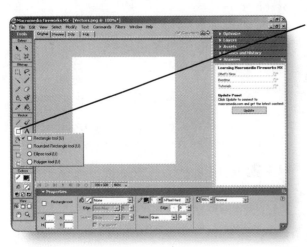

1. In the Tools panel, click on the small triangle in the Rectangle tool. The Rectangle tool pop-up menu will appear.

DRAWING OBJECTS BY USING TOOLS 55

2. In the Rectangle tool pop-up menu, click on the Ellipse tool. The shape of the mouse pointer will change to a crosshair pointer.

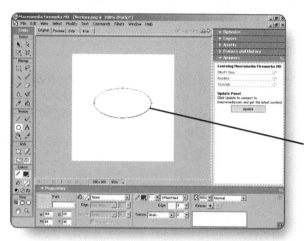

TIP
Alternatively, you can press U to shuffle among the tools present in the Rectangle tool pop-up menu.

3. In the Document window, press and hold the mouse button and drag the mouse pointer to draw an ellipse. The ellipse will appear in the Document window.

TIP
You can also use the Ellipse tool to draw a circle. To do so, press and hold the Shift key while performing Step 3.

Drawing a Polygon

You use the Polygon tool (also found in the Rectangle tool pop-up menu) to draw a polygon. You can set the properties of this tool to specify the number of sides of the polygon. Additionally, you can use this tool to create a star. To create a polygon, follow these steps:

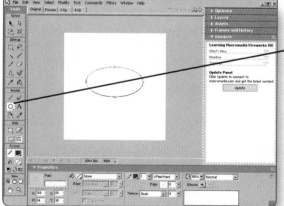

1. In the Rectangle tool pop-up menu, click on the Polygon tool. The shape of the mouse pointer will change to a crosshair pointer.

2. In the Property Inspector, in the Shape drop-down menu, click on Polygon, if necessary. You will draw a polygon.

CHAPTER 5: WORKING WITH VECTOR GRAPHICS

TIP

To draw a star, click on Star in the Shape drop-down menu.

3. In the Property Inspector, in the Sides box, type the number of sides required in the polygon. The polygon will have the specified number of sides.

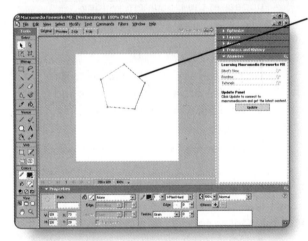

4. In the Document window, press and hold the mouse button and drag the mouse pointer to draw the polygon. The polygon will appear in the Document window.

TIP

You can modify the width, height, and position of an ellipse or a polygon as you can for a rectangle by using the Property Inspector. See "Modifying the Dimensions of a Rectangle" in this chapter for more information.

You may need to include curved paths in your graphics. For example, you may need to create a leaf. The following section provides detailed instructions on creating curved paths.

Drawing Curved Paths

You use the Pen tool to create curved paths. However, you can also create straight paths by using the Pen tool. Using this tool is simple, you need to create only the points; the path connecting these points is created automatically. The curves that you create using the Pen tool are called Bezier curves.

Bezier Curves

Bezier Curves are named after the Frenchman, Pierre Bezier, who invented them. You need to plot points to draw a Bezier curve. To plot the points, you use the Pen tool. A Bezier curve comprises a number of elements.

The following list explains these elements:

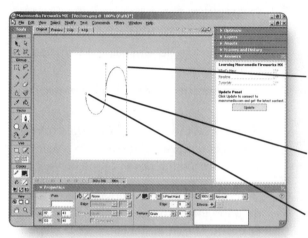

- **Anchor points**. Each point that you create on a path is called an anchor point.

- **Handles**. When you select an anchor point, it displays one or two handles. You use these handles to manipulate the size and shape of the curve.

- **Curve points**. The anchor points that have a curve on either side are called curve points.

- **Corner points**. The anchor points that have a straight path on at least one side are called corner points.

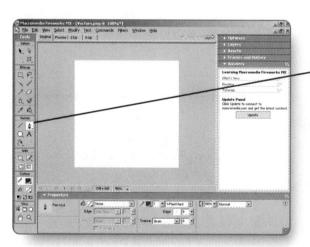

To draw a curve by using the Pen tool, follow these steps:

1. In the Tools panel, click on the Pen tool. The shape of the mouse pointer will change to a pen.

TIP
You can also press P to select the Pen tool.

58 CHAPTER 5: WORKING WITH VECTOR GRAPHICS

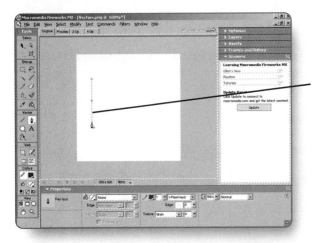

2. Click on the Document window to mark the first curve point. This curve point will determine the starting point of the curve.

3. Press and hold the mouse button and drag the mouse pointer in the downward direction. A handle will appear.

TIP
This handle determines the direction of the curve.

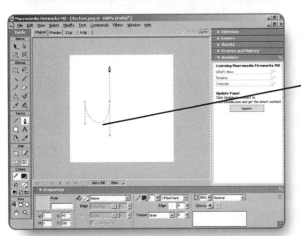

4. Click on the Document window to mark the second curve point. This curve point will determine the depth of the curve.

5. Press and hold the mouse button and drag the mouse pointer in the direction opposite to that of the curve. A C-shaped curve will appear.

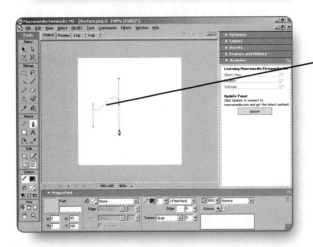

TIP
If you drag the mouse pointer in the direction of the curve, an S-shaped curve will be created.

6. If you need to create a new curve, double-click on the last curve point to end the curve.

DRAWING OBJECTS BY USING TOOLS   59

> **TIP**
> Alternatively, to end the curve, you can press and hold Ctrl and click anywhere in the Document window.

In addition to creating curves by plotting points, you can simply draw the required shape. The following section provides details on creating such shapes.

Drawing Freeform Objects

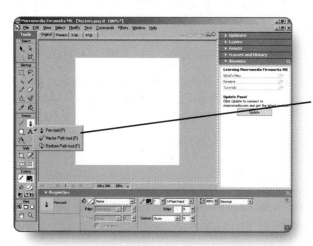

You use the Vector Path tool to draw freeform objects. This tool is available in the Pen tool pop-up menu. To draw a freeform object:

1. Click on the small triangle in the Pen tool. The Pen tool pop-up menu will appear.

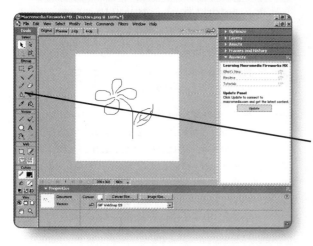

> **TIP**
> You can also press P to shuffle between the various menu items present in the Pen tool pop-up menu.

2. In the Pen tool pop-up menu, click on the Vector Path tool. The shape of the mouse pointer will change to depict the size of stroke.

CHAPTER 5: WORKING WITH VECTOR GRAPHICS

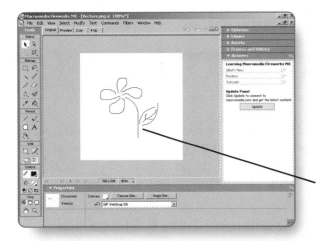

TIP

See "Applying Strokes to an Object" for more information on strokes.

3. In the Document window, point at the position from where you need to start the object.

4. Press and hold the mouse button and drag the mouse pointer to draw the object. The desired object will appear.

After you create an object, you may need to manipulate its shape. For example, you may need to bend a straight line or reshape a polygon. The next section provides details on manipulating objects.

Manipulating Objects

Manipulating an object means making changes to the path of the object. Fireworks MX provides you with a number of tools that help you in changing the path of an object. The following list mentions some of these tools:

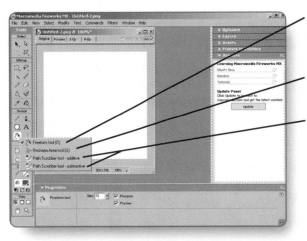

- **Freeform tool**. Lets you to make changes to the path of an object by pushing or pulling it.

- **Reshape Area tool**. Lets you pull the area of a selected path.

- **Path Scrubber tools**. Lets you enhance the appearance of a path by modifying its stroke's properties, such as angle, ink, hue, and saturation. See "Using Advanced Stroke Options" in Chapter 7, "Working with Colors," for more information on stroke properties.

DRAWING OBJECTS BY USING TOOLS   61

All these tools are available in the Freeform tool pop-up menu. In addition to these tools, Fireworks MX provides the Knife tool, which lets you cut an object in two or more pieces. In this section, you'll learn to use the Freeform and Knife tools.

Using the Freeform Tool

As mentioned previously, the Freeform tool allows you to make changes to the appearance of an object by pushing or pulling its path.

In this section, you'll learn to manipulate objects by pushing and pulling them.

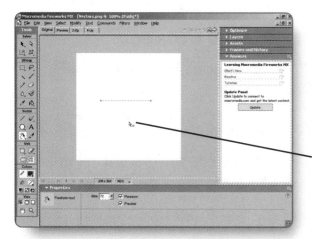

PUSHING AN OBJECT

To manipulate an object by pushing its path, follow these steps:

1. Click on the object that you want to modify by using the Pointer tool. The object will appear selected.

2. Click on the Freeform tool in the Tools panel. The shape of the mouse pointer will change to an arrow and a small circle toward the bottom, which indicates that the Freeform tool is in use.

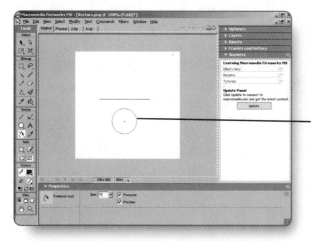

> **TIP**
> You can also press O to select the Freeform tool.

3. Click on the Document window. The shape of the mouse pointer will change to the push pointer.

CHAPTER 5: WORKING WITH VECTOR GRAPHICS

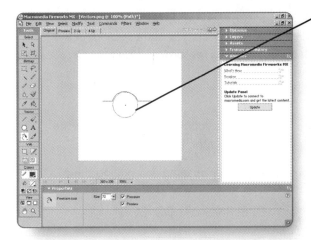

4. Press and hold the mouse button and drag the mouse pointer to push the path of a vector object. The shape of the object will change.

PULLING AN OBJECT

To manipulate an object by pulling its path, follow these steps:

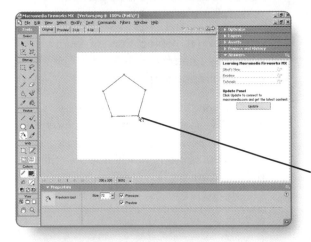

1. Select the object that you want to modify. The object will appear selected.

2. Select the Freeform tool. The shape of the mouse pointer will change to an arrow with a small circle.

3. Point at the position of the selected object that you want to modify. The shape of the mouse pointer will change to the pull pointer.

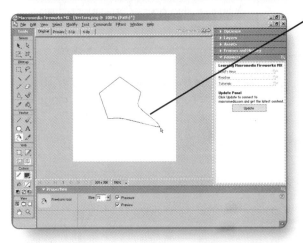

4. Press and hold the mouse button and drag the mouse pointer to pull the path of a vector object. The shape of the object will change.

DRAWING OBJECTS BY USING TOOLS 63

Using the Knife Tool

You use the Knife tool to cut the path of an object into two or more paths. To cut a path, follow these steps:

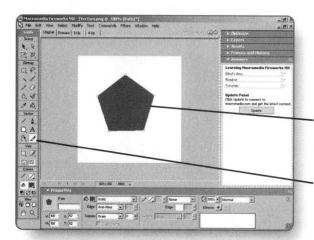

1. Click on the object that you want to cut by using the Pointer tool in the Document window. The object will appear selected.

2. Click on the Knife tool in the Tools panel. The mouse pointer will change to a knife.

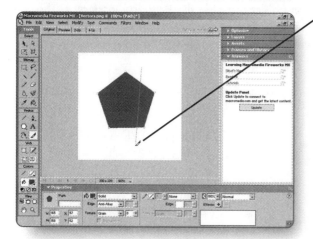

3. Press and hold the mouse button and drag the mouse pointer over the selected object. A line will appear, indicating that the path has been cut.

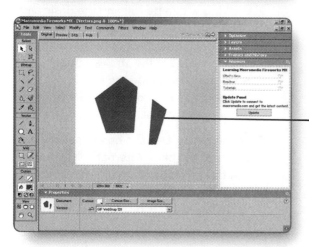

4. Select the Pointer tool. The shape of the mouse pointer will change to an arrow.

5. Click on the Document window. The object will be deselected.

6. Click on one of the two paths. The path will be selected.

7. Press and hold the mouse button and drag the mouse pointer to separate the two paths. The two paths will be separated.

After you've drawn the object that you require, you may need to enhance its appearance by changing the color of its outline or filling it up with a color. The following section provides the details of adding colors to your objects.

Adding Colors to Objects

Fireworks MX provides you with a number of tools to apply strokes and fills to the objects. In this section, you'll learn to apply stroke and fill colors to the objects that you create.

Applying Strokes to an Object

You can change stroke settings for an object by using the Property Inspector. The Property Inspector provides you with a number of options to apply and manipulate the strokes of a vector object. However, you need to select the appropriate vector object to see these options.

The following list explains the options provided by the Property Inspector to apply strokes:

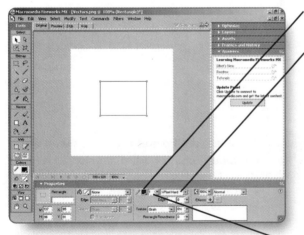

- **Stroke color box**. Use this box to specify a color for a path.

- **Stroke category list**. This list provides you with a number of stroke categories, such as Pencil, Basic, and Air Brush. The Pencil category helps you simulate drawing with a pencil, and the Basic and Air Brush categories help you simulate commonly used brushes for painting. You can also set the stroke category to none, which will hide the path. Moreover, doing so hides other options (listed next) as well.

- **Tip size box**. Use this box to specify the width of the path. Alternatively, you can use the corresponding slider to specify a value. If you adjust the slider to specify a value, the value is displayed in the box.

ADDING COLORS TO OBJECTS   65

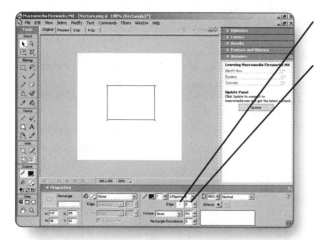

- **Tip preview box**. Use this box to preview the width of the tip.

- **Edge softness box**. Use this box to specify a value for making the edge of a stroke soft or hard. You can also use the adjacent slider to specify a value.

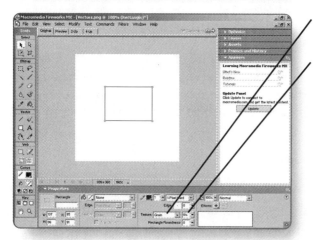

- **Texture name list**. Use this list to apply a texture to a stroke.

- **Amount of texture box**. Use this box to specify the degree of texture in percentage. You can also use the slider to specify a value.

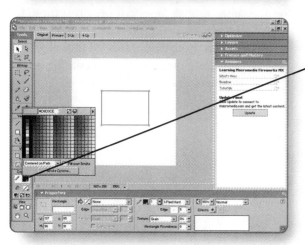

TIP
You can also access the Stroke color box from the Tools panel.

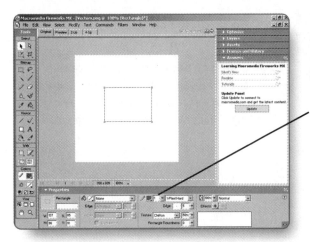

To apply a stroke to a vector object, follow these steps:

1. Click on an appropriate vector object. The object will appear selected.

2. In the Property Inspector, make appropriate Stroke settings. The path of the selected object will contain the applied stroke.

Applying Fills to an Object

Like stroke settings, you can make fill settings for an object by using the Property Inspector. The Property Inspector shows a number of options that help you apply fill to a vector object. However, these options are enabled only when you select an appropriate fill category.

The following list explains these options:

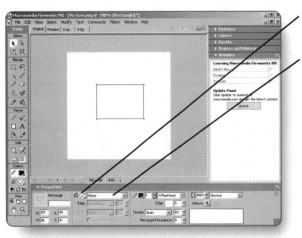

- **Fill color box**. Use this box to specify a color to be filled inside a path.

- **Fill category list**. Use this list to apply a suitable fill category. It provides three fill categories: Solid, Web Dither, and Pattern. In addition, this list also provides a number of gradient fills, such as Linear, Radial, and Cone.

ADDING COLORS TO OBJECTS 67

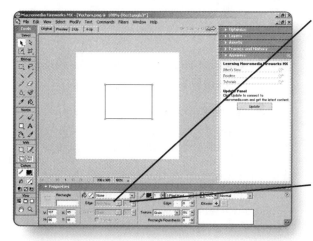

- **Edge of fills list.** Use this list to specify the type of edge for the fill. It provides three options: Hard, Anti-Alias, and Feather. Hard refers to the regular hard line; Anti-Alias refers to making an object appear smoother by blending its color into the background on which it is placed; and Feathering produces a glow by giving a softened effect on the edge.

- **Amount of feather box.** Use this box to specify the degree of feathering if your fill has a feathered edge. Alternatively, you can use the adjacent slider to specify a value.

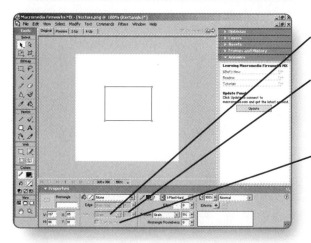

- **Texture name list.** Use this list to apply a texture to a fill.

- **Amount of texture box.** Use this box to specify the degree of texture in percentage. You can also use the adjacent slider to specify a value.

- **Transparent texture check box.** Use this check box to control the transparency of the fill. Check this box to see through the lighter parts of the texture.

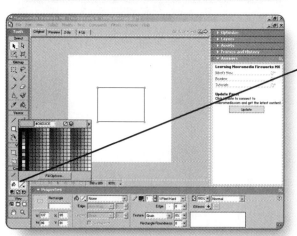

TIP
You can also access the Fill color box from the Tools panel.

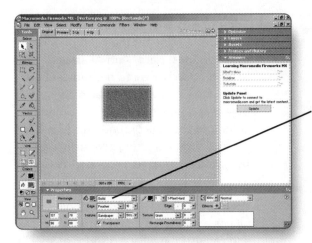

To apply fill to a vector object, follow these steps:

1. Click on an appropriate vector object. The object will appear selected.

2. In the Property Inspector, make appropriate fill settings. The selected object will contain the fill you applied.

With this, you've learned to create and modify vector graphics. In the next chapter, you will learn to work with bitmap objects.

6

Working with Bitmaps

A bitmap consists of a grid of numerous tiny squares, called pixels. Each pixel stores individual color information. You can view these pixels by zooming in on a bitmap object. See "Using the Zoom Tool" in Chapter 4, "Getting Started with Graphics," to learn more about zooming an object.

Bitmap objects are resolution dependent, unlike vector objects. As a result of this, resizing a bitmap object leads to loss in its quality. You use bitmap images when working with digital media, such as scanned images, images captured using digital camera, or images created using any graphics software. Bitmaps are also known as *raster images*.

Fireworks MX provides you with various tools that you can use to work with bitmap objects. In this chapter, you'll learn how to:

- Import bitmap objects
- Draw, paint, and erase bitmap objects
- Select a part of a bitmap object
- Modify bitmap objects

Importing Bitmap Objects

Before using any of the bitmap tools, you need to import the bitmap object in the Document window. You can use Fireworks MX to import images from various file formats, such as JPEG and GIF.

To import a bitmap object, follow these steps:

1. Click on File. The File menu will appear.

2. Click on Import. The Import dialog box will open.

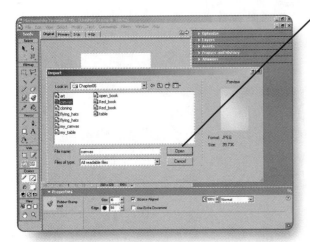

3. Click on Open after selecting the appropriate file. The shape of the mouse pointer will change to the insertion pointer.

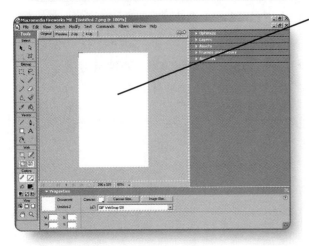

4. Click on the Document window. The imported bitmap will appear in the document.

DRAWING, PAINTING, AND ERASING BITMAP OBJECTS   71

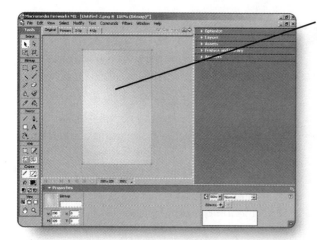

5. Save the file.

In addition to importing a bitmap, you can create your own bitmaps. You will learn to create your own bitmaps in the following section.

Drawing, Painting, and Erasing Bitmap Objects

Fireworks MX provides you with several tools to work with bitmap objects. In this section, you will learn to use the Pencil, Brush, and Eraser tools.

Using the Pencil Tool

You use the Pencil tool to draw freeform one-pixel curves. The Property Inspector provides a number of options to set the Pencil tool as per your requirements. The following list explains these options:

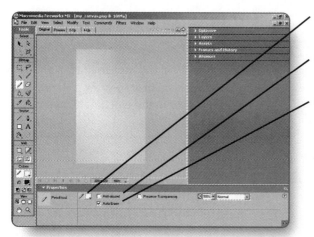

- **Color box.** Use this box to specify a color for the curve.

- **Anti-aliased check box.** Check this box to create a curve with smooth edges.

- **Auto Erase check box.** Check this box to use fill color for drawing strokes instead of stroke color. This takes effect when the Pencil tool is clicked over the strokes drawn in the Document window. See Chapter 7, "Working with Colors," to learn more about fill and stroke colors.

CHAPTER 6: WORKING WITH BITMAPS

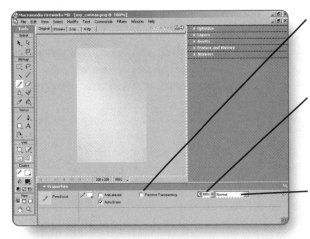

- **Preserve Transparency check box.** Check this box to prevent drawing on the transparent parts of the bitmap object.

- **Opacity box.** Use this box to specify an opacity value for the curve—either by typing in a value or by using the slider. Opacity value specifies the amount of transparency for the curve.

- **Blend Mode list.** Use this list to specify a blending mode for the curve.

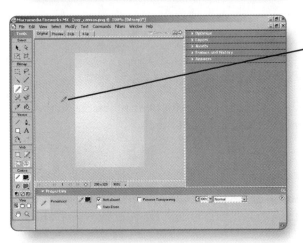

To draw a curve, follow these steps:

1. Click on the Pencil tool in the Tools panel. The shape of the mouse pointer will change to a pencil.

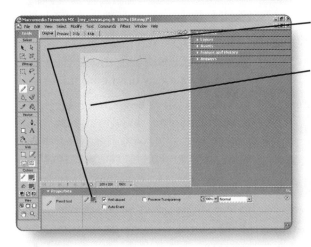

2. Make the required changes in the Property Inspector.

3. Press and hold the mouse button and drag the mouse pointer to draw a curve. The curve will appear in the Document window.

TIP

You can press and hold Shift while dragging the mouse pointer to constrain the curve to 45 degrees.

DRAWING, PAINTING, AND ERASING BITMAP OBJECTS   73

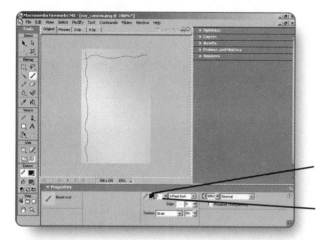
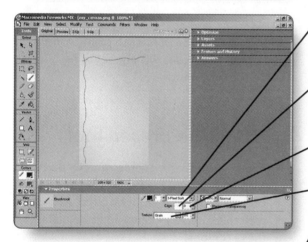
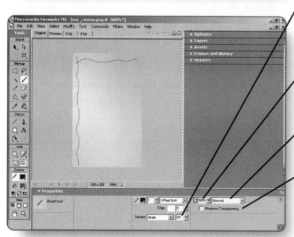

Using the Brush Tool

You use the Brush tool to paint strokes. Like the Pencil tool, the Property Inspector provides you with a number of options to set the Brush tool depending on your requirements. The following list explains the options available with the Brush tool:

- **Color box**. Use this box to specify a color for the stroke.

- **Tip size box**. Use this box to specify the tip weight for the stroke—either by typing in a value or by using the slider.

- **Stroke category list**. Use this list to choose from various available brush types, such as Air Brush and Oil.

- **Tip preview box**. Use this box to view a preview of the brush tip based on current size and edge settings.

- **Edge softness box**. Use this box to specify the softness of the brush tip.

- **Texture list**. Use this list to choose from various available texture types.

- **Texture amount box**. Use this box to specify the amount of the currently selected texture that is to be applied to the stroke.

- **Opacity box**. Use this box to specify an opacity value for the curve—either by typing in a value or using the slider.

- **Blend Mode list**. Use this list to specify a blending mode for the curve.

- **Preserve Transparency check box**. Check this box to prevent painting strokes on the transparent parts of the bitmap object.

To paint a brush stroke, follow these steps:

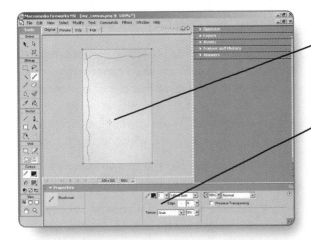

1. Click on the Brush tool in the Tools panel. The shape of the mouse pointer will change to depict the currently selected tip size.

2. Make the required changes in the Property Inspector.

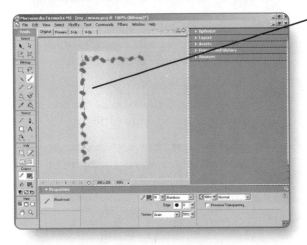

3. Press and hold the mouse button and drag the mouse pointer to paint a brush stroke. The stroke will appear in the Document window.

Using the Eraser Tool

You use the Eraser tool to remove parts of a bitmap object. The Property Inspector provides a number of options for working with this tool. The following list explains these options:

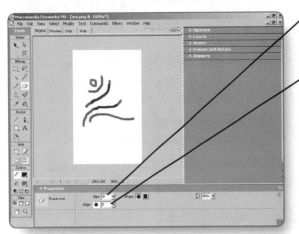

- **Eraser size box**. Use this box to specify the size of the eraser tip—either by typing in a value or by using the slider.

- **Edge softness box**. Use this box to specify the softness of the eraser tip.

DRAWING, PAINTING, AND ERASING BITMAP OBJECTS   75

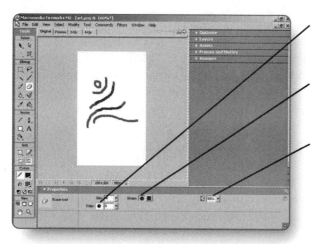

- **Tip preview box**. This box displays a preview of the eraser tip based on current size and edge settings.

- **Shape button**. Use this button to select either square or round shape for the eraser.

- **Opacity box**. Use this box to specify an opacity value for the eraser—either by typing in a value or using the slider.

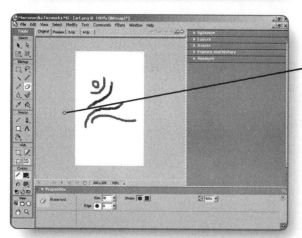

To erase a part of a bitmap object, follow these steps:

1. Click on the Eraser tool in the Tools panel. The shape of the mouse pointer will change to depict the currently selected tip size and shape.

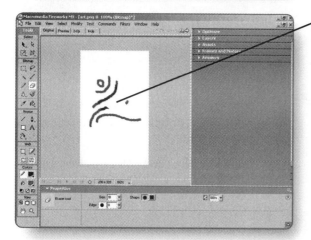

2. Press and hold the mouse button and drag the mouse pointer over the area to be removed. The specific area will be erased.

CHAPTER 6: WORKING WITH BITMAPS

After you've created the bitmap object, you may need to edit it. Fireworks MX provides you with various professional level photo editing and retouching techniques. You can either edit the entire bitmap object or specify a particular part of the bitmap object. If you need to work with a specific part of a bitmap object, you need to select it. For doing so, you can use the various selection techniques provided by Fireworks MX. The following section discusses these techniques in detail.

Selecting Parts of Bitmap Objects

There might be situations in which you want to edit just a part of a bitmap and not the entire object. For example, in a bitmap containing a number of books, you may need to highlight one particular book. In such situations, you can use the following tools to select the required area:

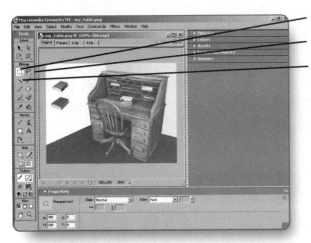

- The Marquee tool
- The Lasso tool
- The Magic Wand tool

In the following sections, you'll learn to use these tools.

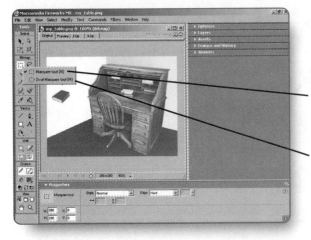

Using the Marquee Tool

Fireworks MX provides you with two types of Marquee tools:

- **Rectangular Marquee tool**. Use this Marquee tool to create a rectangular selection area.

- **Oval Marquee tool**. Use this Marquee tool to create an oval selection area.

SELECTING PARTS OF BITMAP OBJECTS 77

> **NOTE**
> Both these tools are a part of the Marquee tool group. To display all the items of the tool group, click and hold the mouse button on the Marquee tool group. See Chapter 2, "Getting Started with Fireworks MX," to learn more about accessing tools from a tool group.

You can make the Marquee tool work as per your requirements by setting various options present in the Property Inspector. The following list explains these options:

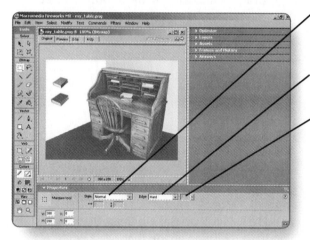

- **Style list**. Use this list to select from the three constraint options: Normal, Fixed ratio, and Fixed size.

- **Edge list**. Use this list to specify the edge type for the selection.

- **Feather amount box**. Use this box to specify the amount of feather to be applied to the selection. This box becomes available only if you select Feather as the edge type from the edge list.

> **NOTE**
> See "Modifying the Selection Marquees" later in this chapter for more information on feathering.

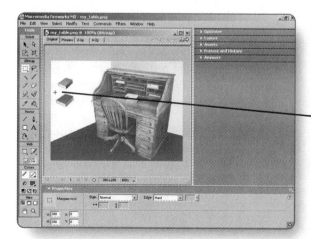

To create a rectangular selection marquee, follow these steps:

1. Click on the Marquee tool in the Tools panel. The shape of the mouse pointer will change to the crosshair pointer.

CHAPTER 6: WORKING WITH BITMAPS

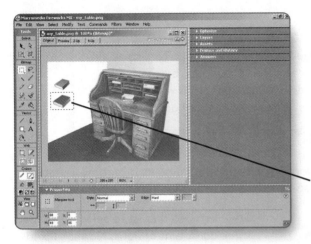

TIP

You can select Anti-alias from the Edge list to ensure that the selection marquee has smooth edges. This option is available with all the bitmap-selection tools.

2. Press and hold the mouse button and drag the mouse pointer to draw a selection marquee. The specific area of the bitmap object will be selected.

TIP

You can draw a square or circular selection marquee by holding Shift while you drag the mouse pointer with the Rectangular or Oval Marquee tool.

Using the Magic Wand Tool

There might be situations when you need to select a part of a bitmap that has a particular color range. For example, you have a bitmap image that has a white border, and you need to remove the white border. In such situations, you can use the Magic Wand tool to select the white border and remove it.

Using the Magic Wand tool, you can select all the contiguous pixels that are in a similar color range. This tool also provides you with a number of options, which are present in the Property Inspector. The following list explains these options:

- **Tolerance box**. Use this box to specify the color tolerance for the Magic Wand tool.

SELECTING PARTS OF BITMAP OBJECTS   79

> **TIP**
>
> *Color tolerance* is the value that specifies a color range for the pixels to be included in the selection marquee. A lower tolerance value will cause fewer pixels to become a part of the selection, as compared to a higher tolerance value.

- **Edge list**. Use this list to specify the edge type for the selection.
- **Feather amount box**. Use this box to specify the amount of feather to be applied to the selection. This box becomes available only if you specify the edge type as Feather.

To select a part of a bitmap object based on a color range, follow these steps:

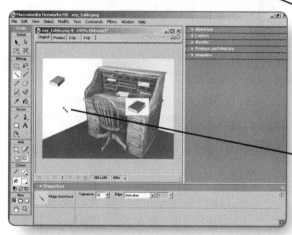

1. Click on the Magic Wand tool in the Tools panel. The shape of the mouse pointer will change to a magic wand.

2. Make the required changes to the tolerance level and edge type in the Property Inspector.

3. Click on the color that you want to select. All the surrounding pixels that are in the same color range will be selected.

CHAPTER 6: WORKING WITH BITMAPS

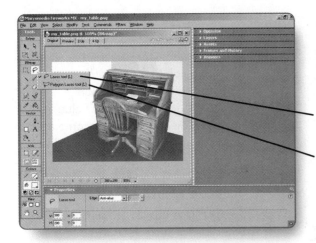

Working with Lasso Tools

You use the Lasso tool to draw freeform selection areas. Fireworks MX provides you with two types of Lasso tools:

- **Lasso tool**. This tool allows you to draw a freehand selection area.
- **Polygon Lasso tool**. This tool allows you to draw a selection area by plotting points.

> **NOTE**
> See Chapter 2, "Getting Started with Fireworks MX," to learn more about accessing tools from a tool group.

The Property Inspector provides the following options to set the Lasso tool:

- **Edge list**. Use this list to specify the edge type for the selection.
- **Feather amount box**. Use this box to specify the amount of feather to be applied to the selection. This box becomes available only if you select Feather as the edge type from the Edge list.

Using the Lasso Tool

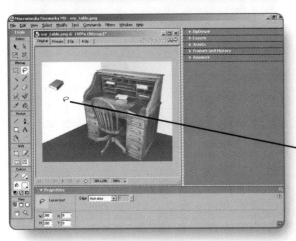

To draw a freehand selection area using the Lasso tool, follow these steps:

1. Click on the Lasso tool in the Tools panel. The shape of the mouse pointer will change to a lasso pointer.

SELECTING PARTS OF BITMAP OBJECTS 81

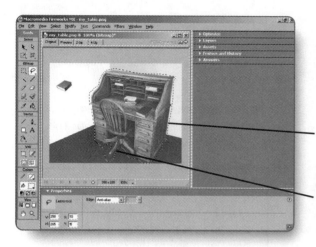

> **NOTE**
> I will refer to this pointer as the Lasso tool pointer.

2. Press and hold the mouse button and drag the mouse pointer around the area to be selected.

3. Release the mouse button when you've covered the area to be selected. A freehand selection marquee will appear around your selection.

Using the Polygon Lasso Tool

You might want to create a straight-edged freeform selection marquee instead of the continuous marquee that is created using the Lasso tool. For example, you might need to select a book in your graphic. In such situations, you use the Polygon Lasso tool. This tool allows you to define the perimeter of the area to be selected by repeatedly plotting points.

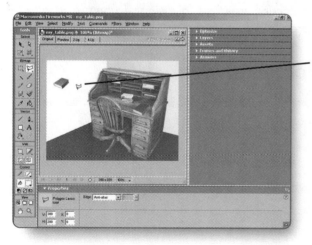

To draw a freehand selection area using the Polygon Lasso tool, follow these steps:

1. Click on the Polygon Lasso tool in the Tools panel. The shape of the mouse pointer will change to a polygon.

> **NOTE**
> I will refer to this pointer as the Polygon Lasso tool pointer.

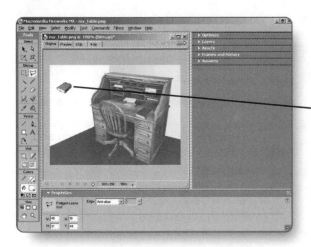

2. Click on the document to plot the points that define the perimeter of the selection area. The object will appear selected.

3. Double-click on the document or click on the first point that you plotted. The selection area will be closed.

> **TIP**
>
> You can move the selection marquee that you created in two ways. First, point with any of the selection tools within the selection marquee. Then, press and hold the mouse button and drag the mouse pointer. Second, use the arrow keys on the keyboard to move the marquee.

The selection area that you create by using the selection tools may not be precise. For example, it does not cover the entire area that is to be selected. In such situations, you need to modify the selection area. The following section provides details on modifying the selection area.

Modifying the Selection Marquees

Fireworks MX allows you to make precise selection areas by modifying a marquee drawn using any of the selection tools. The following list explains the ways in which you can edit selection marquees:

- By adding to or subtracting from a selection marquee
- By inverting an existing selection marquee
- By feathering edges of a selection marquee

Now you'll learn these techniques in detail.

- To add to an existing selection marquee, press and hold Shift and then draw another marquee. The newly selected area will also become a part of the selection marquee.

SELECTING PARTS OF BITMAP OBJECTS   83

- To subtract from an existing selection marquee, press and hold Alt and then draw another marquee covering the part to be removed. The selection marquee will be modified accordingly.

> **TIP**
> You can press and hold Alt and Shift to create a new marquee that covers just the intersecting area of two existing marquees.

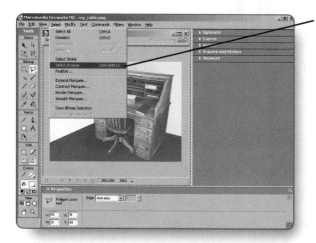

- To invert a selection marquee, click on Select and then choose Select Inverse from the drop-down menu that appears.

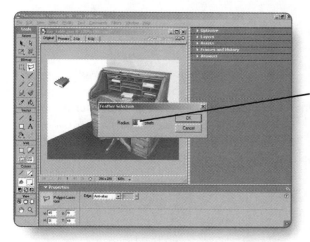

You can apply feather to selection edges to create a selection marquee with smooth edges, which blends very well with the surrounding image area.

- To give feather to a selection marquee, click on Select and then choose Feather from the drop-down menu that appears. Enter a feather amount in the Feather dialog box that opens.

> **TIP**
> You can also set the amount of feather for a selection marquee before creating it. To do so, use the feather setting available with all the selection tools.

You will also need to release the selection marquee after applying the desired changes to the selected area.

Any selected area can be deselected using any of the following ways:

- Create a new selection using any of the available selection tools.
- Click outside the selection marquee with the marquee or lasso tool.
- Click on Select and choose Deselect from the drop-down menu that appears.
- Press Ctrl+D.

Retouching Bitmap Objects

Fireworks MX provides various retouching tools that help you to enhance the appearance of a bitmap object. Fireworks MX provides various image-editing techniques, such as adjusting focus, lightening or darkening, smudging, and cloning. You will learn about these techniques in the following sections.

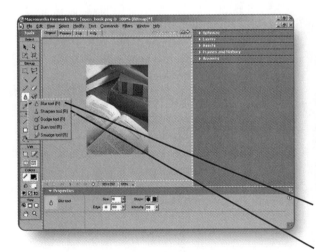

Adjusting Focus of a Bitmap Object

You might want to draw a viewer's attention to a specific part of an image. You can do so in two ways, either by sharpening that particular part or by blurring the rest of the image. Fireworks MX provides the following two tools that serve this purpose:

- **Blur tool**. Use this tool to blur parts of an image.
- **Sharpen tool**. Use this tool to sharpen parts of an image.

RETOUCHING BITMAP OBJECTS 85

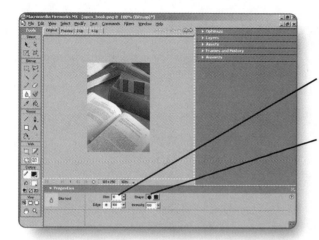

The following list explains the options available with Blur and Sharpen tools that can be set using the Property Inspector:

- **Brush tip size box**. Use this box to specify brush tip weight—either by typing in a value or by using the slider.

- **Shape button**. Use this button to select either a square or a round shape.

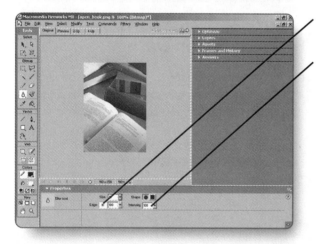

- **Edge softness box**. Use this box to specify the softness of the brush tip.

- **Intensity box**. Use this box to specify the intensity with which blurring or sharpening is applied to the image.

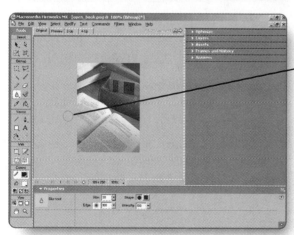

To use the Blur or Sharpen tool, follow these steps:

1. Click on the Blur or Sharpen tool in the Tools panel. The shape of the mouse pointer will change to depict the currently selected tool.

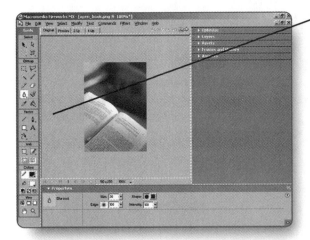

2. Press and hold the mouse button and drag the mouse pointer to apply the effect. The image will get blurred or sharpened accordingly.

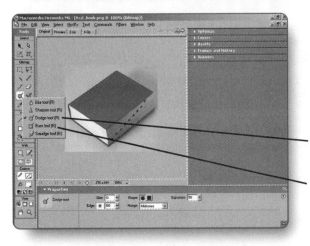

Making a Bitmap Object Lighter or Darker

Fireworks MX allows you to edit tones of an image. You can either lighten or darken parts of an image using the following tools:

- **Dodge tool**. Use this tool to lighten parts of an image.
- **Burn tool**. Use this tool to darken parts of an image.

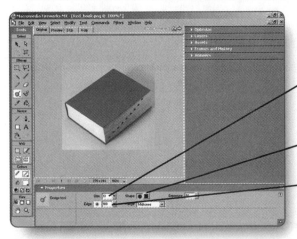

The following list explains the options available with Dodge and Burn tools that you can set using the Property Inspector:

- **Brush tip size box**. Use this box to specify brush tip weight—either by typing in a value or by using the slider.
- **Shape button**. Use this button to select either a square or round shape.
- **Edge softness box**. Use this box to specify the softness of the brush tip.

RETOUCHING BITMAP OBJECTS   87

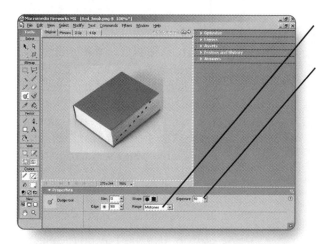

- **Range list**. Use this list to specify the tone to be affected.
- **Exposure box**. Use this box to specify the intensity with which blurring or sharpening is applied to the image.

A continuous tone image, such as a digital photograph, contains various color tones or ranges, as discussed in the following list:

- **Shadows**. The dark areas of the image.
- **Midtones**. The areas having a middle range of gray.
- **Highlights**. The light areas on the image.

You can select the desired color tone of an image to be affected by the Dodge and Burn tools, by using the Range list in the Property Inspector.

To use the Dodge or Burn tool, follow these steps:

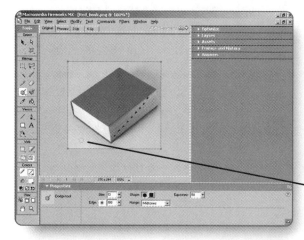

1. Click on the Dodge or Burn tool in the Tools panel. The shape of the mouse pointer will change to depict the currently selected tool.

2. Press and hold the mouse button and drag the mouse pointer to apply the effect. The image will be lightened or darkened accordingly.

CHAPTER 6: WORKING WITH BITMAPS

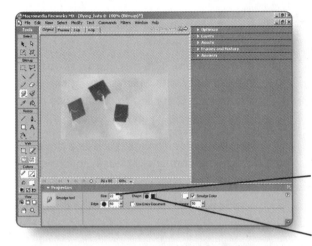

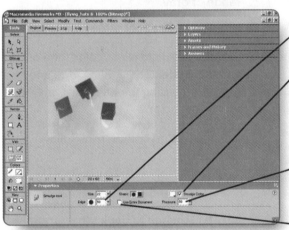

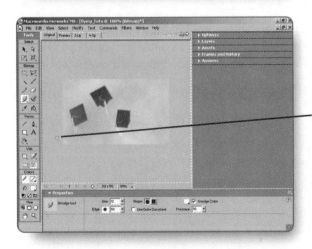

Smudging a Bitmap Object

Smudging on an image gives the effect of dragging a finger through wet paint. The Smudge tool picks the color of the pixel from where you start dragging and blends it with surrounding pixels in the direction in which you drag. The following list explains the options available with the Smudge tool:

- **Brush tip size box**. Use this box to specify brush tip weight—either by typing in a value or by using the slider.

- **Shape button**. Use this button to select either a square or a round shape.

- **Edge softness box**. Use this box to specify the softness of the brush tip.

- **Smudge Color check box**. Use this box to specify the color to be used while smudging, if you want a color other than the color of the pixel from where you start dragging.

- **Pressure box**. Use this box to specify the intensity with which smudging is applied to the image.

- **Use Entire Document check box**. Use this box to use the entire document as a whole for smudging, instead of just the currently selected bitmap object.

To use the Smudge tool, follow these steps:

1. Click on the Smudge tool in the Tools panel. The shape of the mouse pointer will change to depict the currently selected brush tip size.

RETOUCHING BITMAP OBJECTS 89

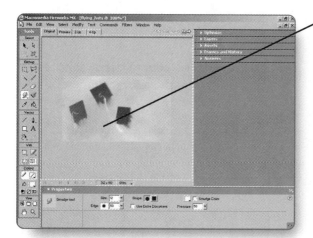

2. Press and hold the mouse button and drag the mouse pointer to apply the effect. The pixels will get smudged.

Cloning a Bitmap Object

You can clone images for fixing minor defects in scanned images, such as scratches on an old photograph or a blemish on a model's face. Cloning involves copying pixels from one part of the image and stamping them over the undesired parts. Cloning can also be used to create special effects. Fireworks MX provides you with the Rubber Stamp tool for cloning images. The following list explains the options available with the Rubber Stamp tool that you can set using the Property Inspector:

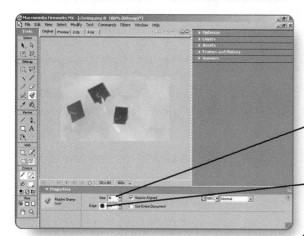

- **Stamp size box**. Use this box to specify the stamp size either by typing in a value or by using the slider.

- **Edge softness box**. Use this box to specify the softness of the brush tip.

- **Source Aligned check box**. Check this box to align the sampling cursor with the stamp cursor.

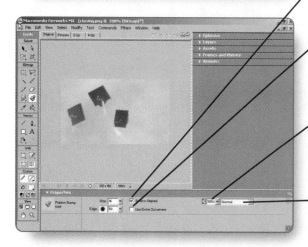

- **Use Entire Document check box**. Use this box to use the entire document as a whole for cloning, instead of just the currently selected bitmap object.

- **Opacity box**. Use this box to specify an opacity value for the stamped pixels— either by typing in a value or by using the slider.

- **Blend Mode list**. Use this list to specify a blending mode for stamping.

To clone pixels using the Rubber Stamp tool, follow these steps:

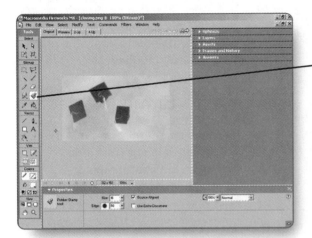

1. Click on the Rubber Stamp tool in the Tools panel. The shape of the mouse pointer will change to the sampling pointer.

> **TIP**
> You can adjust the shape and size of the stamp by using the Property Inspector.

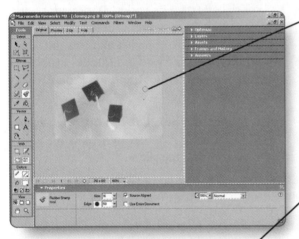

2. Click on the area from where you have to copy pixels. The shape of the mouse pointer will change to the crosshair pointer and another pointer will appear for the stamp. The shape of the stamp pointer will depend on the currently selected stamp size.

3. Point to the part of the image where you want to stamp the pixels.

4. Press and hold the mouse button and drag the mouse pointer to stamp pixels. The pixels from the source will be copied to this location.

> **TIP**
> To select a different part of the image as the source, press Alt and click on that particular area.

In this chapter, you learned the various bitmap tools available in Fireworks MX. You'll learn about controlling colors of bitmap and vector graphics in the next chapter.

7

Working with Colors

Fireworks MX allows you to manage colors in your documents by using various options available in the Tools panel, the Colors panel group, and the Property Inspector. The Tools panel contains various tools, such as the Paint Bucket tool, which allow you to apply color to both bitmap and vector objects. The Colors panel group contains the Swatches panel and the Color Mixer panel, which allow you to select or modify colors in your Fireworks MX document. The Property Inspector and the Tools panel provide you with several types of fill and stroke settings, such as brush strokes and pattern fills, that you can use to enhance the appearance of vector objects. You have already learned the basics of applying stroke and fill colors to vector objects by using the Property Inspector in Chapter 5, "Working with Vector Graphics." This chapter discusses the enhancements that you can make to stroke and fill colors.

In this chapter, you'll learn how to:

- Use the Tools panel for applying colors
- Use the Colors panel group
- Use fill options
- Use stroke options

Using the Tools Panel for Applying Colors

The Colors section in the Tools panel contains various controls for applying and modifying colors to vector objects. In addition, the Bitmap section in the Tools panel contains some tools that are used to apply colors to vectors as well as bitmap objects. These tools include the Eyedropper tool, the Paint Bucket tool, and the Gradient tool. In this section, you'll learn to use the Colors section of the Tools panel and the Eyedropper and Paint Bucket tools.

> **NOTE**
> The Gradient tool is used to apply gradient fills. Therefore, I'll cover this tool in "Using Fill Options" later in this chapter.

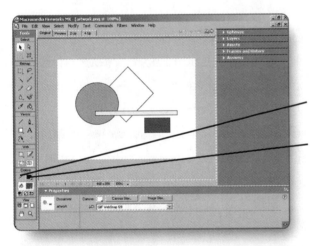

Using the Colors Section

The Colors section of the Tools panel contains the following controls:

- **Stroke Color icon.** Activates the Stroke Color box.

- **Stroke Color box.** Opens the Stroke Color pop-up window. You can use the Stroke Color pop-up window to set stroke options.

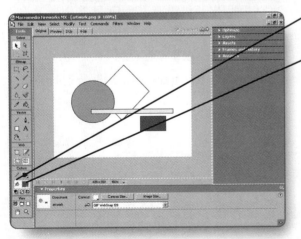

- **Fill Color icon.** Activates the Fill Color box.

- **Fill Color box.** Opens the Fill Color pop-up window. You can use the Fill Color pop-up window to set fill options.

> **TIP**
> You can also access the Stroke Color box and the Fill Color box from the Property Inspector.

USING THE TOOLS PANEL FOR APPLYING COLORS 93

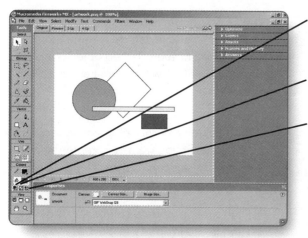

- **Set Default Stroke/Fill Color button**. Sets the stroke color to black and the fill color to white.

- **No Fill or Stroke button**. Sets the stroke or fill color to none.

- **Swap Stroke/Fill Colors button**. Interchanges the stroke and fill colors.

> **TIP**
> While working with vector objects, you can specify stroke and fill color settings before creating a vector object or after selecting an existing vector object.

Using the Eyedropper Tool

You use the Eyedropper tool to pick a color from anywhere inside the Fireworks MX document, and apply it to an object's fill or stroke color. This process of picking a color is also called *sampling*. You can set the Eyedropper tool to sample colors in the following ways:

- **1-Pixel**. Samples color of a single pixel.

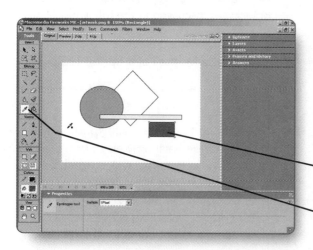

- **3x3 Average**. Samples the average color value of a 3x3 pixel area.

- **5x5 Average**. Samples the average color value of a 5x5 pixel area.

To sample a stroke or fill color and apply it to a vector object using the Eyedropper tool, follow these steps:

1. Select a vector object in the Document window.

2. Click on the Eyedropper tool in the Tools panel. The mouse pointer will change to an eyedropper.

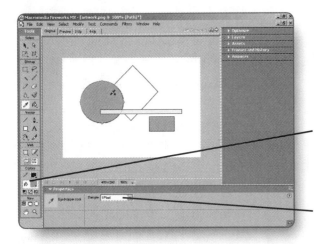

3a. Click on the Stroke Color icon in the Tools panel, if you want to sample the stroke color of the selected object. The Stroke Color box will become active.

OR

3b. Click on the Fill Color icon in the Tools panel, if you want to sample the fill color of the selected object. The Fill Color box will become active.

4. Set an appropriate color sampling setting in the Property Inspector.

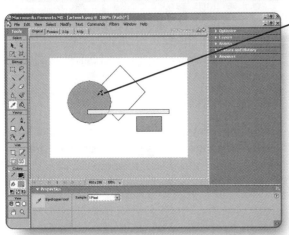

5. Click anywhere in a Fireworks MX document. The color will be sampled and applied to the stroke or fill of the selected object.

Using the Paint Bucket Tool

The Paint Bucket tool can be used to apply color to bitmap objects. In addition to the fill color options, the Property Inspector displays a few more options specific to the Paint Bucket tool. These options control the way Paint Bucket applies color to bitmap objects, as discussed in the following list:

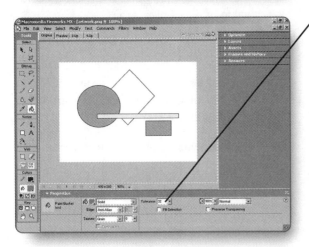

- **Tolerance box.** Specifies the color tolerance for the Paint Bucket tool.

> **NOTE**
>
> The color tolerance value specifies a color range for the pixels to be included in the area, which would be painted with the Paint Bucket tool. See "Using the Magic Wand Tool" in Chapter 6, "Working with Bitmaps," to learn more about color tolerance.

USING THE TOOLS PANEL FOR APPLYING COLORS 95

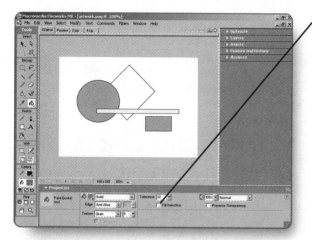

- **Fill Selection box.** Allows you to fill color in the selected areas of a bitmap object, instead of using the tolerance value, to calculate the area to be filled.

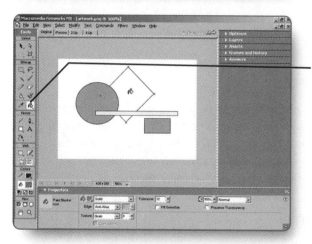

To apply color to a bitmap object using the Paint Bucket tool, follow these steps:

1. Click on the Paint Bucket tool in the Tools panel. The mouse pointer will change to a paint bucket.

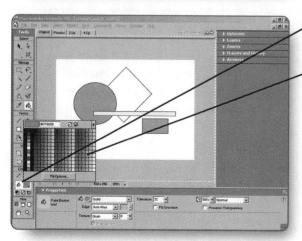

2. Click on the Fill Color box in the Tools panel. The Color pop-up window will open.

3. Select a color swatch from the Color pop-up window. The Fill Color box will display the selected color.

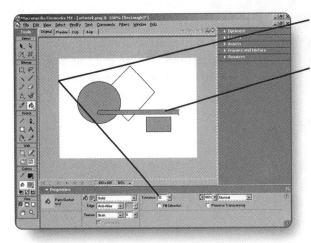

4. Make the appropriate settings for the Paint Bucket tool in the Property Inspector.

5. Click on the area to be filled. The fill color will be applied to the area.

Using the Colors Panel Group

The Colors panel group contains the Swatches panel and the Color Mixer panel. These panels allow you to apply color to a vector object. The following sections discuss these two panels in detail.

Exploring the Swatches Panel

The Swatches panel displays colors as swatches. A collection of all the color swatches is called a *color set* or a *swatch group*. You can change the stroke or fill color of a vector object by choosing any of the color swatches. Furthermore, you can also customize the Swatches panel according to your requirements. The following sections provide instructions on working with the Swatches panel.

Using the Swatches Panel

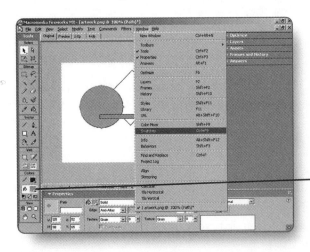

To apply stroke or fill color to a selected vector object, follow these steps:

1a. Click on the Stroke Color icon in the Tools panel, if you want to change the stroke color of the selected object. The Stroke Color box will become active.

OR

1b. Click on the Fill Color icon in the Tools panel, if you want to change the fill color of the selected object. The Fill Color box will become active.

USING THE COLORS PANEL GROUP   97

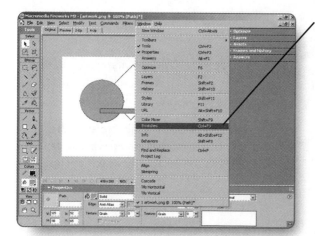

2. Select Swatches from the Window menu. The Swatches panel will open.

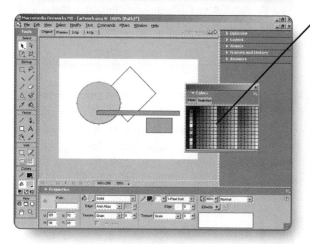

3. Click on any of the swatches in the Swatches panel. The selected color will be applied to the object.

Modifying the Swatches Panel

Fireworks MX allows you to change the color set that appears in the Swatches panel as well as individual color swatches. The following subsections provide instructions on modifying the Swatches panel.

MODIFYING A SWATCH GROUP

There might be a situation when you want to restrict the colors that you are using in a document to a particular color set. For example, you might want to use only the default Windows System colors. In such a situation, you can load the required color set in the Swatches panel.

CHAPTER 7: WORKING WITH COLORS

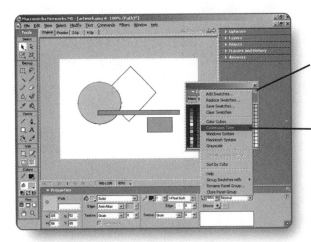

To select a swatch group, follow these steps:

1. Click on the Options menu icon in the Swatches panel. The Swatches panel Options pop-up menu will appear.

2. Select any of the available swatch groups. The Swatches panel will display the swatches in the selected swatch group.

> **TIP**
> Some of the available swatch groups are Color Cubes, Continuous Tone, Macintosh System, Windows System, and Grayscale.

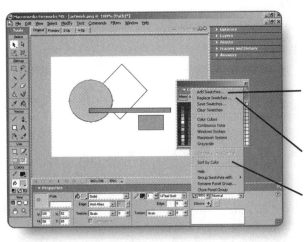

The Swatches panel Options pop-up menu also provides several other options that allow you to arrange or modify the swatch group, as discussed in the following list:

- **Add Swatches**. Appends swatches from a custom swatch group to the current swatches.

- **Replace Swatches**. Loads a custom swatch group in the Swatches panel.

- **Sort by Color**. Sorts the swatches in the Swatches panel according to their color values.

USING THE COLORS PANEL GROUP

ADDING SWATCHES

You can add colors to an existing swatch group as well as remove colors from it. To add a color to the current color set, follow these steps:

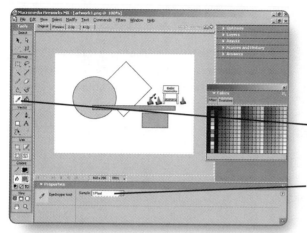

1. Click on the Eyedropper tool in the Tools panel. The mouse pointer will change to an eyedropper.

2. Select a sample setting for the Eyedropper tool in the Property Inspector.

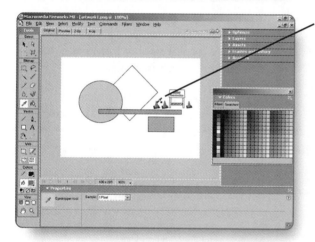

3. Click on the color to be added in the Document window.

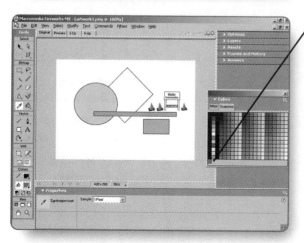

4. Click on the empty space after the last swatch in the Swatches panel. The sampled color will be added to the Swatches panel.

CHAPTER 7: WORKING WITH COLORS

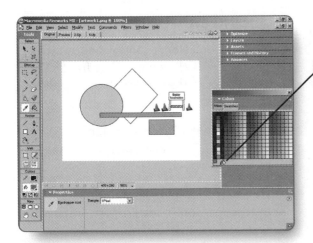

TIP
When you point to empty space after the last swatch in the Swatches panel, the shape of the mouse pointer changes to a paint bucket.

REMOVING SWATCHES

To remove a color swatch from the current color set, follow these steps:

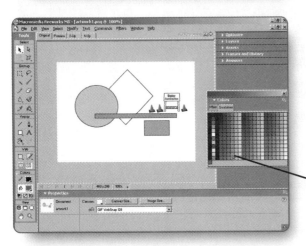

1. Press and hold Ctrl and move the mouse pointer to a swatch in the Swatches panel. The mouse pointer changes to a scissor.

2. Click on the swatch. The swatch is removed from the color set.

NOTE
You can't undo the addition or deletion of a swatch from the Swatches panel.

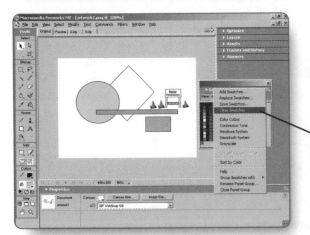

TIP
Select Clear Swatches from the Swatches panel Options pop-up menu to remove all the swatches from the Swatches panel.

USING THE COLORS PANEL GROUP 101

Using the Color Mixer Panel

You can use the Color Mixer panel to create new colors and apply them to objects. Before you learn to create colors, however, you need to understand the basics of *color models*.

Understanding Color Models

A *color model* is a scheme for calculating color values. The following list describes the color models available in Fireworks MX:

- **RGB**. Creates colors by combining varying values of Red, Green, and Blue. These values can range from 0-255 for each of the three RGB color components. If you set red, green, and blue to 0, you'll get black. Similarly, if you set red, green, and blue to 255, you'll get white.

- **Hexadecimal**. Expresses RGB color values in the hexadecimal number system. For example, white is expressed as 000000 and black as FFFFFF.

- **CMY**. Creates colors by combining varying values of Cyan, Magenta, and Yellow. These values can range from 0-255 for each of the three CMY color components. If you set cyan, magenta, and yellow to 0, you'll get white. Similarly, if you set cyan, magenta, and yellow to 255, you'll get black.

- **HSB**. Creates colors based on the Hue, Saturation, and Brightness values. Hue represents the color, and can have a value ranging from 0 to 360 degrees. Saturation represents the purity of the color, and can have a value ranging from 0% to 100%. Brightness represents the relative lightness or darkness of the color, and can have a value ranging from 0% to 100%.

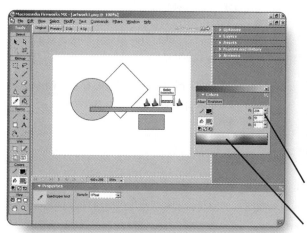

- **Grayscale**. Creates colors in shades of gray by using a percentage of black.

Applying Colors Using the Color Mixer

To apply colors by using the Color Mixer panel, you can perform any of the following tasks:

- Create a color by entering values for the selected color model's components.

- Pick a color from the color bar.

CHAPTER 7: WORKING WITH COLORS

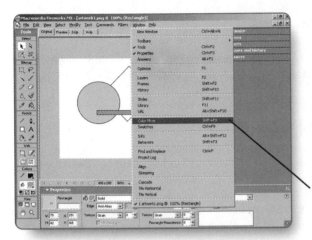

In the following subsections, you'll learn to perform both the tasks.

CREATING AND APPLYING COLORS BY USING A COLOR MODEL

To create and apply a color to a selected object by using a color model, follow these steps:

1. Select Color Mixer from the Window menu. The Color Mixer panel will open.

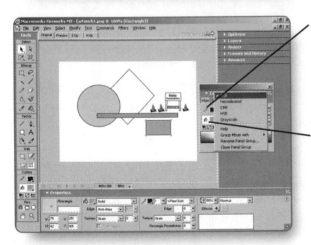

2a. Click on the Stroke Color icon in the Color Mixer panel, if you want to change the stroke color of the selected object. The Stroke Color box will become active.

OR

2b. Click on the Fill Color icon in the Color Mixer panel, if you want to change the fill color of the selected object. The Fill Color box will become active.

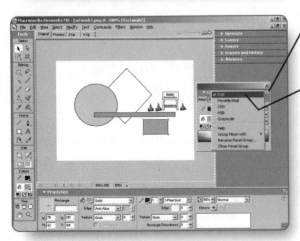

3. Click on the Options menu icon in the Color Mixer panel. The Color Mixer panel options will appear.

4. Select a color model. The Color Mixer panel will display the settings for the selected color model.

USING THE COLORS PANEL GROUP   103

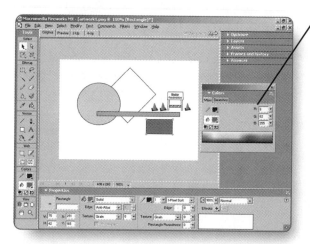

5. Enter appropriate values for each color model component. The new color will be created and applied to the selected object.

APPLYING COLORS BY USING THE COLOR BAR

To apply color to a selected object by using the color bar, follow these steps:

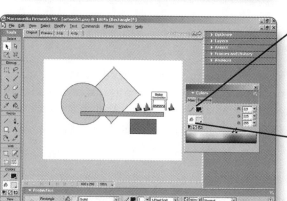

1a. Click on the Stroke Color icon in the Color Mixer panel, if you want to change the stroke color of the selected object. The Stroke Color box will become active.

OR

1b. Click on the Fill Color icon in the Color Mixer panel, if you want to change the fill color of the selected object. The Fill Color box will become active.

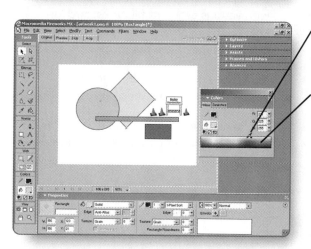

2. Move the mouse pointer to the color bar. The mouse pointer will change to an eyedropper.

3. Click anywhere in the color bar to pick a color. The color that you pick will be applied to the selected object.

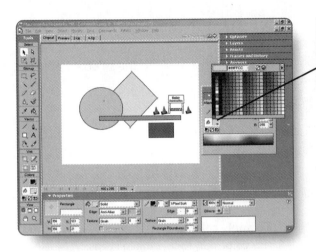

TIP
You can also use the Fill and Stroke color box in the Color Mixer panel to apply color using the color pop-up window.

Using Fill Options

Fireworks MX allows you to apply a fill color to vector objects. In addition, you can apply colors to bitmap objects. You can also apply gradients, patterns, and Web-safe fills to vector objects. Furthermore, you can transform the fill applied to a vector object. In this section, you will learn to apply various types of fills to an object.

Applying Gradient Fills

A gradient is a smooth transition between colors. The Bitmap section of the Tools panel contains the Gradient tool. It allows you to apply gradient fills to vector and bitmap objects. Fireworks MX provides you with various gradient fill types, such as linear and radial. You can access these gradient types from the Property Inspector.

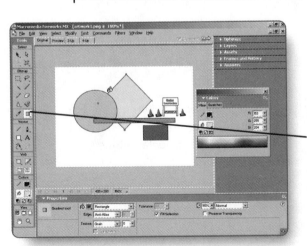

To apply a gradient fill by using the Gradient tool, follow these steps:

1. Select the Gradient tool from the Tools panel. The mouse pointer will change to a paint bucket.

USING FILL OPTIONS **105**

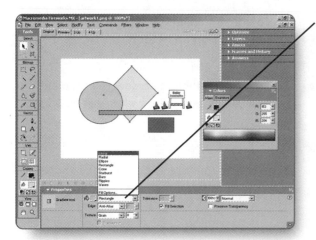

2. Select a gradient type from the Gradient type list in the Property Inspector.

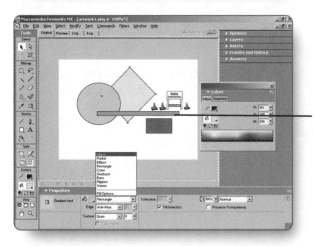

3a. Click on the selected bitmap area with the Gradient tool. The gradient will be applied to the selected area of a bitmap.

OR

3b. Click on a vector object with the Gradient tool. The gradient will be applied to the vector object.

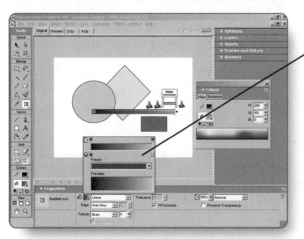

Editing Gradients

You can modify the current gradient by using the Edit Gradient pop-up window. You can access the Edit Gradient pop-up window by clicking on a Fill Color box either in the Tools panel or the Property Inspector.

To edit a gradient by using the Edit Gradient pop-up window, follow these steps:

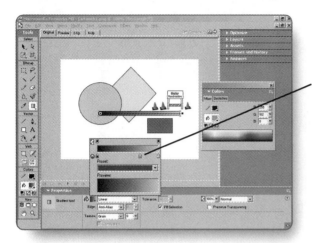

1. Click on the area below the gradient preview. A new color swatch will be added.

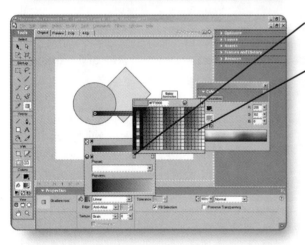

2. Click on the color swatch. The Color pop-up window will open.

3. Select a color from the Color pop-up window. The color of the color swatch will change.

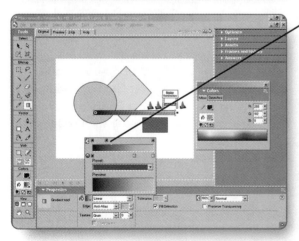

4. Click on the area above the gradient preview. An opacity swatch will be added.

NOTE

An *opacity swatch* defines the opacity of the gradient.

USING FILL OPTIONS   107

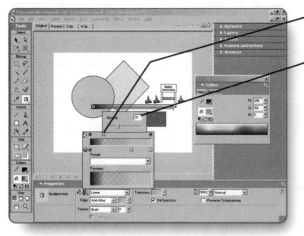

5. Click on the opacity swatch. The Opacity box appears.

6. Set a value for opacity. The transparency of an opacity swatch will change: A higher value of opacity will make the gradient more opaque and a lower value will make it more transparent.

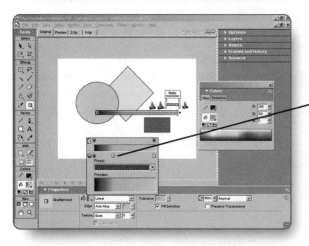

7. Click and drag a color or opacity swatch outside the Edit Gradient pop-up window. The swatch will be removed from the gradient.

8. Drag the color and opacity swatches left or right. The transition between colors will change accordingly.

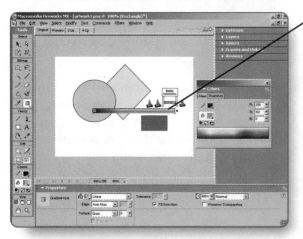

9. Press Enter when you have finished editing the gradient. The new gradient will become the active gradient.

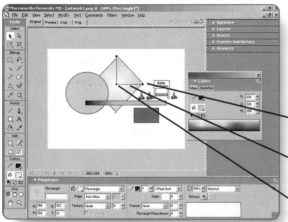

Transforming Gradient Fills

When an object with a gradient is selected, a set of handles appears on the object. These handles can be used to transform the object's fill, as discussed in the following list:

- **The Square Handle.** Click and drag to modify the width of the fill.
- **The Connecting Lines.** Click and drag to rotate the fill.
- **The Round Handle.** Click and drag to move the fill.

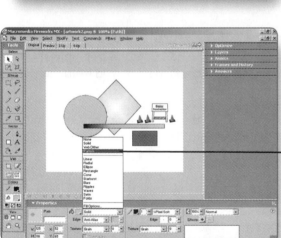

Applying Pattern Fills

Fireworks MX allows you to apply a bitmap image as a pattern to vector objects. To apply a pattern fill to a selected vector object, follow these steps:

1. Select Pattern from the Fill Options category list in the Property Inspector.

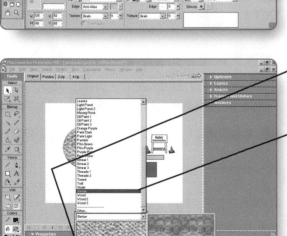

2. Click on the Color pop-up box in the Tools panel. The Pattern name pop-up window will open.

3. Select a pattern from the Pattern name pop-up list. The Pattern name pop-up window will display the preview of the selected pattern and the pattern will be applied to the selected object.

USING FILL OPTIONS 109

> **TIP**
> You can transform the pattern fills just as you transform the gradient fills. See the section, "Transforming Gradient Fills," earlier in this chapter for more information.

Applying Web Dither Fills

You should ideally use Web-safe colors while creating graphics for the Web. *Web-safe colors* is a set of default colors that Web browsers use regardless of the platform. But there might be a situation where you have to use a non Web-safe color. In such a situation, you can apply Web Dither fills. A *Web Dither fill* creates an illusion of a non Web-safe color, when viewed from a distance, by using two Web-safe colors.

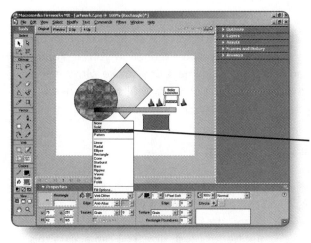

> **NOTE**
> See Chapter 11, "Optimizing and Exporting Graphics," to learn more about dithering and Web-safe colors.

To apply a Web Dither fill to a selected object containing a non Web-safe color, select Web Dither from the Fill category list in the Property Inspector.

You can use the Web Dither fill Options pop-up window to edit Web Dither fill options. Click on the Color pop-up box either in the Property Inspector or the Tools panel to open the Web Dither fill pop-up window.

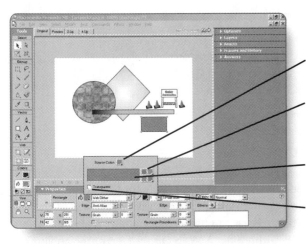

The Web Dither fill pop-up window displays the following options:

- **Source Color box**. Displays the non Web-safe color.
- **Web-safe Dither Color boxes**. Displays the two Web-safe colors that are used to create the Web Dither fill.
- **Preview Area**. Displays a preview of the Web Dither fill.
- **Transparent check box**. Creates an illusion of a transparent dither fill.

Using Stroke Options

Fireworks MX provides you with a wide variety of stroke options, such as calligraphy and watercolor, which helps you create visually appealing strokes. In addition to these options, there are some advanced stroke options available that allow you to create custom strokes. Furthermore, you can adjust the placement of a stroke with respect to the object outline to control the overall size of the object to which the stroke is applied. In the following sections, you'll learn about these advanced options.

Using Advanced Stroke Options

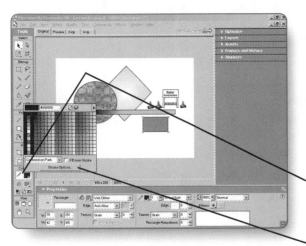

Fireworks MX provides you with the Edit Stroke dialog box. It allows you to precisely define stroke characteristics, such as the number of brush tips. You can access this dialog box either from the Tools panel or from the Property Inspector.

To open the Edit Stroke dialog box using the Tools panel, follow these steps:

1. Click on the Stroke Color box in the Tools panel. The Stroke Color pop-up window will appear.

2. Click on the Stroke Options button. The Stroke Options pop-up window will open.

USING STROKE OPTIONS 111

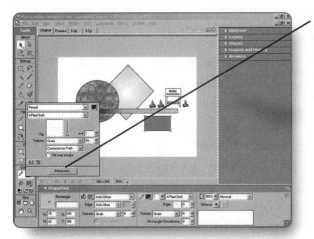

3. Click on the Advanced button. The Edit Stroke dialog box will open.

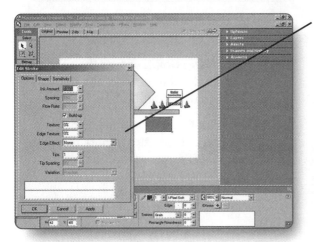

The Edit Stroke color box provides you with the Options, Shape, and Sensitivity tabs. In the following subsections, you'll learn to use these tabs.

NOTE
You can view the effect of the settings that you make in the preview area of the Edit Stroke dialog box.

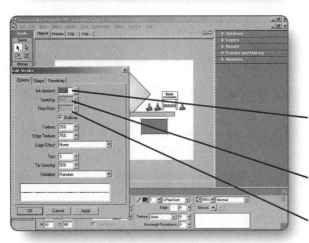

Exploring the Options Tab

The Options tab contains various general stroke options, as discussed in the following list:

- **Ink Amount box**. Specifies the percentage amount of the ink that the stroke uses.

- **Spacing box**. Specifies the distance between the brush marks in the stroke.

- **Flow Rate box**. Controls the speed at which the brush stroke is applied.

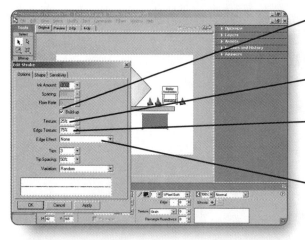

- **Build-up check box**. Causes brush strokes to overlap to create dense strokes.
- **Texture box**. Controls the amount of texture that is applied to the stroke.
- **Edge Texture box**. Controls the amount of texture that is applied at the stroke edges.
- **Edge Effect list**. Contains a list of special effects that can be applied to the stroke edges.

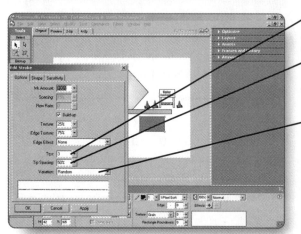

- **Tip box**. Specifies the number of tips that the brush stroke will have.
- **Tip Spacing box**. Controls the spacing of brush tips if more than one tip is specified using the Tip box.
- **Variation list**. Controls the color variation of brush tips if more than one tip is specified using the Tip box.

Exploring the Shape Tab

The Shape tab contains various options that control the shape of the brush tip, as discussed in the following list:

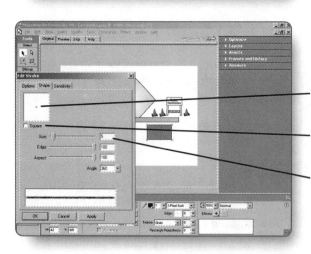

- **Tip Preview area**. Displays the effect of current shape settings on the brush tip.
- **Square check box**. Sets the brush tip to a square instead of circle.
- **Size box**. Specifies the size of the brush tip.

USING STROKE OPTIONS

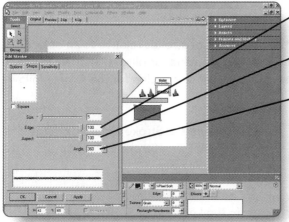

- **Edge box**. Controls the edge softness of the brush tip.
- **Aspect box**. Specifies the width of the brush tip.
- **Angle box**. Controls the brush tip angle.

Exploring the Sensitivity Tab

The Sensitivity tab contains options for controling the effect of speed and pressure on the stroke, when you are using a pressure-sensitive Wacom tablet and pen. These options are discussed in the following list:

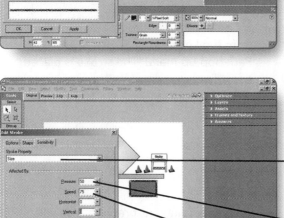

- **Stroke Property list**. Selects the stroke property that will be affected by the following options.
- **Pressure box**. Controls the effect of pressure on the selected property.
- **Speed box**. Controls the effect of drawing speed on the selected property.

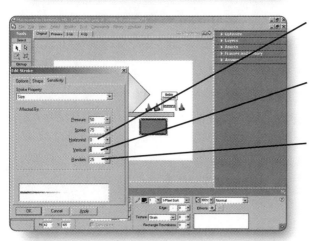

- **Horizontal box**. Controls the effect of horizontal drawing on the selected property.
- **Vertical box**. Controls the effect of vertical drawing on the selected property.
- **Random box**. Controls the overall randomness.

Placing Strokes

Fireworks MX allows you to specify the placement of strokes relative to an object's outlines. You can center the stroke to an object's outline, or place the stroke inside or outside an object's outline. To change the placement option for the stroke, follow these steps:

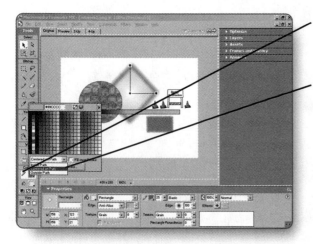

1. Click on the Stroke Color box in the Tools panel. The Stroke Color pop-up window will open.

2. Select the required placement option from the Location of Stroke Relative to Path pop-up menu. The stroke is placed accordingly.

In this chapter, you learned to apply colors to objects in your graphics. You will need to try out the options discussed in this chapter to see their effects. In the next chapter, you will learn to use text in your graphics.

8

Using Text in Graphics

A company can advertise its products by presenting a number of attractive images on its Web site. However, for presenting its profile, the company needs to use text. To retain the customer's interest, this text should be equally attractive. Fireworks MX enables you to use text in your graphics with ease. It gives you the option of typing the text on your own or importing it from some other file. You can format this text like you format text in most of the word processors. Additionally, you can combine text with paths and apply various effects to make the text attractive. In this chapter, you'll learn how to:

- Add text to a graphic
- Enhance the appearance of the text

Adding Text to a Graphic

Fireworks MX enables you to add text to a graphic in two ways:

- Using the Text tool
- Importing the text

In this section, you'll learn to add text by using both of these methods.

Using the Text Tool

Fireworks MX provides you with the Text tool to add text to a graphic. The text that you add to a Fireworks MX document is held in a rectangular container, called a text block. By default, the text block is autosizing, which means the size of the text block increases or decreases depending on the size of the text. However, Fireworks MX also provides you with the option of creating a fixed-width text block, which arranges the text depending on the width of the text block.

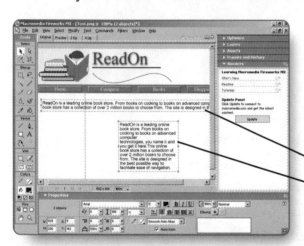

- Auto size text block
- Fixed-width text block

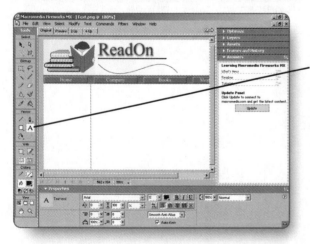

To add text to a graphic, follow these steps:

1. Click on the Text tool in the Tools panel. The shape of the mouse pointer will change to an I-beam.

> **TIP**
> You can also press T to select the Text tool.

ADDING TEXT TO A GRAPHIC   117

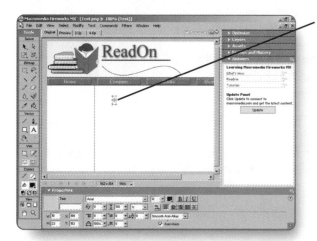

2a. Click on the document. An autosize text block will appear.

> **TIP**
>
> An auto size text block contains an empty circle in the top-right corner.

OR

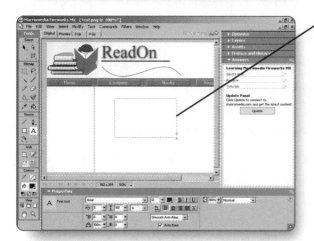

2b. Press and hold the mouse button and drag the mouse pointer to draw a marquee. A fixed-width text block will appear.

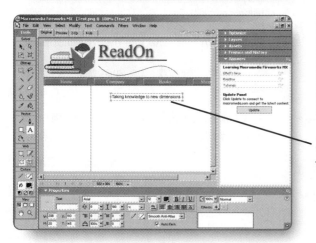

> **TIP**
>
> A fixed-width text block contains an empty rectangle in the top-right corner.

3. Type the text into the text block. The text will appear in the document.

> **TIP**
> To shuffle between an auto sizing and a fixed-width text block, double-click on the empty circle or rectangle in the upper-right corner.

In addition to typing text, Fireworks MX enables you to import text from other files. In the following section, you'll learn to import text.

Importing Text

You need to include some text related to your company in the company's official Web site. This text is available as an external file, such as RTF (Rich Text Format) or plain text. What will you do? You have three options:

- Type the entire text, which may not be efficient if the text is lengthy.

- Copy and paste the text from the file to the Fireworks MX document. However, doing so doesn't copy the formatting instructions.

- Import the file, which is quicker and does include formatting instructions.

Fireworks MX provides you with the option to import an RTF or an ASCII (plain text) file. If you import an RTF file, various formatting instructions, such as font, size, style, and alignment, are also copied. If you import an ASCII file, the text is set to the default font. This text has a font size of 12.

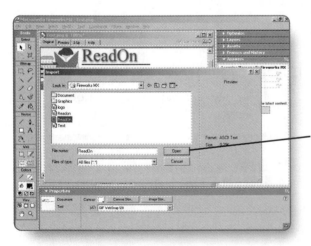

To import a file that contains text, follow these steps:

1. Click on File. The File menu will appear.

2. Click on Import. The Import dialog box will open.

3. Click on Open after you select the required file.

ENHANCING THE APPEARANCE OF TEXT 119

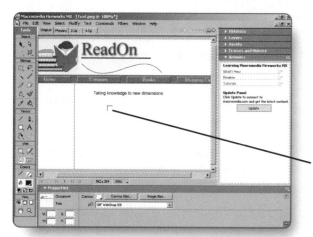

TIP

To view the text files, you may need to choose the All Files option from the Files of Type list in the Import dialog box.

The mouse pointer will change to the insertion pointer.

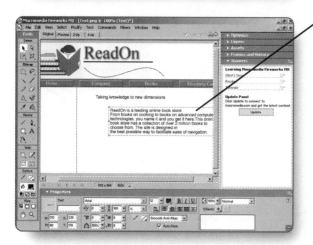

4. Click on the document. The text block containing the text from the file will appear.

After you have added text to a graphic, you may want to enhance its appearance. Fireworks MX provides a number of features that help you do so. I discuss these features in the next section.

Enhancing the Appearance of Text

Text forms an important part of a Web page. Therefore, to make your Web page appealing, you need to enhance the appearance of the text as well. Fireworks MX provides you with a number of options that enable you to modify text. For example, you can apply the bold or the italics style to mark important pieces of information, and make headings appear bigger than the rest. You can also change the alignment of text as per your requirements. In addition, you can specify spacing between characters and paragraphs. Last but not the least you can attach text to a path to make the text flow along the path.

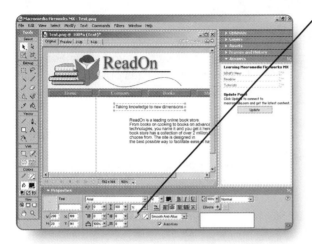

All the options to modify text are located in the Property Inspector. However, to view these options, you need to select a text block first.

In this section, you'll learn to format text. Then, you'll learn to specify spacing between characters. You'll also learn to apply stroke and fill to text. Finally, you'll learn to attach text to a path.

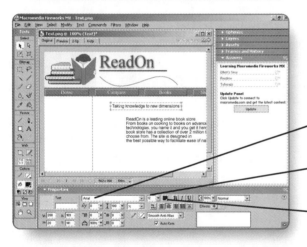

Formatting the Text

The Property Inspector contains a number of options, such as Font list and Size list, for formatting text. The following list explains these options:

- **Font list**. Use this list to specify a font for the text.

- **Size list**. Use this list to specify a size for the text.

- **Color box**. Use this box to specify a color for the text.

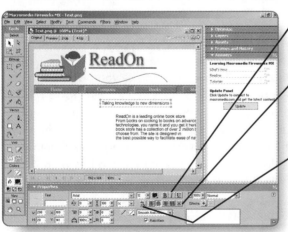

- **Bold, Italic, and Underline buttons**. Use these buttons to apply a suitable style to the text.

- **Alignment buttons**. Use these buttons to left-, right-, or center-align the text. You can also make the text justified and stretched.

- **Text Orientation button**. Use this button to specify an appropriate orientation for the text, such as horizontal left to right or horizontal right to left.

ENHANCING THE APPEARANCE OF TEXT   121

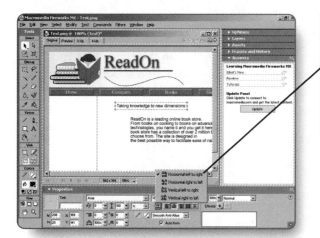

NOTE

When you click on the Text Orientation button, a pop-up menu appears. Select the appropriate option from this menu.

To format text, follow these steps:

1. Click on the text block. The text block will be selected.

TIP

Selecting a text block formats the entire text. However, if you need to format only selective text, you can use the Text tool to highlight the text and make the changes.

2. Make the required changes to font, size, style, alignment, and orientation. The appearance of the font will change.

TIP

You can also set these options by using the Text menu.

After you've formatted the text, you might want to improve its readability. The following section provides you details on specifying space settings for the text.

Spacing the Text

You can specify the amount of space to be inserted between the characters and between the lines of text. You can also specify space information about paragraphs. The Property Inspector contains a number of options that help you to do so. The following list explains these options:

- **Kerning box**. Use this box to specify the amount of space between characters. You can also use the adjacent slider to specify a value.

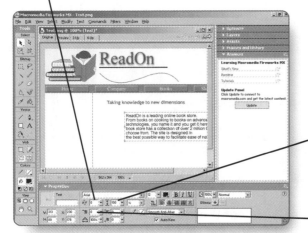

> **TIP**
> To specify spacing between two characters, select the Text tool and click between the characters. To specify spacing for a number of characters, select the characters by using the Text tool. Finally, to specify spacing for all the characters, select the text block.

- **Leading box**. Use this box to specify the amount of space between the adjacent lines of a paragraph. You can also use the adjacent slider to specify a value.

- **Paragraph Indent box**. Use this box to specify the indent value for the first line of a paragraph. You can also use the adjacent slider to specify a value.

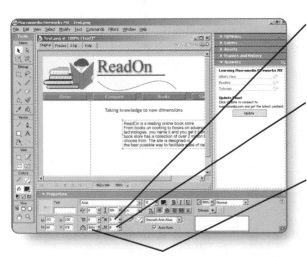

- **Space Preceding Paragraph box**. Use this box to specify the amount of space preceding a paragraph. You can also use the adjacent slider to specify a value.

- **Space After Paragraph box**. Use this box to specify the amount of space following a paragraph. You can also use the adjacent slider to specify a value.

- **Horizontal Scale box**. Use this box to expand or contract the width of your horizontal text. You can also use the adjacent slider to specify a value.

ENHANCING THE APPEARANCE OF TEXT   123

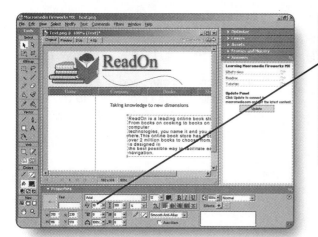

TIP
By default, each font that you use specifies the amount of space between characters. If you need to specify your own value, uncheck the Auto-Kern check box and specify a value in the Kerning box.

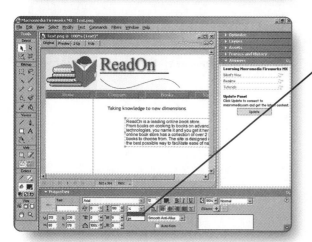

TIP
You can specify the leading value in percentage or pixels. To specify a unit of leading space, choose an appropriate value from the Leading Units list.

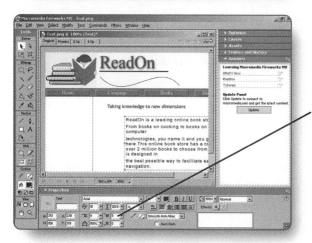

To specify the spacing for the text, follow these steps:

1. Click on the text block. The text block will be selected.

2. Enter appropriate values in the boxes mentioned previously and press Enter. The spacing of the text will change.

You can further enhance the appearance of the text by applying strokes and fills. The next section provides information about applying strokes and fills to text.

Applying Strokes and Fills to Text

You can apply strokes and fills to the text by using the Stroke color box and the Fill color box in the Tools panel. To apply stroke and fill to the text, follow these steps:

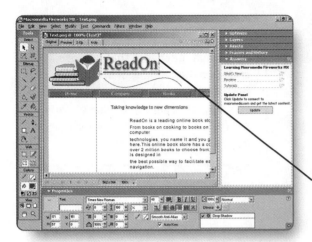

1. Click on the text block. The text block will be selected.

2. Click on the appropriate color in the Stroke color box. The stroke color of the text will change to the selected color.

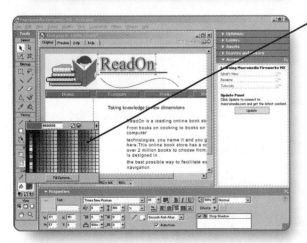

3. Click on the appropriate color in the Fill color box. The fill color of the text will change to the selected color.

ENHANCING THE APPEARANCE OF TEXT   125

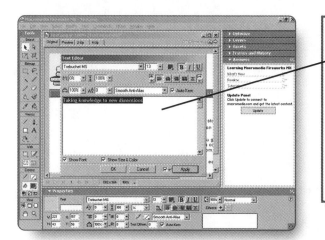

TIP

Fireworks MX also provides a Text Editor that provides you with most of the options present in the Property Inspector. It is advantageous to use the Text Editor if the text is substantial. To display the Text Editor, click on the Editor menu item in the Text menu.

You may want to further highlight the text in your graphic by making it appear different. For example, making your company slogan look wavy on the Web site is an effective way of attracting the attention of the visitor. The next section provides information on making text appear in different shapes.

Attaching Text to a Path

You can make the text in your document appear curvy to make it appear different from the rest. For doing so, create a path, which represents a curve, and then attach text to this path. See "Drawing Curved Paths" in Chapter 5, "Working with Vector Graphics," for more information on creating paths. To attach text to a path, follow these steps:

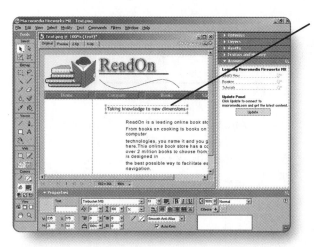

1. Click on the text block. The text block will be selected.

2. Press and hold Shift and click on the path. The path will also be selected.

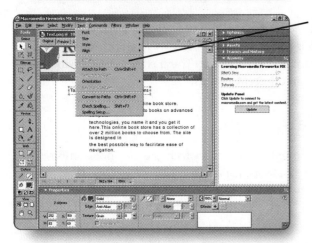

3. Click on the Text menu. The Text menu will appear.

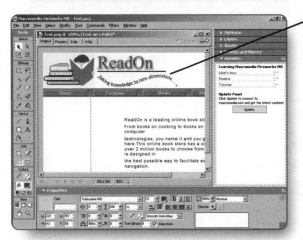

4. Click on Attach to Path. The text will be attached to the path.

TIP
Alternatively, select both the text and the path, and then press Ctrl+Shift+Y to attach them.

ENHANCING THE APPEARANCE OF TEXT   127

A spelling error will white wash all the hard work that you did to make graphics appealing. Fireworks MX provides you with a Check Spelling command to check spelling in your graphic. The next section explains how to use this command.

Spell-Checking the Text

To spell check the text, follow these steps:

1. Click on the text block. The text block will be selected.

2. Click on the Text menu. The Text menu will appear.

3. Click on Check Spelling. A message box prompting you to select a dictionary will open.

4. Click on OK. The Spelling Setup dialog box will open.

5. Click on the appropriate dictionary. A check will be placed in the corresponding check box.

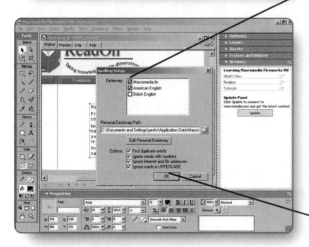

TIP
If you have specified the dictionary once, the Check Spelling dialog box will open instead of the Spelling Setup dialog box. You can change the settings later by clicking on the Spelling Setup menu item in the Text menu.

6. Click on OK after you select a dictionary. The Check Spelling dialog box will open.

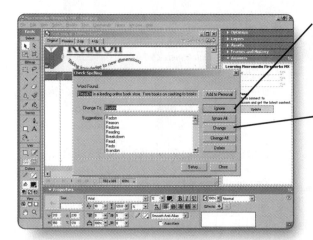

7a. Click on Ignore. The suggested change will not be applied, and the spell checker will move to another word.

OR

7b. Click on Change. The spelling will change.

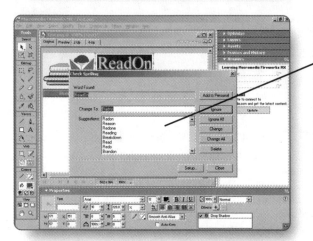

TIP

Step 7 will be repeated for all incorrect spellings. After the spelling check is complete a message box opens, informing you that the current selection has been spell checked, and asks you whether you would like to continue with the rest of the document.

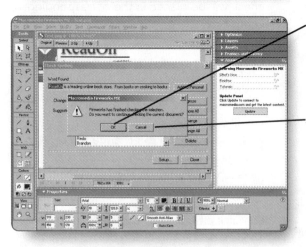

8a. Click on OK. The spell checker will continue checking the text in the remaining document.

OR

8b. Click on Cancel. The spell checker will end.

With this you have learned to use text in your graphics. In the next chapter, you'll learn about the concepts of layers.

9

Managing Images Using Layers

The dictionary meaning of layer is a coating on a surface, and it is not much different in Fireworks MX's perspective. You can also consider layers to be a stack of papers, which you can see through. In Fireworks MX, each object that you create resides on a layer. The layers help you arrange these objects in a desired manner. For example, you may need to create a graphic for the Web site of a company selling books. The graphic should contain a collage of books in the background and there should be some text related to the company on top of it. Moreover, this image should also contain the logo of the company and various buttons to navigate the site. Thanks to layers, you can place each object—such as the collage of books, logo, and buttons—on a different layer and arrange these layers to make your graphic mind-blowing.

To ease your working with layers, Fireworks MX provides the Layers panel. In this chapter, you'll learn how to:

- Use the Layers panel
- Create new layers
- Work with layers

Using the Layers Panel

Fireworks MX provides the Layers panel that helps you work with layers in your graphics. The Layers panel lists all the layers present in your graphic starting from the topmost layer moving down to the bottom layer. The Layers panel also contains another layer named *Web Layer*. This layer contains various Web objects, such as hotspots and slices, and is the topmost layer. An interesting fact about the Web Layer is that you cannot change its position.

> **TIP**
> See Chapter 12, "Creating Hotspots and Slices," for more information about hotspots and slices.

The Layers panel represents each layer as a folder, which further contains all the objects present on the layer. For example, a Buttons layer may contain all the button objects present in the graphic. The beauty of Fireworks MX is that you can use the Layers panel to work with either the entire layer or with a specific object present on the layer. In this chapter, I will refer to the layer folder as a layer and the objects contained in this folder as objects.

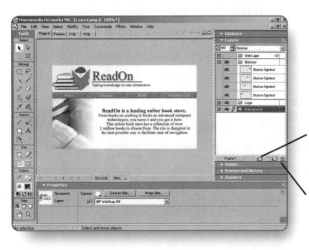

The Layers panel lets you create, delete, and manipulate layers. To do so, it provides you with buttons and the Layers Options pop-up menu. The following list explains some of the most commonly used buttons present in the Layers panel:

- **New/Duplicate Layer**. Use this button to create new layers or duplicate the existing ones.
- **Delete Selection**. Use this button to delete the selected layer or object.

Looking at the Layers Options Pop-up Menu

The Layers Options pop-up menu provides options to create, duplicate, show, and hide layers. To display this pop-up menu, click on the icon in the upper-right corner of the Layers panel.

The following list explains some of the options present in the Layers Options pop-up menu:

- **New Layer**. Creates a new layer.
- **Duplicate Layer**. Duplicates a selected layer.
- **Share This Layer**. Shares a layer across all the frames in a graphic.
- **Flatten Selection**. Merges all the selected vector and bitmap objects with the bitmap object that lies next to the bottommost selected object.
- **Single Layer Editing**. Protects the objects on layers, other than the selected one, from unwanted changes.
- **Hide All**. Hides all the layers.
- **Show All**. Shows all the layers.
- **Lock All**. Locks all the layers to prevent them from editing.
- **Unlock All**. Unlocks all the layers.

In the next section, I discuss creating new layers.

Creating Layers

In Fireworks MX, whenever you create an object, it is created on the currently selected layer. All the objects that you create further are added on to this layer, and will be displayed under the folder representing the layer. For example, you have a layer named Background in your graphic and it contains a bitmap object. Now, if you add a rectangle object, by default it will be added to the Background layer.

However, Fireworks MX provides you with an option of creating different objects on different layers. To do so, you need to create a new layer. When you create a new layer it is added on the top of the currently selected layer.

132 CHAPTER 9: MANAGING IMAGES USING LAYERS

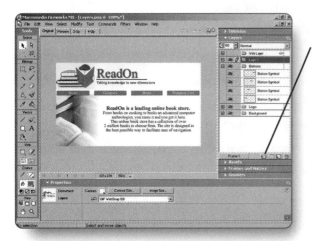

To create a new layer, follow these steps:

1. Click on the New/Duplicate Layer button at the bottom of the Layers panel. A new layer will appear, in the Layers panel, at the top of the selected layer.

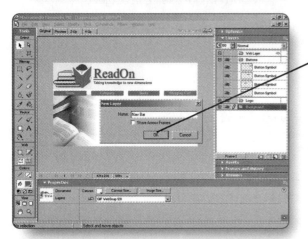

TIP

Alternatively, you can choose New Layer from the Layers Options pop-up menu. When you do so, the New Layer dialog box opens. Specify a name for the new layer and click on OK. The new layer is added on top of the currently selected layer.

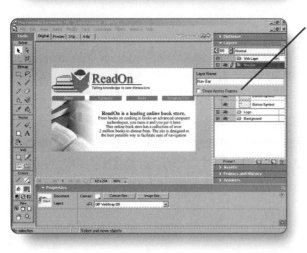

2. Double-click on the layer that you added in Step 1. A pop-up window will appear.

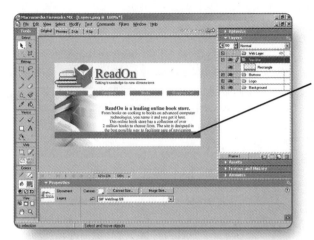

3. Type a new name in the Layer Name box and press Enter. The name of the layer will change.

4. Create the object that you require. The object will be added to the new layer that you created.

5. Double-click on the object in the Layers panel. A text box will open.

6. Type a name for the object in the text box and press Enter. The name of the object will change.

After you've created layers, you may need to manipulate them. In the next section, I discuss manipulating layers.

Working with Layers

Your graphic may contain a number of layers and each layer may contain different objects. For example, one layer contains navigation buttons and the other contains background images. While trying to move the button, you may move the background images. To avoid such situations, you can lock the layer containing background image and then move the button. Not only that, you can hide all the layers that contain objects not required at the time of creating the graphic. You can also duplicate existing layers and make changes to them. In the following sections, I discuss all these ways of manipulating images.

Locking a Layer

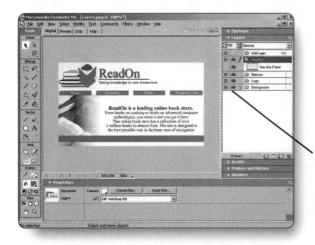

You lock a layer to prevent making any unintentional changes to its content. When you lock a layer, you cannot edit or select the objects present on the layer. To lock a layer, follow these steps:

1. Click on the square to the left of the layer name. A padlock icon will appear.

2. Click on any object present on the layer that you locked in Step 1. The object will not be selected indicating that the layer is locked.

3. Make appropriate changes to other objects. The changes will appear in the graphic. For example, I moved the rectangle upwards.

Arranging a Layer

You may want to change the order of layers. For example, you create a book on one layer and after that you add another layer and create a table. The layer containing the table lies on top of the one containing the book. Hence, the book is not visible. In such situations, you can arrange layers by changing their order. To change the order of layers, follow these steps:

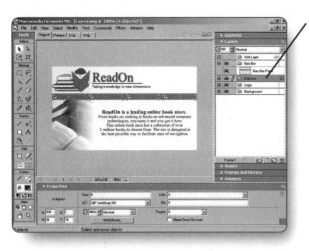

1. Click on the required layer in the Layers panel. The layer will be selected.

WORKING WITH LAYERS 135

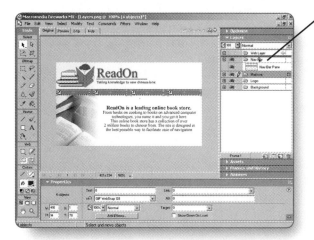

2. Press and hold the mouse button and drag the mouse pointer. The selected layer will move to the new position.

Compositing Images

After you arrange the layers in your document, some objects may overlap each other. In such situations, you can change the transparency or specify the color interaction of these objects. This process of specifying the transparency and color interaction of objects in an image is called *compositing*. To help you create composite images, the Layers panel contains the Opacity slider and the Blend Mode list. The following list explains the functions of these elements:

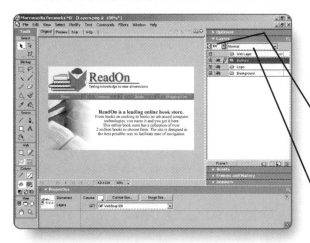

- **Opacity slider**. Specifies the transparency of an object. A value of zero makes an object 100% transparent and vice versa.

- **Blend Mode list**. Specifies how the color of an object appears when placed on top of another object.

To specify the transparency and color interaction settings, follow these steps:

1. Select the object in the Document window.

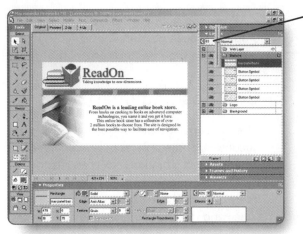

2. Specify an appropriate transparency setting by using the Opacity slider in the Layers panel.

3. Specify an appropriate color interaction by using the Blend Mode list in the Layers panel.

Hiding a Layer

If an image contains a large number of objects, it is difficult to work with. For example, while working with the background image, the buttons may hide some portion of the image. In such situations, you can hide the layer containing the buttons and then continue working with the background image. To hide a layer, follow these steps:

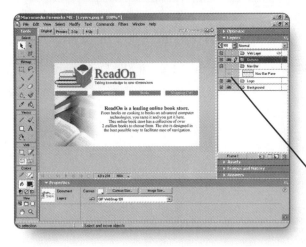

1. Click on the eye icon to the left of the layer name in the Layers panel. The eye icon will disappear and all the objects on the corresponding layer will be hidden.

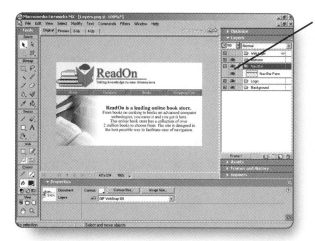

2. Click on the same location as in Step 1. The eye icon and all the objects on the corresponding layer will appear again.

Duplicating a Layer

Your graphic contains the image of a book. You need another copy of the book with some minor modifications. In such situations, you can duplicate the layer containing the book and then make changes to the duplicated copy. To duplicate a layer, follow these steps:

1. Click on the layer name in the Layers panel. The layer will be selected.

> **TIP**
>
> If you need to copy only one object contained in a layer, you can select the object in the Layers panel and then perform the following steps.

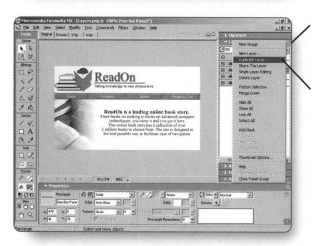

2. Click on the icon in the upper-right corner of the Layers panel. The Layers Option pop-up menu will appear.

3. Click on Duplicate Layer. The Duplicate Layer dialog box will open.

CHAPTER 9: MANAGING IMAGES USING LAYERS

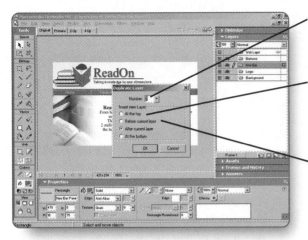

4. Type the number of copies you require in the Number box. The specified number of copies of the layer will be created.

5a. Click on At the top. The duplicated layer will become the topmost layer.

OR

5b. Click on Before current layer. The duplicated layer will be placed on top of the current layer.

OR

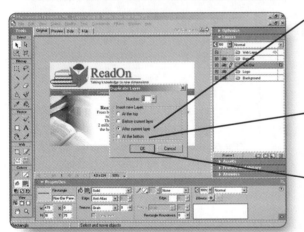

5c. Click on After current layer. The duplicated layer will be placed below the current layer.

OR

5d. Click on At the bottom. The duplicated layer will become the bottommost layer.

6a. Click on OK. The duplicate layer will be created.

OR

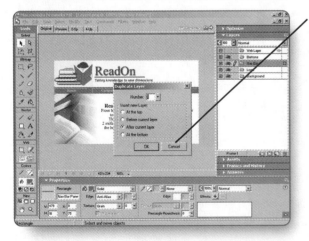

6b. Click on Cancel. The duplicate layer will not be created.

WORKING WITH LAYERS 139

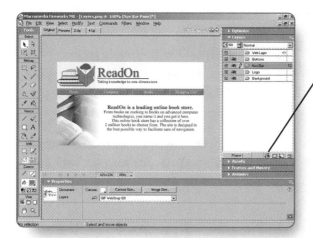

TIP

Alternatively, to create a duplicate layer, drag the appropriate layer to the New/Duplicate Layer button. In such a situation, a duplicated layer is created on top of the current layer.

Deleting a Layer

If you don't require the objects present on a layer, you can delete the layer. To delete a layer, follow these steps:

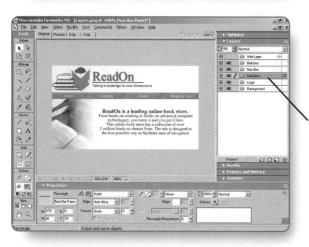

1. Click on the layer or object name in the Layers panel. The layer will be selected.

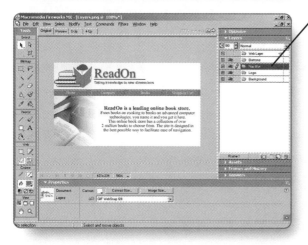

2. Click on the Delete Selection button. The selected layer or object will be deleted.

TIP

Alternatively, you can drag the appropriate layer or object to the Delete Selection button.

With this, you have learned to use layers in your graphics. You can now go ahead and create complex graphics easily.

10

Enhancing the Appearance of Objects

You created an image after putting in a lot of sweat. However, the image looks flat and lacks visual appeal. For example, in your Web site, you created a number of buttons, but they lack body and, hence, are difficult to identify. To make these buttons livelier, you can apply effects to them. Fireworks MX provides you with a number of effects and styles that help you make images vivid. It also allows you to use some third-party filters, such as Eye Candy 4000 LE, to make your graphics eye-catching. In addition to applying effects, you can combine two images to make them appear as one by applying masks. In this chapter, you'll learn how to:

- Use effects to beautify objects
- Use masks to combine objects

Using Effects to Beautify Objects

Fireworks MX provides you with a number of categories of effects, such as Bevel and Emboss, Blur, Shadow and Glow, and Sharpen. Each category further contains a number of effects. For example, the Bevel and Emboss category contains the Inner Bevel and Outer Bevel effects that help add a 3-D look to an object. In Fireworks MX, these effects are called *Live Effects* because you can edit them at any time.

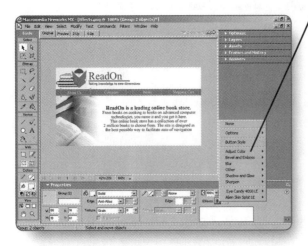

You use the Property Inspector to apply effects to an object. It contains the Add Effects button, which displays the Effects pop-up menu, from which you can select the required effect. I will discuss various options available in the Effects pop-up menu when they are used.

In Fireworks MX, you can apply the existing effects or edit the effects and save them as styles for later use. You can also apply third-party image filters to the images for additional effects. In this section, I will discuss all these tasks.

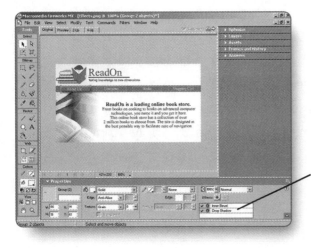

Applying Effects to an Object

The Effects pop-up menu contains various categories of effects. To apply an effect to an object, first select the object and then select the appropriate effect. You can apply multiple effects to an object.

All the effects that you apply to an object are added to the Effects list, which is also present in the Property Inspector.

USING EFFECTS TO BEAUTIFY OBJECTS   143

To apply effects to an object, follow these steps:

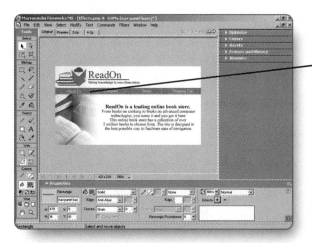

1. Click on the object. The object will be selected.

2. Click on the Add Effects button in the Property Inspector. The Effects pop-up menu will appear.

3. Point to the required effect category and click on appropriate effect.

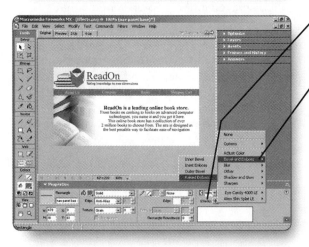

The effect will be applied to the object with some default settings and a pop-up window will appear displaying these settings.

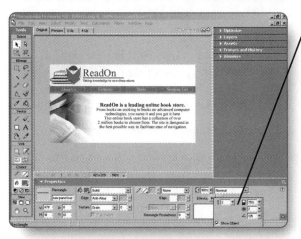

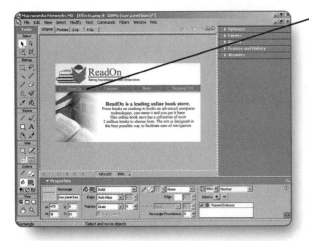

4. Click on the Document window. The pop-up window will close and the applied effect will appear in the Effects list.

After you apply an effect to an object, you may need to edit it. I discuss editing an effect in the next section.

Editing Effects

Each effect has settings, and when you apply an effect to an object, it contains the default settings. These settings are displayed in the pop-up window that appears when you apply an effect. However, the default settings may not suit your taste. In such situations, you can edit the applied effect. To edit the effects applied to an object, follow these steps:

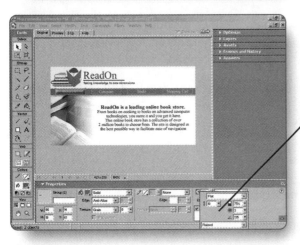

1. Double-click on the effect in the Effects list. A pop-up window will appear.

TIP
Alternatively, to display the pop-up window, you can click on the i icon next to the name of the effect in the Effects list.

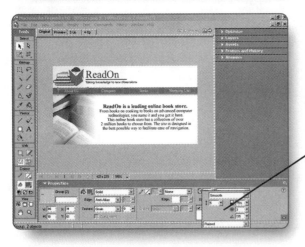

2. Make appropriate changes to the effect. The effect will be applied to the selected object.

3. Close the pop-up window.

Fireworks MX lets you save the effects that you create for reuse later. I discuss saving effects in the next section.

Removing Effects

You may need to remove the effect that you applied to an object. You can do so by:

- Turning off the effect
- Deleting the effect

To turn off the effect applied to an object, follow these steps:

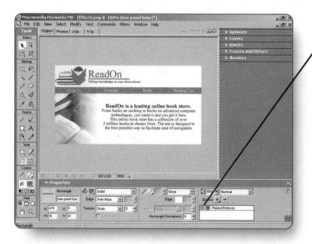

1. Select the object.

2. Click on the check mark next to the effect name in the Edit and arrange effects list present in the Property Inspector. A red cross mark indicates that the effect has been removed from the object.

To reapply the effect, click on the red cross mark and a check mark will appear, thus indicating that the effect has been applied.

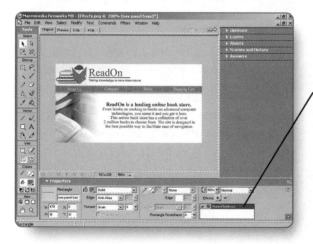

To delete the effect applied to an object, follow these steps:

1. Select the object.

2. Click on the effect in the Edit and arrange effects list. The effect will be selected.

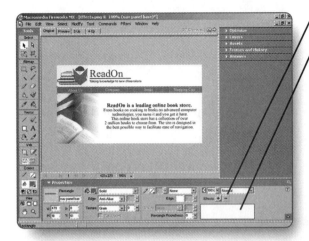

3. Click on the Delete Effects button.

The effect will be removed from the selected object and will be deleted from the Effects list.

Saving Effects for Future Use

You may need to apply a similar effect to a number of objects. For example, you applied the Inner Bevel effect to a button with some customized settings. You need to apply this effect to all the buttons that you create. In such situations, you can save this effect as a style and use it later. To save effects, follow these steps:

1. Select the object with the effects you need to save.

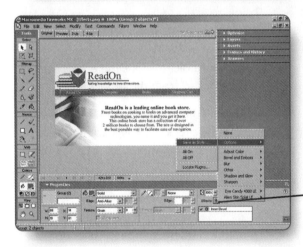

2. Click on the Add Effects button. The Effects pop-up menu will appear.

3. Point to Options and click on Save as Style. The New Style dialog box will open.

4. Type an appropriate name for the effect in the Name box. The effect will be saved with the specified name.

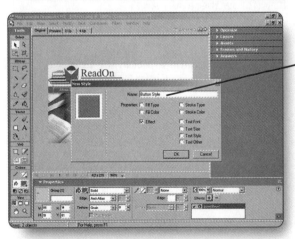

USING EFFECTS TO BEAUTIFY OBJECTS 147

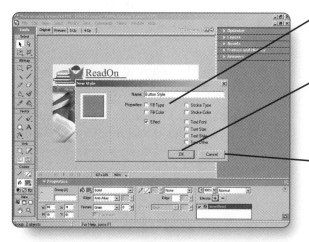

5. Make appropriate changes to the properties of the effect. The effect will be saved with the selected properties.

6a. Click on OK. The effect will be saved as a style.

OR

6b. Click on Cancel. The effect will not be saved.

Now, you might be eager to learn how to apply the style that you created. I discuss the steps to apply a style in the following section.

Applying Styles

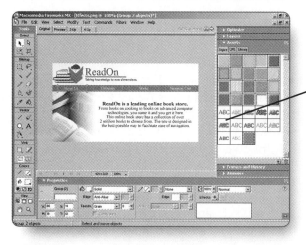

You use the Styles panel to apply styles to an object. This panel lists the styles that you create along with some predefined styles.

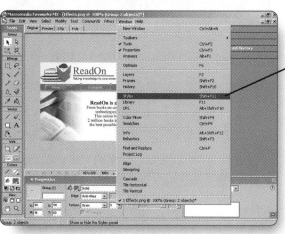

To apply a style to an object, follow these steps:

1. Select the object.

2. Click on Window. The Window menu will appear.

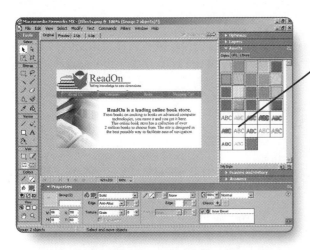

3. Click on Styles. The Styles panel will open.

4. Click on the required style. The style will be applied to the selected object.

In addition to effects and styles, Fireworks MX also provides third-party filters to apply additional effects. I discuss these filters in the next section.

Applying Third-party Filters

You might have come across images showing a running man or a paper blowing away by wind. You too can create such effects by using filters. In Fireworks MX, the Filter menu provides you with several categories of filters, such as Adjust Color, Blur, and Sharpen. You will be glad to know that most of these filters are also available as effects in the Effects pop-up menu. However, there is a marked difference between the two. When you apply a filter to a vector object, the object is converted to a bitmap, which is not the case with effects.

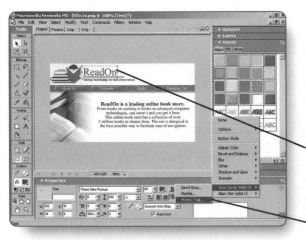

In this section I will discuss the Eye Candy 4000 LE filter. The Eye Candy 4000 LE filter is comprised of a number of filters, such as Bevel Boss, Marble, and Motion Trail. Using the Motion Trail filter, you can make an object appear to be moving. To use Eye Candy 4000 LE, follow these steps:

1. Select the object.

2. Click on the Add effects button. A pop-up menu will appear.

3. Point to Eye Candy 4000 LE and click on Motion Trail. The Motion Trail window will open.

USING EFFECTS TO BEAUTIFY OBJECTS 149

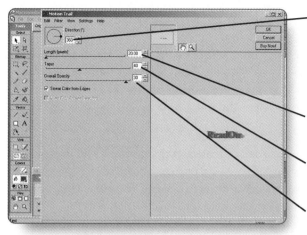

4. Type the direction value in the Direction box. The direction of the trail of the selected object will change. Also, the preview of the selected object will change as per the settings.

5. Type the length value in the Length box. The length of the trail will change.

6. Type the taper value in the Taper box. The trail will be tapered accordingly.

7. Type the opacity value in the Overall Opacity box. The opacity of the trail will change.

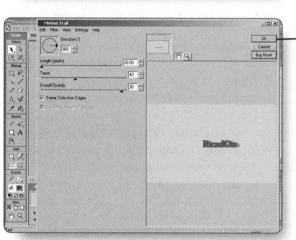

8. Click on OK.

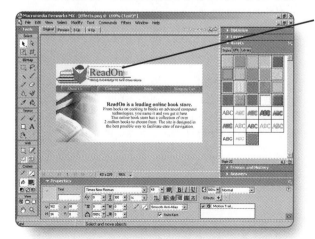

The motion trail effect will be applied to the selected object.

Using Masks to Combine Objects

While surfing the Web, you will probably come across eye-catching images with wavy corners or a big image cut out in the shape of text. Creating masks lets you do that with ease. Masking is a technique in which an object (lying on the top) filters the underlying object. The object on top is called the *mask object*, and the two objects together form the *mask group*.

Fireworks MX allows you to create two types of masks, bitmap masks and vector masks. As the name suggests, a *bitmap mask* uses a bitmap object to mask the underlying object. A *vector mask* uses a vector object to mask the underlying object. In this section, I discuss both these masking techniques.

Creating Bitmap Masks

You can use the Layers panel to create a bitmap mask. The Layers panel contains the Add Mask button. When you click this button, an empty mask object is added on top of the object being masked. Also, a mask thumbnail, which represents the empty mask object, appears in the Layers panel. You can then use any bitmap tool to enhance the mask object. The Property Inspector then displays the properties of the mask object and the bitmap tool you select.

You can apply a bitmap mask using its alpha channel or grayscale appearance.

- Applying a bitmap mask using its alpha channel creates a cut-out effect on the object being masked.

- Applying a bitmap mask using the grayscale appearance determines the visibility of the mask object by the lightness of the pixels. Light pixels display the mask object, whereas the dark pixels hide the mask object and display the background. By default, the bitmap masks are applied using their grayscale appearance.

USING MASKS TO COMBINE OBJECTS   151

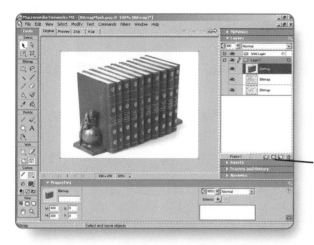

To create a bitmap mask, follow these steps:

1. Select the underlying object.

2. Click on Window. The Window menu will appear.

3. Click on Layers. The Layers panel will open.

4. Click on the Add Mask button present at the bottom of the Layers panel. A canvas sized mask object will be added on top of the selected object. Also, a mask thumbnail will appear in the Layers panel.

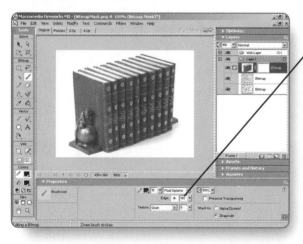

5. Select a bitmap tool.

6. Optionally, make changes to the settings of the bitmap tool.

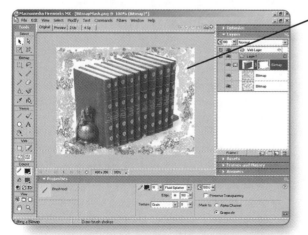

7. Create any shape on the mask. The underlying object will be masked.

Creating Vector Masks

A vector mask uses a vector object to apply the mask. A vector mask can be applied using its path outline or grayscale appearance. When you create a vector mask using its path outline, the underlying object appears cut out. Applying a vector mask using its grayscale appearance is similar to the bitmap masks.

152 CHAPTER 10: ENHANCING THE APPEARANCE OF OBJECTS

See the section "Creating Bitmap Masks" to learn more about grayscale appearance.

To create a vector mask, follow these steps:

1. Select a vector tool. For example, I selected the Ellipse tool.

2. Create a shape.

3. Select the shape that you created.

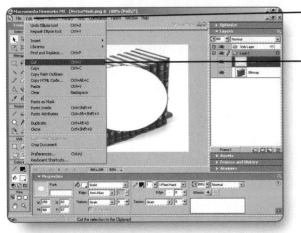

4. Click on Edit. The Edit menu will appear.

5. Click on Cut. The selected shape will disappear.

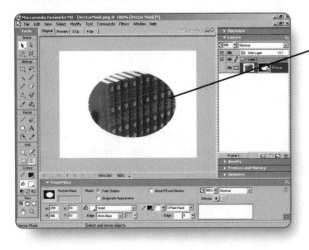

6. Select the object being masked.

7. Choose Paste as Mask from the Edit menu. The underlying object will be cut out in the shape of the vector object. Also, a mask thumbnail with a pen icon will appear in the Layers panel.

You can now enhance the appearance of the objects in your graphics by applying effects and styles to them. Furthermore, you can merge two images by using the concept of masking. In the next chapter, you will learn to optimize and export graphics.

11

Optimizing and Exporting Graphics

The major concern that Web developers and designers face is the time that a Web page takes to download on a viewer's Web browser. To ensure faster download, you should keep the size of your Web pages as small as possible. As digital media constitutes a major part of the Web page, you need to focus on reducing the file size of the images that you use on the Web page. At the same time, you have to maintain a fair level of image quality. This process of striking a balance between file size and image quality is known as optimization. Fireworks MX allows you to optimize graphics and export them to the Web.

In this chapter, you'll learn how to:

- Optimize graphics
- Export graphics
- Use the Export Wizard

Optimizing Graphics

Fireworks MX provides you with effective control for compressing the file size of an image while maintaining an optimum display quality. The process of optimizing graphics for the Web using Fireworks MX involves the following steps:

- Choosing a suitable file format.
- Selecting appropriate color and compression settings for the chosen file format.
- Previewing the optimization settings.

You can try various optimization settings and preview their effects on the image quality and file size. Once you are satisfied with the resultant optimized image, you can go ahead and export it.

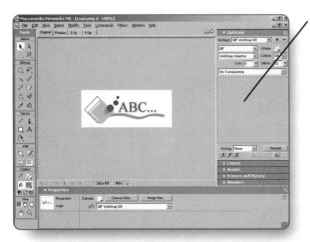

Fireworks MX provides you with the Optimize panel to optimize graphics for the Web.

The various optimization settings that you can apply using the Optimize panel include specifying a color palette, compression setting, and other file format specific settings.

In the following section, you will learn the details of various steps involved in the optimization process.

Choosing a File Format

The first step for optimizing an image is to decide on a suitable file format, depending on the image's characteristics, such as colors and tone. Some of the commonly used file formats for Web graphics are described in the following list:

- **GIF or Graphics Interchange Format**. The GIF file format supports 8-bit color and can have a maximum of 256 colors. You should use this file format for exporting images that have flat colors, such as cartoons, line arts, and logos. In addition to still GIF graphics, you can create animated GIF files.

- **JPEG or Joint Photographic Experts Group**. The JPEG file format supports 24-bit color. You should use this format for exporting continuous-tone images, such as photographs.

OPTIMIZING GRAPHICS   155

- **PNG or Portable Network Graphic.** The PNG file format supports up to 32-bit color. You can specify 8-bit color depth for exporting flat color images, and 24-bit or 32-bit color depth for exporting continuous-tone images. Depending on the color depth, the file format is known as PNG-8 (for 8-bit color depth), PNG-24 (for 24-bit color depth), or PNG-32 (for 32-bit color depth). However, only the browser versions above Netscape Navigator 4.04 and Microsoft Internet Explorer 4.0 support the PNG file format.

The GIF and PNG file formats support transparency. As a result, you can view the background of the Web page through the transparent areas in these images. However, the JPEG file format doesn't support this feature.

> **NOTE**
> The PNG file format that is used to export images is different from the PNG file format that is used by Fireworks MX to save its source files. The Fireworks MX PNG source files save application-specific information, which is not preserved in the exported PNG files.

> **TIP**
> In addition to the previously discussed file formats for Web graphics, Fireworks MX allows you to export graphics in other formats, such as TIFF and BMP.

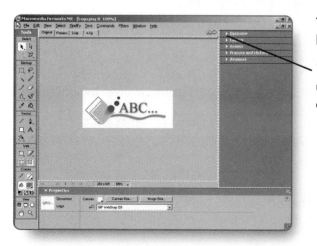

To specify a file format for the graphic to be exported, follow these steps:

1. Click on the expander arrow on the upper-left corner of the Optimize panel to expand it. The Optimize panel expands.

156 CHAPTER 11: OPTIMIZING AND EXPORTING GRAPHICS

2. Click on the Export File Format list in the Optimize panel. A pop-up list of the supported file formats appears.

3. Select a file format from the pop-up list. The Optimize panel will display the options related to the selected file format.

Specifying File Format Specific Settings

Each file format has certain settings related to it, such as color palette and transparency. You can set these options by using the Optimize panel. In the following subsections, you will learn about the settings for each file format.

GIF and PNG-8 Optimization Settings

The Optimize panel allows you to apply the following optimization settings to GIF and PNG-8 file formats:

- Color palette
- Transparency
- Compression
- Interlacing

You will learn more about these settings in the following subsections.

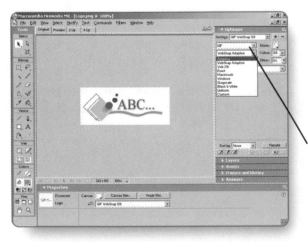

MAKING COLOR PALETTE SETTINGS

The GIF and PNG-8 file formats allow you to precisely optimize the number of colors used in the exported image. You can reduce the file size of a graphic by reducing the number of colors used in the graphic.

You can reduce the number of colors in a graphic by selecting an appropriate color palette (for the image) from the Indexed Palette list in the Optimize panel.

> **TIP**
> If you are creating a graphic to be used on the Web, try using as few colors as possible.

The following list describes various color palettes available in the Indexed Palette list:

- **Adaptive**. Contains the actual colors present in the image.
- **Web 216**. Contains the colors that are common to both Windows and Mac system palettes. These colors are also referred to as Web-safe colors.
- **WebSnap Adaptive**. Converts colors that are close to Web-safe colors to their closest Web-safe alternatives.
- **Exact**. Contains the exact colors used in the image. You can use this palette only if the image has a maximum of 256 colors. Otherwise, you need to use the Adaptive color palette.
- **Macintosh**. Contains the standard Mac OS system colors.
- **Windows**. Contains the standard Windows system colors.
- **Grayscale**. Contains a maximum of 256 shades of gray.
- **Black and White**. Contains only black and white color.
- **Uniform**. Creates a palette by uniformly sampling colors from RGB pixel values.
- **Custom**. Opens a customized palette by importing an external color palette file.

After you've selected a color palette, you may need to modify it for optimization.

Modifying a Color Palette

The Optimize panel displays the color palette if your image contains a maximum of 256 colors. You can select a color in the palette by clicking on it.

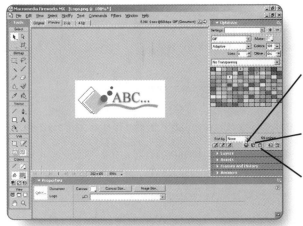

You can now modify the selected color using the following controls present in the Optimize panel:

- **Edit color.** Opens the color dialog box, which you can use to edit the selected color.
- **Snap to Web safe.** Converts the color to its closest value in the Web-safe palette.
- **Lock color.** Prevents the color from any modification.

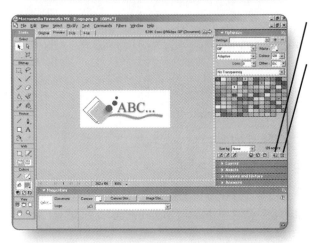

- **Add color.** Adds a new color to the current palette.
- **Delete color.** Deletes the selected color.

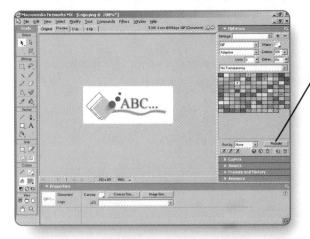

TIP

The Optimize panel displays the number of colors in an image. However, in some situations, you might see the Rebuild button instead. This indicates that you need to rebuild the color table.

OPTIMIZING GRAPHICS   159

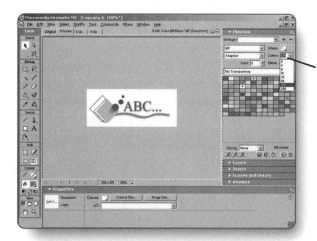

Restricting and Removing Colors from a Color Palette

You can restrict the number of colors used in the current color palette by specifying the number of colors and by removing the unused colors. To restrict the number of colors, select a value for the maximum number of colors in the image from the Colors list.

To remove unused colors from the current palette, follow these steps:

1. Click on the Options menu in the Optimize panel. The Optimize panel's menu appears.

2. Select Remove Unused Colors from the Optimize panel's menu.

Dithering an Image

The modifications that you apply to the color palette may lead to a loss of color information. Some colors present in the image might not be in the current color palette. To account for this loss of color information, you can apply dithering to the exported graphic. Dithering simulates a color by changing the adjacent pixels in such a way that when viewed from a distance, an illusion of the required color is produced.

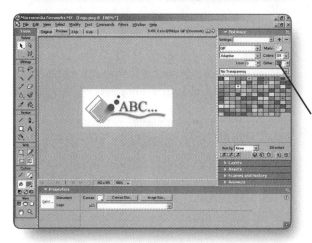

To apply dithering to an image, enter the required dither percentage in the Dither box in the Optimize panel. Higher dither values can simulate more colors, but lead to an increase in the file size. You can experiment with different dither amounts to achieve the optimum output.

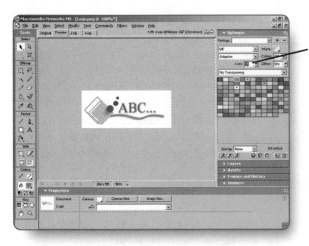

COMPRESSING THE IMAGE

You can further compress the size of a GIF or PNG-8 file by specifying the percentage loss in quality while exporting the image. To compress an image, enter the loss percentage in the Loss GIF Compression box.

TIP
In most of the situations, a loss percentage between 5–15% will result in a sufficiently reduced file size without much loss in the image quality.

SPECIFYING TRANSPARENCY IN THE IMAGE

By default all pixels in an image are opaque. You can specify a part of an image to be transparent.

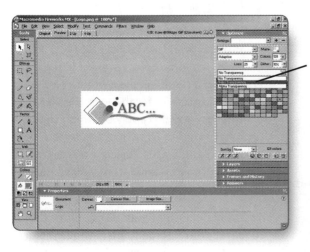

To make parts of an image transparent, follow these steps:

1a. When exporting a GIF file, select Index Transparency from the Type of Transparency list.

OR

1b. When exporting a PNG file, select either Index or Alpha Transparency from the Type of Transparency list.

NOTE
You can't use the JPEG file format for exporting images with transparent areas.

If you are using Index Transparency as the transparency type, the canvas color becomes transparent by default. The Optimize panel provides you with the following controls when you select the Index Transparency type:

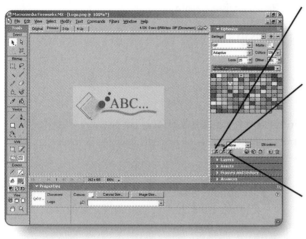

- **Add color to transparency**. Use this button to sample a color from the image. All the color pixels in the image of the same color become transparent.

- **Remove color from transparency**. Use this button to sample a color from the image, which is currently a part of transparency. All the color pixels in the image having the same color are no longer transparent.

- **Select transparent color**. Select a color, other than the default canvas color, which is to become transparent.

INTERLACING

Interlacing is a technique in which an image is displayed at a lower resolution in a Web browser while the full resolution image downloads. This is beneficial because viewers can see some aspects of your site while the larger images download. Fireworks MX allows you to export interlaced images.

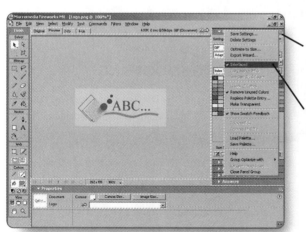

To specify interlacing, follow these steps:

1. Click on the Options menu in the Optimize panel. The Optimize panel's menu appears.

2. Select Interlaced from the Optimize panel's menu.

JPEG Optimization Settings

You can specify the following optimization settings for the JPEG file format:

- Quality
- Smoothing
- Sharp edges
- Progressive display
- Selective compression

ADJUSTING QUALITY

You can specify the amount of compression for a JPEG image by setting the percentage of quality that is to be maintained in the exported image. A lower quality value leads to smaller file size.

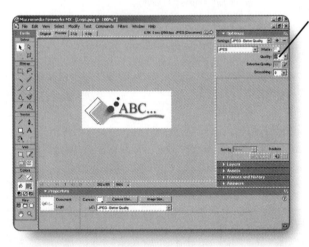

To specify the JPEG image quality, enter the desired quality percentage in the JPEG Quality box.

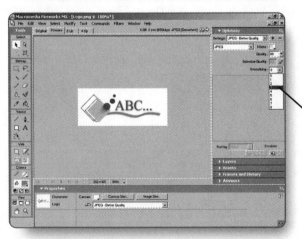

APPLYING SMOOTHING

Smoothing is the process of blurring hard edges in an image. It further reduces the file size.

To apply smoothing, enter the desired smoothing amount in the Smoothing box.

MAINTAINING SHARPNESS

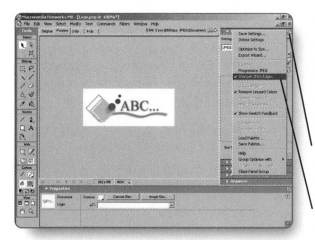

There might be a situation where you want to maintain hard edges in the exported image. In such a situation, you can preserve the sharpness of an image by following these steps:

1. Click on the Options menu icon in the Optimize panel. The Optimize panel's Options pop-up menu appears.

2. Select Sharpen JPEG Edges from the Optimize panel's menu.

TIP

Selecting Sharpen JPEG Edges will cause the file size to increase. Therefore, you should use this option only when you want to preserve the sharpness of an image with text or buttons.

DISPLAYING IMAGES PROGRESSIVELY

As in interlaced GIFs, JPEG files can also be displayed at a lower resolution in a Web browser while the full resolution image downloads. Such JPEG images are called *Progressive JPEGs*.

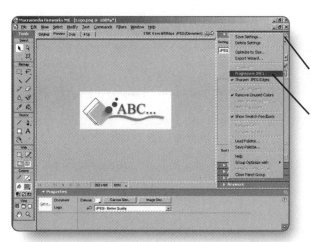

To set progressive display for JPEG images, follow these steps:

1. Click on the Options menu. The Optimize panel's menu appears.

2. Select Progressive JPEG from the Optimize panel's menu.

COMPRESSING IMAGES SELECTIVELY

Fireworks MX also allows you to apply different compression settings to specified parts of an image. To selectively compress an image, follow these steps:

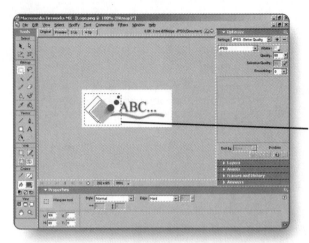

1. Select the area to be compressed by using any of the bitmap selection tools.

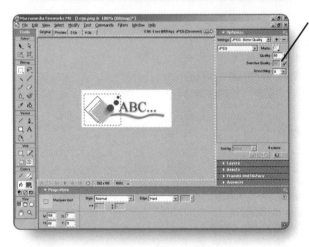

2. Click on the Edit Selective Quality Options button in the Optimize panel. The Selective JPEG Settings dialog box will open.

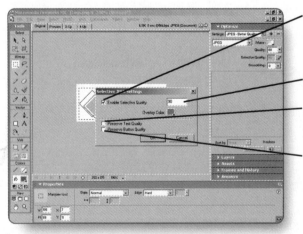

3. Check the Enable Selective Quality check box. The compression settings will be enabled.

4. Enter the compression quality value.

5. Check the Preserve Text Quality check box to preserve text quality.

6. Check the Preserve Button Quality check box to preserve button quality.

Using Preset Optimization Settings

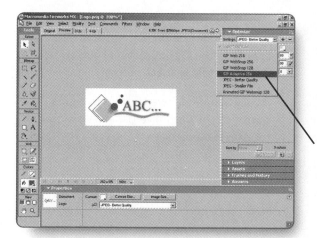

In addition to specifying custom settings, the Optimize panel allows you to specify preset optimization settings.

To use a preset optimization setting, select any of the available settings from the Saved Settings list in the Optimize panel.

Following are the Optimization settings that you can select from the Saved settings list:

- **GIF Web 216**. Restricts the image's color palette to the Web-safe palette.
- **GIF WebSnap 256**. Converts all non Web-safe colors in the image to their closest color value in the Web-safe palette.
- **GIF WebSnap 128**. Converts all non Web-safe colors in the image to their closest color value in the Web-safe palette, which contains a maximum of 128 colors.
- **GIF Adaptive 256**. Creates a custom color palette (maximum 256 colors) that contains only the colors used in the graphic.
- **JPEG – Better Quality**. Sets the JPEG file Quality to 80% of the original file quality.
- **JPEG – Smaller File**. Sets the JPEG file Quality to 60% of the original file quality.
- **Animated GIF Websnap 128**. Sets the exported file type to Animated GIF. In addition, converts all non Web-safe colors in the image to their closest color value in the Web-safe palette, which contains a maximum of 128 colors.

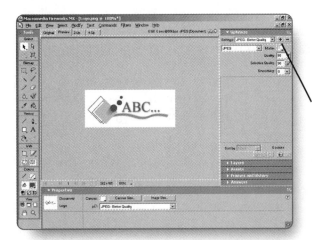

Fireworks MX allows you to save the custom optimization settings that you specify in the Optimize panel as a preset. To do so, follow these steps:

1. Click on the Save Current Settings button in the Optimize panel. A dialog box for preset name opens.

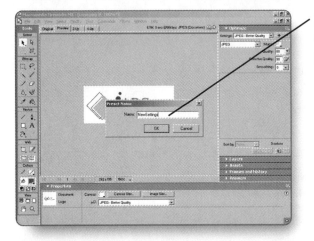

2. Type a name for the preset and click on OK. The current settings will be saved as a preset.

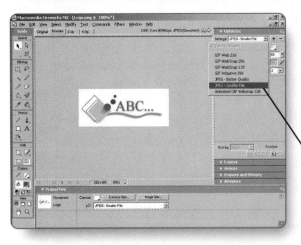

You can access the optimization settings that you have saved from the Saved Settings list in the Optimize panel.

You can remove a preset optimization setting from the Saved Settings list by following these steps:

1. Select the undesired optimization preset from the Saved Settings list in the Optimize panel.

OPTIMIZING GRAPHICS   167

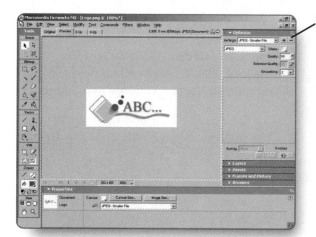

2. Click on the Delete Saved Setting button in the Optimize panel. The optimization preset will be removed from the Saved Settings list.

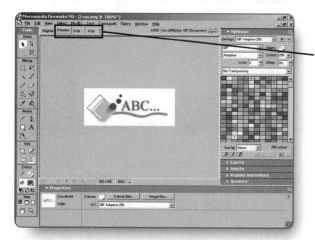

Previewing the Document

Fireworks MX allows you to simultaneously preview the effect of the optimization settings by using the Preview tabs in the Document window.

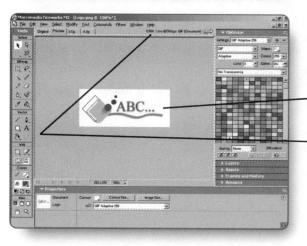

You can click on the Preview tab to view the effect of the current optimization settings on an image. The Preview tab displays the following information:

- **Image Preview.** A preview of the image that will be exported.

- **File size and estimated download time.** The resultant file size of the exported image and the estimated time the image will take to download on a Web browser.

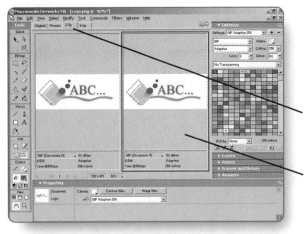

You can also compare the effect of different optimization settings on the image by selecting the 2-Up or 4-Up preview tabs. To work with different optimization settings, follow these steps:

1. Click on the 2-Up or 4-Up preview tab. The preview area will split to display the image at different settings.

2. Click on any of the views to make it the active view. The Optimize panel displays the settings related to the currently selected view.

3. Continue selecting different views and adjusting the settings in the Optimize panel until you decide on the most suitable setting.

Exporting Graphics

Once the graphic is optimized you can export it. To export the optimized graphic, follow these steps:

1. Click on File. The File menu will appear.

2. Click on Export. The Export dialog box will open.

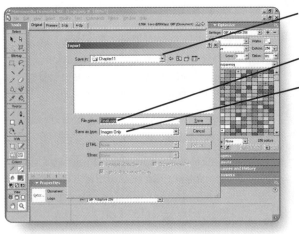

3. Select an appropriate location to export the graphic to.

4. Type a name for the exported graphic.

5. Select Images Only from the Save as type pop-up menu and click on Save. The graphic will be exported.

USING THE EXPORT WIZARD   169

Using the Export Wizard

In addition to manually optimizing and exporting graphics, Fireworks MX allows you to use the Export Wizard. The Export Wizard guides you to optimize and export graphics in a step-by-step manner. You can choose from any of the export settings that the Export Wizard recommends. In addition, you can restrict the file size of the exported graphic to a maximum value. To optimize and export graphics by using the Export Wizard, follow these steps:

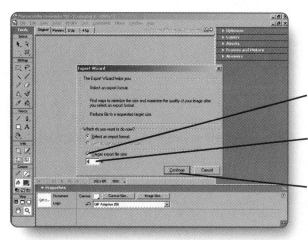

1. Click on File. The File menu will appear.

2. Click on Export Wizard. The Export Wizard window will open.

3. Click on the Target Export File Size. The target export size box is enabled.

4. Enter the upper limit for the file size of the exported graphic.

5. Click on Continue. A dialog box for specifying the destination of the exported graphic opens.

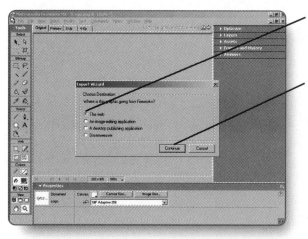

6. Select the intended destination of the exported graphic by using these radio buttons.

7. Click on Continue. The Export Wizard displays the Analysis Results window, which contains the recommended optimization settings.

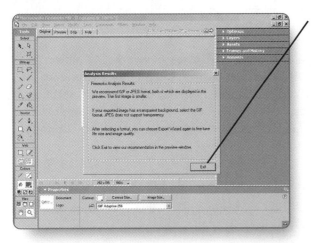

8. Click on Exit. The Export Preview window will open.

The Export Preview window allows you to preview, compare, and modify the optimization settings recommended by the Export Wizard.

The Export Preview window is divided as follows:

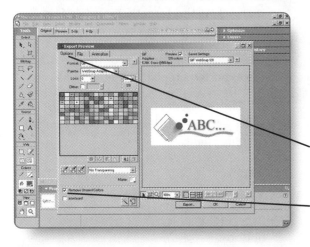

- **Options tab**. View and modify the optimization settings for the selected file format.

- **Remove Unused Colors**. Remove all unused colors from the color palette.

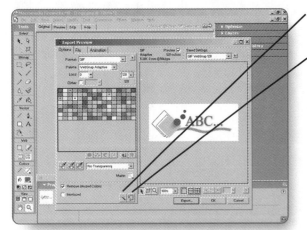

- **Export Wizard button**. Open the Export Wizard.

- **Optimize to Size button**. Open the Optimize to size dialog box, which you can use to specify the target maximum exported file size.

USING THE EXPORT WIZARD   171

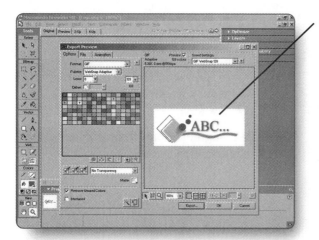

- **Preview area.** View a preview of the exported image.

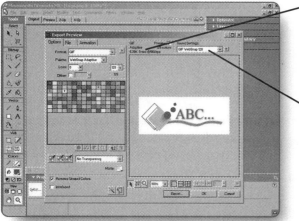

- **File size and estimated download time.** View the resultant file size of the exported image and the estimated time the image will take to download on a Web browser.

- **Saved Settings list.** Select any of the previously saved optimization settings.

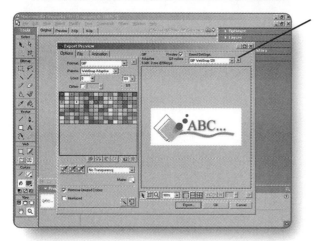

- **Save Current Settings button.** Save the current optimization settings for later use.

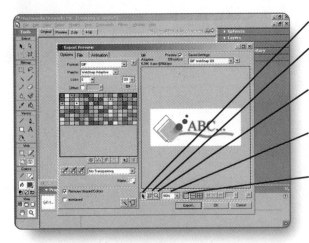

- **Pointer button.** Pan the preview area.
- **Export Area button.** Specify a part of the image to be exported.
- **Zoom tool.** Zoom in and out of the preview area.
- **Set magnification list.** Specify a magnification value.
- **Split view buttons.** Select from one, two, or four previews.

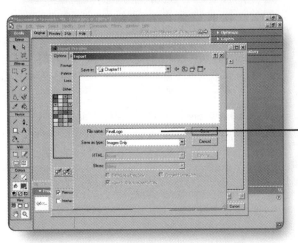

After you have specified the required optimization settings, you can export your image by following these steps:

1. Click on Export. The Export dialog box will open.

2. Select the name and the location to export the graphic to and click on Save. The graphic will be exported.

In this chapter, you learned to optimize Web graphics using Fireworks MX. You also learned to export these optimized graphics in a suitable Web graphics format. You can now use these graphics on your Web site.

PART III

Designing Interactive Web Graphics

Chapter 12
Creating Hotspots and Slices **175**

Chapter 13
Adding Rollovers to Graphics **193**

Chapter 14
Adding Buttons to a Graphic **209**

Chapter 15
Displaying Options Using Pop-up Menus . . . **227**

Chapter 16
Adding Animations to Graphics **243**

Chapter 17
Automating Tasks **259**

Chapter 18
Integrating Fireworks MX with
Macromedia Dreamweaver MX **281**

12
Creating Hotspots and Slices

You may need to provide a number of links in your Web site. For example, the home page of your company's Web site lists various categories of books that your company sells, wherein each category contains a link to the page displaying books related to that category. In addition to providing text links, you can also add links to images. For example, clicking the logo of the company takes users to the home page of the company. To add links to your graphics, you use hotspots. The images used in your Web site may take a long time to download. To avoid such situations, you can cut the image into a number of smaller images by using a technique called *slicing*. In addition, slicing allows you to optimize different parts of an image differently. In this chapter, you will learn how to:

- Create image maps using hotspots
- Cut and optimize images using slices

Creating Image Maps Using Hotspots

An *image map* is a graphic that contains a number of links. For example, to provide details of all bookstores across the United States, you can create an image of the US map and provide links at appropriate locations. Each link on an image map is called a *hotspot*.

In this section, you will learn to create hotspots and image maps.

Creating a Hotspot

Fireworks MX provides you with three tools to create hotspots. These tools are listed in the Web category of the Tools panel. The following list describes these tools:

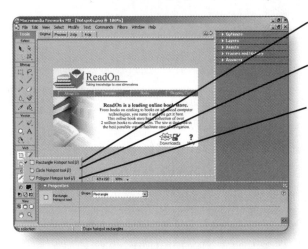

- **Rectangle Hotspot tool**. Use this tool to create a rectangular hotspot.
- **Circle Hotspot tool**. Use this tool to create a circular hotspot.
- **Polygon Hotspot tool**. Use this tool to create an irregular-shaped hotspot.

By default, the Rectangle Hotspot tool is visible. To view the remaining two tools, click on the small triangle to display the Rectangle tool pop-up menu and select the appropriate tool. Creating a hotspot is similar to creating rectangles and ellipses. For more information on creating rectangles and polygons, see "Drawing Rectangles and Polygons" in Chapter 5, "Working with Vector Graphics."

All the hotspots that you create are placed on the Web layer, and appear as a shape lying on top of an object. The hotspots are filled with a color, which is not visible when you preview the image. While working with graphics, you can hide the hotspots. To do so, click on the Hide slices and hotspots button in the Tools panel. To make hotspots reappear, click on the Show slices and hotspots button.

CREATING IMAGE MAPS USING HOTSPOTS 177

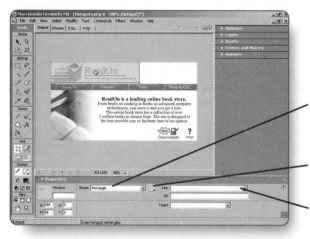

When you create a hotspot, the Property Inspector displays a number of options for it.

The following list explains these options:

- **Shape list**. Use this list to change the shape of the hotspot. The options are Rectangle, Circle, and Polygon.

- **Color box**. Use this box to change the color of the hotspot.

- **Link list**. Use this list to specify a new Uniform Resource Locator (URL) or select from the existing ones.

> **TIP**
>
> A URL is the address of a Web site or page. For example, to access the official site of Premier Press, type **http://www.premierpressbooks.com** in the address bar of your Web browser.

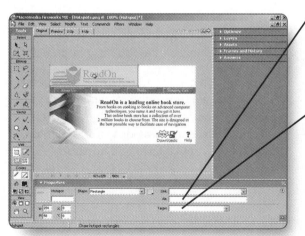

- **Alt box**. Use this box to specify the alternative text that will appear if the browser does not support images. This text is visible as a tool tip when you point at the image.

- **Target list**. Use this list to specify the location of the linked page. Some of the available options are _blank and _self. The _blank option makes the target page appear in a new browser window, and the _self option makes it appear in the same browser window.

In this section, you'll learn to create a rectangular and polygonal hotspot.

Creating a Rectangular Hotspot

To create a rectangular hotspot, follow these steps:

1. Select the Rectangle Hotspot tool. The mouse pointer will change to the crosshair pointer.

2. Draw the hotspot at the appropriate location. The Property Inspector will display the options for the hotspot.

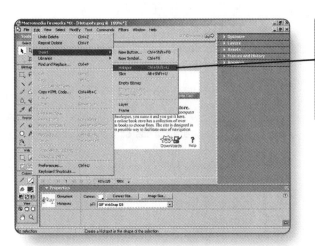

> **TIP**
> Alternatively, you can select the object and choose Hotspot from the Edit, Insert menu.

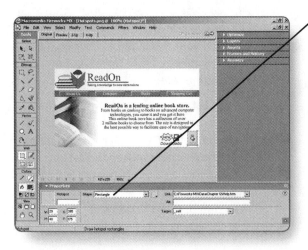

3. Make appropriate changes to the various options in the Property Inspector.

Your graphic may contain irregular objects, and you cannot use the rectangular or circular hotspots for these objects. The following section provides information on creating irregularly shaped hotspots.

Creating a Polygonal Hotspot

A polygonal hotspot is actually an irregularly shaped hotspot. You can create such a polygon by placing vector points at appropriate locations to trace the appropriate object. To create a polygonal hotspot, follow these steps:

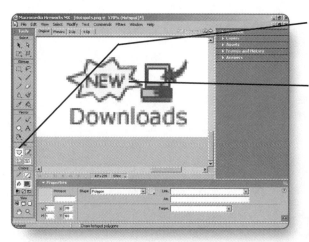

1. Select the Polygon Hotspot tool. The mouse pointer will change to the crosshair pointer.

2. Click on the document to create the first vector point.

> **TIP**
> I've magnified the image to show the vector points clearly.

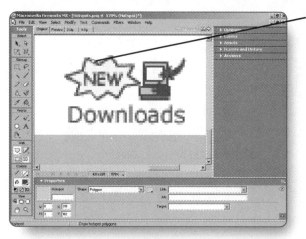

3. Click on the document again to create a second vector point.

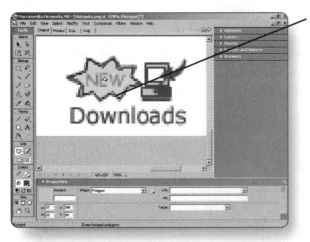

4. Repeat Step 3 to complete the shape. An irregularly shaped hotspot will appear on the top of the object.

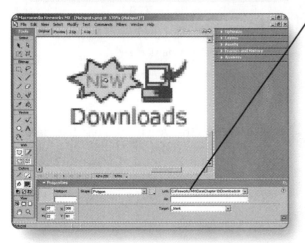

5. Make appropriate changes to various options in the Property Inspector.

After you have created a hotspot, you need to test it. The following section provides details on testing the hotspot.

Testing a Hotspot

Testing a hotspot involves the following two steps:

- Specifying the Web browser
- Previewing the document in the specified Web browser

However, you need to perform the first step only once. In this section, you will learn to perform both the steps.

Specifying a Web Browser

Fireworks MX allows you to test your documents in multiple browsers by specifying primary and secondary browsers. The primary browser is the default browser for all your documents. The secondary browser is the additional browser that you can use for viewing your documents. For example, you can specify Internet Explorer as the primary browser and Netscape Navigator as the secondary browser.

CREATING IMAGE MAPS USING HOTSPOTS   181

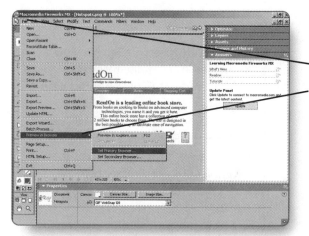

To specify a Web browser, follow these steps:

1. Click on File. The File menu will appear.

2a. Point to Preview in Browser and click on Set Primary Browser. The Locate Browser dialog box will open.

OR

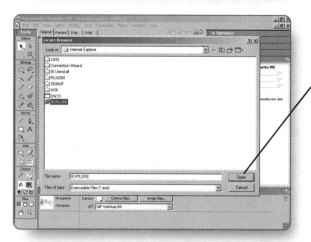

2b. Point to Preview in Browser and click on Set Secondary Browser. The Locate Browser dialog box will open.

3. Click on Open after selecting the executable file of the browser. The browser will be set as your default browser for viewing Fireworks MX documents.

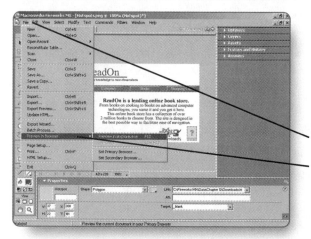

Previewing a Document in the Browser

To preview a document containing a hotspot in a Web browser, follow these steps:

1. Click on File. The File menu will appear.

2. Point to Preview in Browser and click on Preview in iexplore.exe. The browser window containing your document will appear.

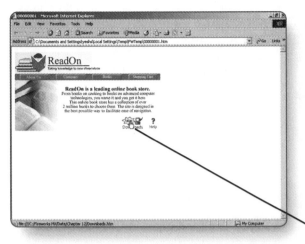

> **TIP**
>
> Alternatively, press F12 to preview a document in the default Web browser, which is Internet Explorer in this case. To preview your document in the secondary browser, select Preview in XX from the File, Preview in Browser menu, where XX is the name of the .EXE file of the secondary browser.

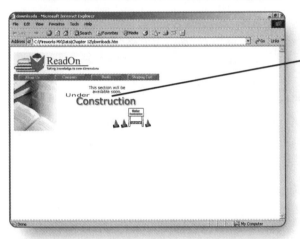

3. Point to a hyperlink that you created. The mouse pointer will change to a hand indicating that the image contains a hyperlink.

4. Click on the hyperlink. The target page will appear.

After you have created and tested the required hotspots, your graphic is ready to be exported as an image map. The following section provides instructions on creating an image map.

Creating an Image Map

To create an image map, follow these steps:

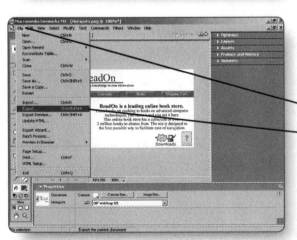

1. Click on File. The File menu will appear.

2. Click on Export. The Export dialog box will open.

CREATING IMAGE MAPS USING HOTSPOTS   183

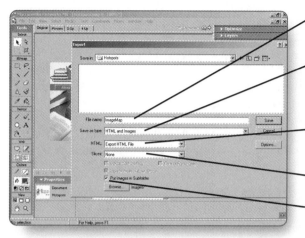

3. Type a file name in the File name box. This will be the name of the image map.

4. Choose HTML and Images from the Save as type list. The graphic you created will be saved as an HTML file.

5. Choose Export HTML File from the HTML list.

6. Choose None from the Slices list.

7. Click on Put Images in Subfolder. A check will be placed in the check box, and all the images used in the graphic will be saved in a separate folder called Images.

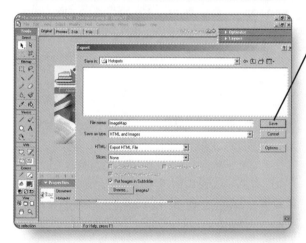

8. Click on Save. The Export dialog box will close.

9. Click on Start and point to Programs. The Programs menu will appear.

10. Click on Internet Explorer. The Internet Explorer will be launched.

> **TIP**
> Launch Netscape if you need to test your files in Netscape Navigator.

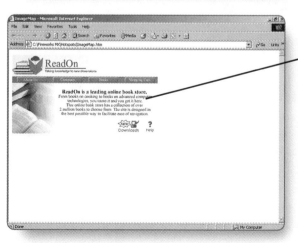

11. Open and test the image map that you created.

This was all about creating hotspots and image maps. In the next section, you will learn to cut images by using the *slicing* method.

Cutting and Optimizing Images Using Slices

Image slicing is a technique in which an image is cut into a number of smaller pieces, called *slices*. An image is sliced due to the following reasons:

- The smaller the image, the easier it is to download. As a result, a Web site user can view the Web page downloaded in parts instead of staring at the blank screen while the larger images download.

- You can optimize different slices differently. For example, you can optimize one slice as a JPEG file and the other one as an animated GIF. This is helpful in situations when you need to have multiple types of images in a graphic.

Like hotspots, slices appear as a shape on top of objects and are added to the Web layer. You can hide and show the slices by using the Hide slices and hotspots button and the Show slices and hotspots button, respectively.

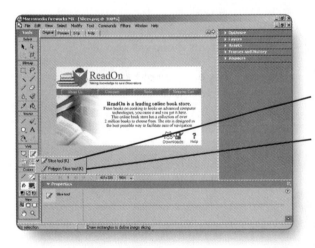

Creating a Slice

Fireworks MX provides you with two tools to create slices. These are:

- **Slice tool**. Use this tool to create rectangular slices.

- **Polygon Slice tool**. Use this tool to create irregular slices.

When you create a slice, Fireworks MX creates additional slices to slice the entire image. In addition, the slice guides appear automatically, which determine the shape and position of a slice. Creating a slice is similar to creating a hotspot. The Property Inspector shows a number of options for the slices that you create.

CUTTING AND OPTIMIZING IMAGES USING SLICES   185

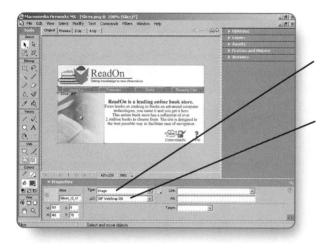

Most of these options are similar to those of hotspots except for the following:

- **Type list**. Use this list to specify the type of slice. In Fireworks MX, you can create image and HTML slices.

- **Slice export settings list**. Use this list to specify the format in which the slice will be exported.

Creating an Image Slice

To create an image slice, follow these steps:

1. Select the object on which you need to create a slice.

> **TIP**
>
> You can also select multiple objects. To do so, press and hold Shift and click on the required objects.

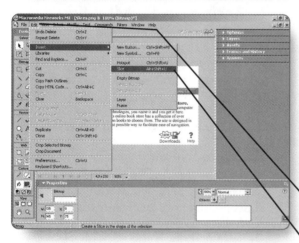

2. Click on Edit. The Edit menu will appear.

3. Point to Insert and click on Slice. A slice appears on top of the selected object.

> **TIP**
>
> Alternatively, you can select the Slice tool or the Polygon Slice tool to create a slice. You use the Polygon Slice tool in a manner similar to the Polygon Hotspot tool. See "Creating a Polygonal Hotspot" earlier in this chapter for more information on creating hotspots.

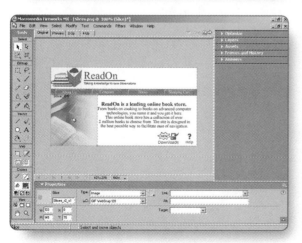

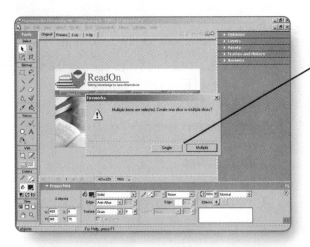

> **NOTE**
> If you've selected multiple objects, a message box opens asking you to create single or multiple slices. Click on Single to create a single slice, and click on Multiple to create multiple slices.

4. Make appropriate changes to the slice by using the Property Inspector.

Creating an HTML Slice

An HTML slice represents the area which, when viewed in a browser, displays HTML text instead of an image. To create an HTML slice, follow these steps:

1. Create a slice object and select it.

2. Choose HTML from the Type list in the Property Inspector. The selected slice will display HTML Slice and an Edit button will appear in the Property Inspector.

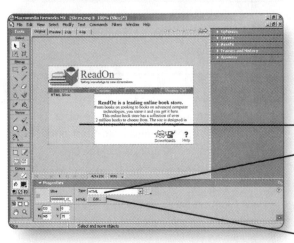

3. Click on Edit. The Edit HTML Slice window will open.

4. Type the text and click on OK.

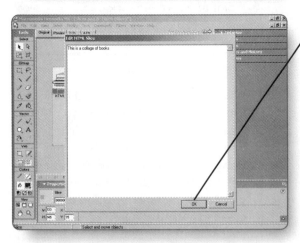

CUTTING AND OPTIMIZING IMAGES USING SLICES   187

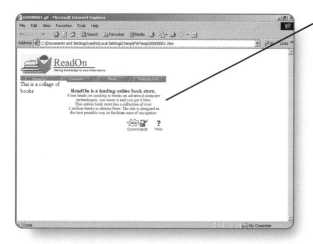

5. Press F12. The document will appear in the browser and HTML slice displays the text you added.

After you have sliced the graphic, it is important to specify a name for the slices. In the next section, you will learn to specify names for slices.

Naming Slices

When you export a sliced document, Fireworks MX generates separate files for all the slices. Therefore, it is important for you to name the slices that you create. You can either specify the slice names yourself (*custom-naming*) or let Fireworks MX do that for you (*auto-naming*). In this section, you will learn about both methods.

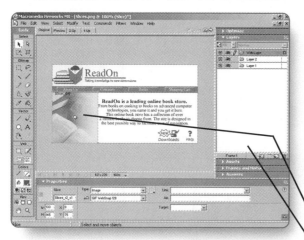

Custom Naming the Slice Files

To specify a custom name for the slice files, follow these steps:

1. Select the required slice.

2. Click on Layers in the Fireworks MX workspace. The Layers panel will open.

3. Expand the Web layer.

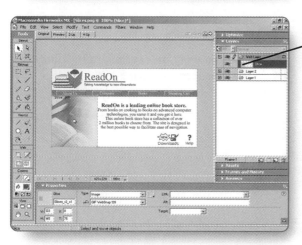

188 CHAPTER 12: CREATING HOTSPOTS AND SLICES

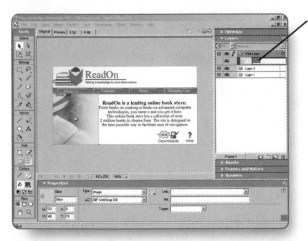

4. Double-click on the appropriate Slice object. A text box will open.

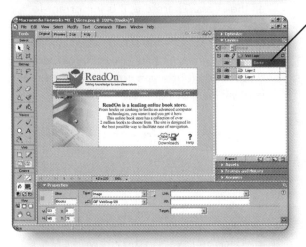

5. Type a name in the text box and press Enter. The name of the slice will change.

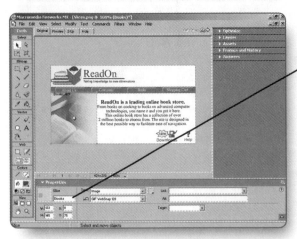

TIP
Alternatively, select the appropriate slice, and type a name in the Object name box in the Property Inspector.

Auto-Naming the Slice Files

When you don't specify a name for the slices, Fireworks MX names the slices on its own. However, Fireworks MX does provide you with an option to specify the naming convention to be used. The naming convention used for slices can consist of six elements. Each of these elements can take one of the following options:

- **None**. Use this option to specify no name for the element.
- **doc.name**. Use this option to specify the name of the document as the element name.
- **"slice"**. Use this option to insert the word slice in the naming convention.
- **Slice #(1,2,3...), Slice #(01, 02, 03), Slice #(A, B, C...)**. Use this option to name the element numerically or alphabetically.
- **row/column(r3_c2, r4_c7...)**. Use this option to specify the rows and columns used by the Web browser to reconstruct the sliced image.
- **Underscore, Period, Space**. Use this option to insert a separator between other elements.

For example, if you specify:

- The first element as doc.name (for example, Books)
- The second element as underscore
- The third element as row/column(r3_c2, r4_c7...)
- The fourth, fifth, and sixth elements as None

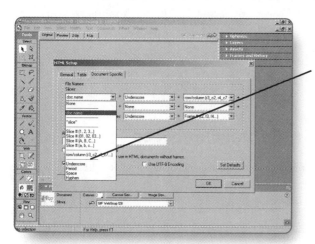

The slice files will be named Books_r1_c1, Books_r1_c2, and so on.

You specify these elements in the HTML Setup dialog box, which contains six lists for each element. Each of these lists contains the required options.

To auto-name the slice files, follow these steps:

1. Choose HTML Setup from the File menu. The HTML Setup dialog box will open.

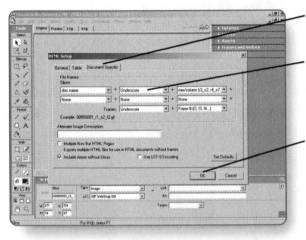

2. Click on the Document Specific tab. The Document Specific tab will be active.

3. Specify the appropriate convention by using the Slices lists. The example of the convention specified will appear in the dialog box.

4. Click on OK. The naming convention will be applied and the HTML Setup dialog box will be applied.

After you have specified a naming convention for the slice files, your document is ready to be exported. The next section provides detail on exporting slices.

Exporting the Slices

When you export a sliced document, a number of images are generated because each slice represents an individual image. Now, when you open this exported Fireworks MX document in a Web browser, the browser reassembles this image in an HTML table. Each slice is placed in a table cell. However, in certain browsers, the cells of the table may not be aligned properly. To help you prevent this, Fireworks MX provides spacer.gif. The spacer.gif is a transparent GIF image that helps you align the cells of a table.

In Fireworks MX, you can either export the complete document containing slices or export specific slices. In the following section, you will learn about both these techniques.

Exporting the Document Containing Slices

While exporting a document containing slices, you need to specify the slicing technique.

CUTTING AND OPTIMIZING IMAGES USING SLICES   191

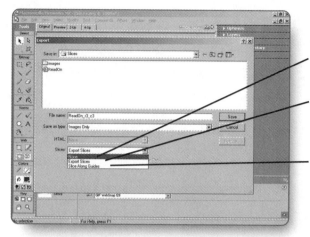

Fireworks MX provides you with three options:

- **None**. Lets you export the complete image in one piece.
- **Export Slices**. Lets you export the slices based on the slice objects created in the document.
- **Slice Along Guides**. Lets you export the slices by using the standard slice guides.

You specify these options by using the Slice list in the Export dialog box.

To export a document containing slices, follow these steps:

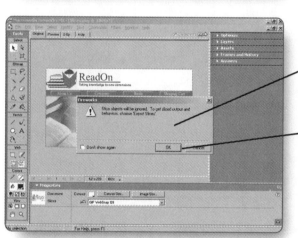

1. Choose Export from the File menu. A message box providing a tip on exporting slices will open.

2. Click on OK. The Export dialog box will open.

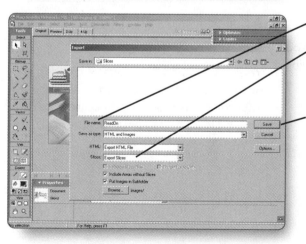

3. Make appropriate settings.

4. Choose Export Slices from the Slices list. The slices in the document will be exported.

5. Click on Save. The entire document will be exported.

CHAPTER 12: CREATING HOTSPOTS AND SLICES

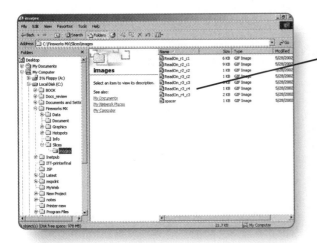

TIP

To view the files generated after exporting, launch Windows Explorer.

Open the folder in which you exported the file and then open the images folder. The folder contains all the slice files with appropriate naming conventions.

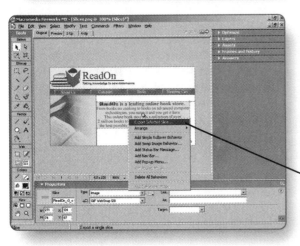

Exporting a Specific Slice

To export a specific slice, follow these steps:

1. Select a slice.

2. Right-click on the document. A shortcut menu will appear.

3. Choose Export Selected Slice. The Export dialog box will open.

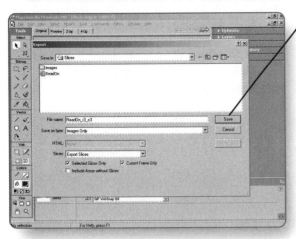

4. Click on Save after you make appropriate changes.

You have learned the basics of creating hotspots and slices. Slices form an important constituent of Web graphics. You will learn more about the use of slices in the following chapters.

13
Adding Rollovers to Graphics

While visiting a Web site, when you point at a button it appears pressed, or when you point at an image, a brief description of the image appears. These effects are called rollovers, and they add to the visual appeal of your Web site. Using Fireworks MX, you can create rollovers with ease.

Using Fireworks MX, you can create two types of rollovers, simple and disjoint. In a simple rollover an image replaces another image on user interaction. In disjoint rollover, user interaction on one part of a graphic leads to a change in some other part. To create both these types of rollover, you need to use either hotspots or slices. In this chapter, you will learn how to:

- Create simple rollovers
- Create disjoint rollovers

Creating a Simple Rollover

A *simple rollover* is an effect in which an object is swapped by another object when a user points or clicks at the first object. I will refer to the object being swapped as the *source object* and the image swapping it as the *target object*. The most common example of a simple rollover is a button that changes its shape when you point or click it.

In a simple rollover, the source object, covered by a slice, is placed on one frame and the target object is placed on the other. A *frame* is a placeholder that contains an image and is used in creating animations. See Chapter 16, "Adding Animations to Graphics," for more information on frames.

In this section, you will learn to create simple rollovers. The process of creating a simple rollover consists of the following four steps:

- Creating the source object
- Creating the target object
- Assigning a behavior
- Testing the rollover

The following sections discuss these steps in detail.

Creating the Source Object

The source object is the object that triggers the rollover. To create a source object, follow these steps:

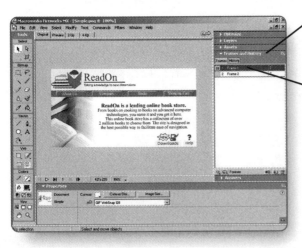

1. Click on Frames and History in the Fireworks MX workspace. The Frames panel will open.

2. Click on the frame containing the source object to make it active. The contents of the frame will be displayed in the Document window.

CREATING A SIMPLE ROLLOVER 195

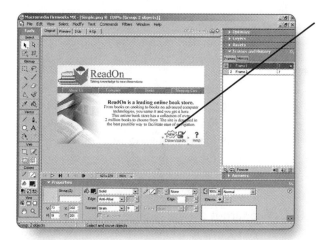

3. Create the source object and select it. For example, I selected the Downloads text object.

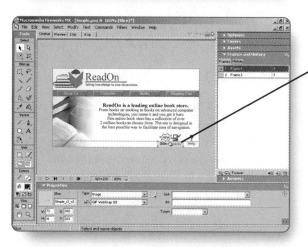

4. Click on Edit. The Edit menu will appear.

5. Point to Insert and click on Slice. A slice will appear on top of the selected object.

After creating the source object, the next step is to create the target object. The following section provides details on creating the target object.

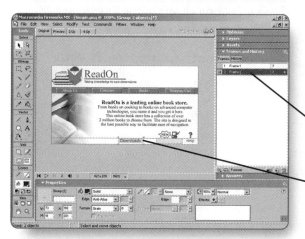

Creating the Target Object

The target object swaps the source object. To create the target object, follow these steps:

1. Click on the frame that will contain the target object in the Frames panel to make it active.

2. Optionally, create the target object.

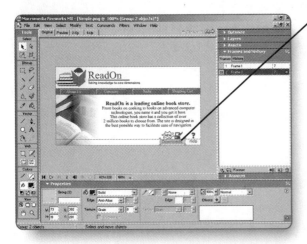

3. Place the target object under the slice that you created in Step 5 of "Creating the Source Object".

After creating the source and target objects, you need to assign a behavior to the source object. You will learn to assign a behavior to a rollover in the following section.

Adding a Frame

The target object, used in a rollover, is present in a different frame. Therefore, you will need to add frames to create rollovers. To add a new frame to a graphic, click on the New / Duplicate Frame button present at the bottom of the Frames panel. A blank frame will be added to the graphic.

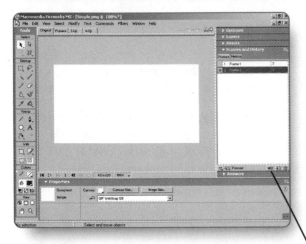

The frame that you add does not contain the background image present in the graphic. To insert the background image in all frames used by a graphic, place the background image in a separate layer and share this layer across the frames of a graphic. To share a layer across frames, follow these steps:

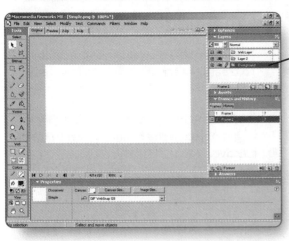

1. Click on Layers in the Fireworks MX workspace. The Layers panel will open.

2. Click on the appropriate layer to select it.

CREATING A SIMPLE ROLLOVER 197

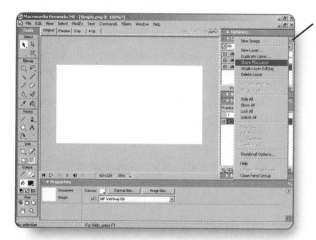

3. Click on the icon present at the top-right corner of the Layers panel. The Layers Option pop-up menu will appear.

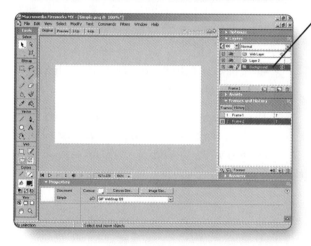

4. Click on Share This Layer. An icon appears to the right of the layer name in the Layers panel.

Assigning a Behavior

A behavior is a combination of an event and an action. For example, an event is clicking the mouse button and the action is swapping the image. The behavior uses the JavaScript code to trap the event and perform the desired action. However, you don't need to write the JavaScript code; Fireworks MX generates this code automatically. In Fireworks MX, you can use the following events:

- onMouseOver. Occurs when you point to an object.
- onMouseOut. Occurs when you move the mouse pointer out of the focus of the object.
- onClick. Occurs when you click an object.
- onLoad. Occurs when the page is loaded in the browser.

You can use the Behavior handle present in a slice or a hotspot to assign behavior to a rollover. To assign a behavior, follow these steps:

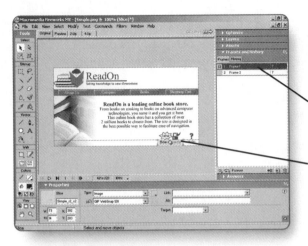

1. Switch to the frame that contains the source object. For example, I switched to Frame 1.

2. Select the slice you created in "Creating the Source Object". A Behavior handle will appear in the center of the slice.

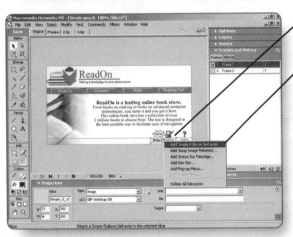

3. Click on the Behavior handle. A pop-up menu will appear.

4. Click on Add Simple Rollover Behavior to create the simple rollover.

The last step in creating a rollover is to test it. The following section provides detail on testing your rollover.

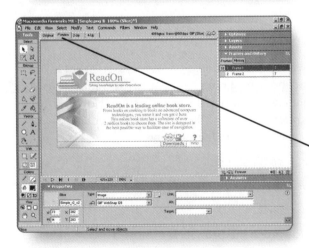

Testing the Simple Rollover

You can test a rollover in the Preview tab or in the Web browser. To test the rollover in the Preview tab, follow these steps:

1. Click on the Preview tab. The Preview tab will become active.

CREATING A SIMPLE ROLLOVER 199

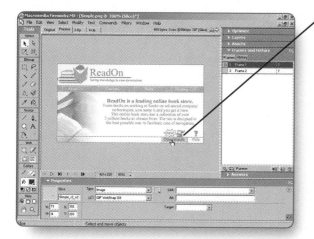

2. Point to the source object. The target object will swap the source object.

> **TIP**
> A simple rollover contains a minimum of two frames. One contains the source object and the other contains the target object. When you preview this document, the frame containing the source object is visible by default. Now, when you point at the source object, the frame containing the target object becomes visible. Thus giving you the effect of a rollover. This procedure, of hiding one frame and displaying the other, uses JavaScript code to produce the desired effect.

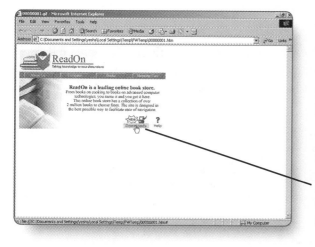

Seeing the JavaScript Code

To view the JavaScript code generated by Fireworks MX for the rollover (in Internet Explorer), follow these steps:

1. Press F12. The Fireworks MX document will open in the primary browser.

2. Point to the source object. The target object will appear giving you a rollover effect.

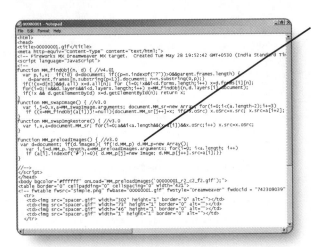

3. Choose Source from the View menu to view the JavaScript code. The source document containing the JavaScript code will appear.

Creating a Disjoint Rollover

While surfing the Internet, you will see Web pages in which when you point to an image, a change occurs at some other location of the Web page. For example, when you point to the image of a product, a description of the product appears in the document. The effects in which an interaction in one part of an image leads to a change in some other part of an image are called *disjoint rollovers*.

Like a simple rollover, a disjoint rollover also contains two objects, one that triggers the rollover and the other that is changed. However, unlike simple rollovers, these two objects are present in different areas of the graphic, and are covered by two separate slices. The area of the graphic containing the object, which triggers the rollover effect, is called the *trigger area*. And, the area in which there is a change is called the *target area*.

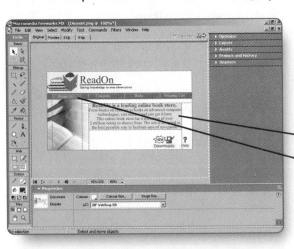

The process of creating a disjoint rollover can be divided into the following four steps:

- Creating the target area
- Creating the trigger area
- Assigning a behavior
- Testing the rollover

Creating the Trigger and Target Areas

The trigger and the target areas are present in different frames of a graphic, and are covered by a slice each. I will refer to the slice covering the trigger area as the *trigger slice* and the one containing the target area as the *target slice*.

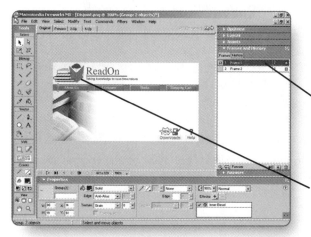

Creating the Trigger Area

To create the trigger area, follow these steps:

1. Open the Frames panel.

2. Click on the frame containing the trigger area to make it active. The frame will appear selected in the Frames panel.

3. Create the source object and select it.

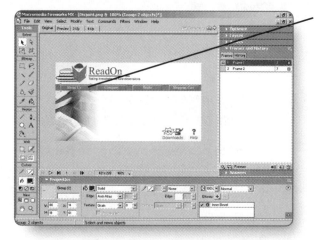

4. Create or insert a slice on top of the trigger area.

Creating the Target Area

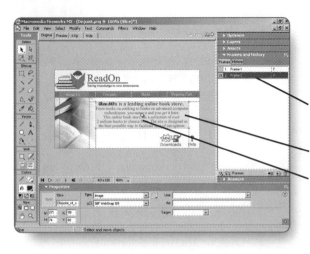

To create the target area, follow these steps:

1. Select the frame containing the target area by using the Frames panel.

2. Create the source object and select it.

3. Create or insert a slice on top of the target area.

After you create the target area, you need to assign a behavior to the trigger area. You will learn to do so in the following section.

Assigning a Behavior

You can assign a behavior to the trigger area in two ways:

- By using the Behavior handle
- By using the drag-and-drop method

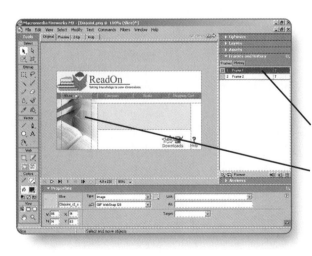

Assigning Behaviors by Using the Behavior Handle

To assign a behavior by using the Behavior handle, follow these steps:

1. Switch to the frame containing the trigger slice.

2. Select the trigger slice. A Behavior handle will appear in the center of the slice.

CREATING A DISJOINT ROLLOVER 203

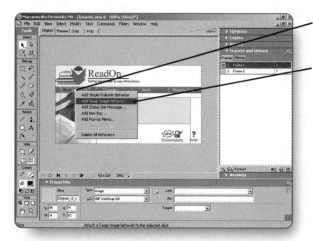

3. Click on the Behavior handle. A pop-up menu will appear.

4. Click on Add Swap Image Behavior. The Swap Image dialog box will appear.

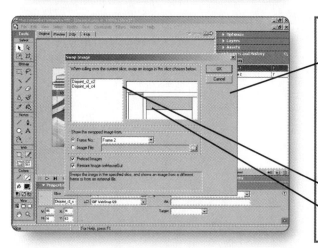

TIP

The Swap Image dialog box contains two lists, one containing the name of the slices and the other displaying the location of the slices in your document. You can select the appropriate slice by clicking any of the two lists.

- Slice names
- Slice locations

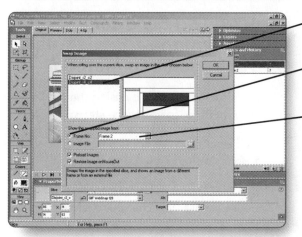

5. Click on the target slice. The slice will appear selected.

6. Optionally, click on Frame No. The Frame No. will be selected.

7. Choose the appropriate frame from the corresponding list.

204 CHAPTER 13: ADDING ROLLOVERS TO GRAPHICS

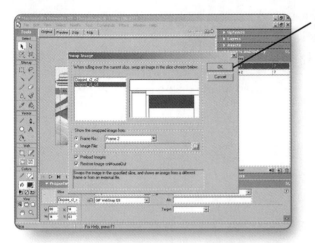

8. Click on OK.

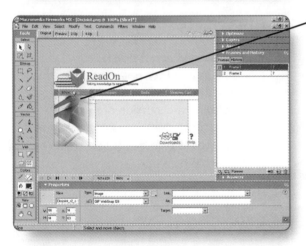

A blue line joining the two slices appears. This line indicates that a swap image behavior has been applied to the two slices.

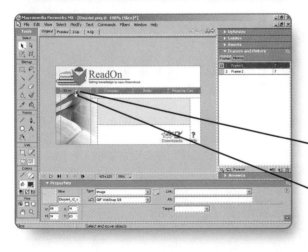

Assigning Behaviors by Using the Drag-and-Drop Method

To assign a behavior by using the drag-and-drop method, follow these steps:

1. Select the slice containing trigger area. A Behavior handle will appear.

2. Point to the Behavior handle. The mouse pointer will change to a hand.

CREATING A DISJOINT ROLLOVER   205

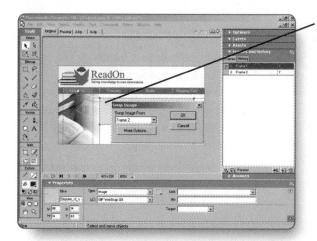

3. Press and hold the mouse button and drag the mouse pointer to the slice containing the target area. The Swap Image dialog box will open.

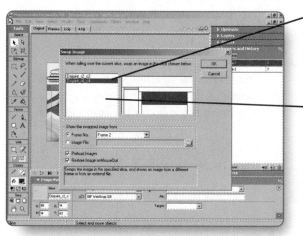

4. Choose the appropriate frame from the Swap Image From list.

> **TIP**
>
> If you are not sure which frame contains the target area, click on More Options. The Swap Image dialog box will expand. Click on the appropriate slice to select it.

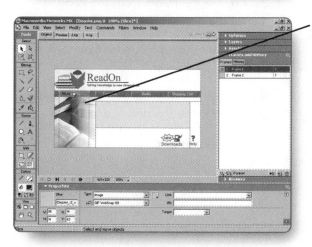

5. Click on OK. A line joining the two slices appears.

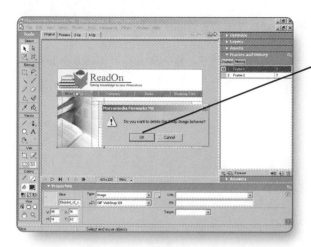

> **NOTE**
>
> You can also delete a behavior. To do so, click on the line joining the two slices. A message box appears asking you to delete the Swap Image behavior. Click on OK to delete the behavior.

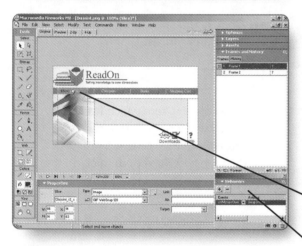

Changing the Event of a Rollover

You may need to change the event that triggers a rollover. For example, instead of triggering the rollover by pointing at a button, you may need to trigger the rollover by clicking on the button. The steps to do so are as follows:

1. Select the slice containing the trigger area.

2. Choose Behaviors from the Window menu. The Behaviors panel will open.

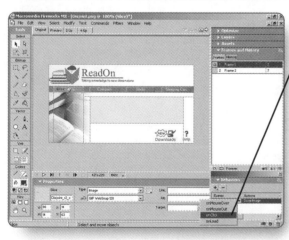

3. Click on the arrow under Events. A pop-up menu will appear.

4. Choose the appropriate event and click anywhere in the Document window.

5. Test the rollover.

Testing a Rollover

You can test a rollover in the Preview tab or in the Web browser. To test the rollover in the Preview tab, follow these steps:

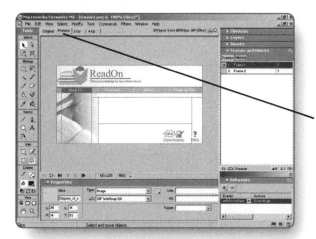

1. Click on the Preview tab. The Preview tab will become active.

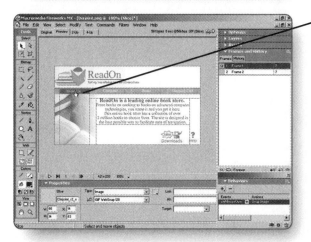

2. Point to the trigger area. The target object will swap the source object.

TIP

You can also test your rollover in a Web browser. To do so, press F12. Your document will open in the primary Web browser. Now, point to the source object to test the rollover.

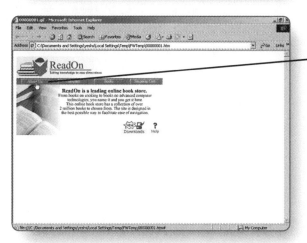

NOTE

You can also test the rollover in a different Web browser. To do so, select Preview in XX from the File, Preview in Browser menu where XX is the name of the .EXE file of the secondary browser. See "Specifying a Web Browser" in Chapter 12, "Creating Hotspots and Slices," for more information on specifying secondary Web browsers.

With this chapter you have learned to add rollovers to your graphics. Go ahead and use rollovers to make your Web sites lively. In the next chapter, you will learn to create buttons, which are also a form of rollovers.

14

Adding Buttons to a Graphic

Buttons are an integral part of a Web site. They help you navigate between different Web pages of the Web site. Moreover, a colorful button with an attractive shape and a 3-D appearance adds to the visual appeal of your Web site. These days, most of the Web sites incorporate a navigation bar (a group of buttons) that helps in navigating the Web site. In this chapter, you will learn how to:

- Create a button
- Create a navigation bar

Creating a Button

A *button* is an object that helps you add interactivity to a Web page. For example, you can create a button that helps a user to move to the next page. In Fireworks MX, a button has four states. The following bulleted points list these states:

- **Up**. The default or at-rest appearance of the button
- **Over**. The state when you point at the button
- **Down**. The state when you click the button
- **Over While Down**. The state when you move the mouse pointer over the button while the button is in the down state

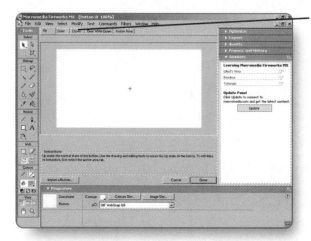

You can use the Button Editor provided by Fireworks MX to create buttons in your graphics. The Button Editor contains four tabs that represent the four states of a button. In addition, the Button Editor contains an Active Area tab, which is used to assign interactivity to a button. You can access the Button Editor by selecting the New Button command from the Edit, Insert menu. Using the Button Editor, you can create a button having two, three, or four states.

The following list describes these buttons:

- **Two-state button**. A button having Up and Over states
- **Three-state button**. A button having Up, Over, and Down states
- **Four-state button**. A button having all the four states

In the following sections, you will learn to create all the states of a button.

Creating the Up State

In Fireworks MX, you can use any object to create a button. For example, you can create a rectangle and then place some text on top of it to create a button containing text, or you can use an image as a button.

CREATING A BUTTON   211

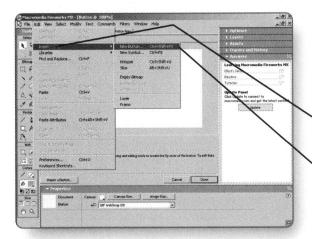

To create a button, you need to create its Up state. You use the Up tab of the Button Editor to design the Up state of a button. To create the Up state of a button, follow these steps:

1. Click on Edit. The Edit menu will appear.

2. Point to Insert and click on New Button. The Button Editor will open.

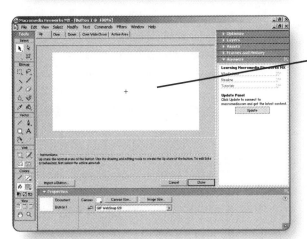

TIP
You can also press the Ctrl, Shift, and F8 keys simultaneously to open the Button Editor.

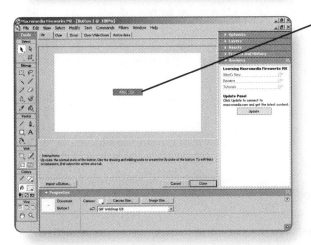

3. Create or insert the object you wish to use as a button. For example, I created a rectangle and placed some text on top of it.

TIP
When you open the Button Editor, the Up tab is active by default.

212 CHAPTER 14: ADDING BUTTONS TO A GRAPHIC

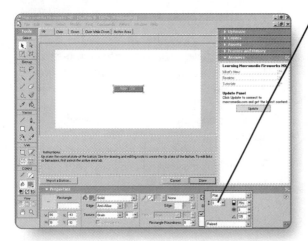

4. Apply suitable effects by using the Property Inspector.

> **TIP**
> See Chapter 5, "Working with Vector Graphics," and Chapter 8, "Using Text in Graphics," for more information on creating objects and text, respectively.

> **TIP**
> See Chapter 10, "Enhancing the Appearance of Objects," for more information on applying effects.

Creating the Over State

A button is said to be in the Over state when you point at it by using the mouse pointer. You create this state by using the Over tab of the Button Editor. To create the Over state of a button, follow these steps:

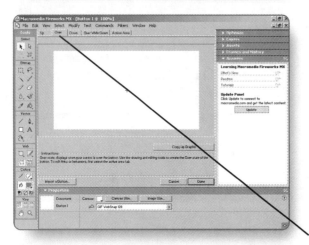

1. Click on Over in the Button Editor. The Over tab will be activated.

2. Click on Copy Up Graphic. A copy of the button in the Up state will appear in the tab.

> **TIP**
> You can also create the object, representing the button, manually.

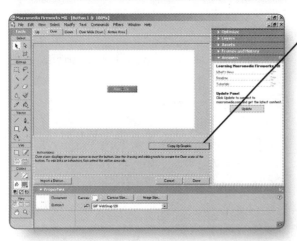

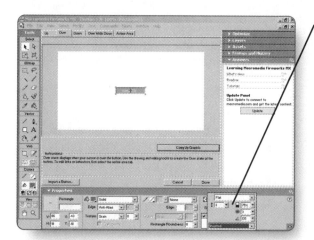

3. Make suitable changes to the appearance of the button.

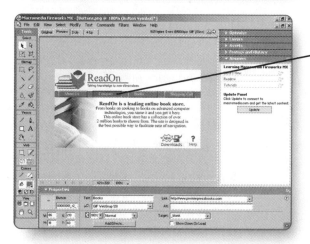

Creating the Down State

A button is said to be in the Down state when you click it. The Down state is used when you are creating the button for a navigation bar. To understand the use of the Down state, consider the following example. A Web site uses the About Us, Company, Books, and Shopping Cart buttons in its navigation bar. By default, the About Us page is displayed when you open the Web site in a browser. When a user clicks the Company button, the Web page containing company details is displayed, and the Company button remains in the Down state. This will help the users identify the currently active Web page.

You create the Down state of a button by using the Down tab of the Button Editor. To create the Down state of a button, follow these steps:

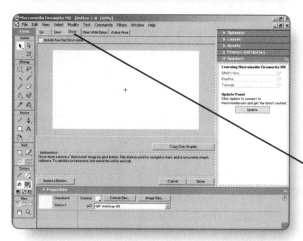

1. Click on Down in the Button Editor. The Down tab will be activated.

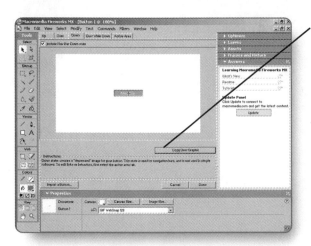

2. Click on Copy Over Graphic. A copy of the button in the Over state will appear in the Down tab.

> **TIP**
>
> Also, a check will be placed next to Include Nav Bar Down State. This is necessary if the button is part of a navigation bar.

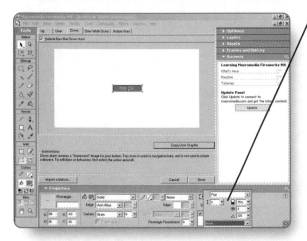

3. Make suitable changes to the appearance of the button to distinguish it from the previous two states. For example, I changed the background color of the button.

Creating the Over While Down State

A button is said to be in the Over While Down state when you move the mouse pointer over it while the button is in the Down state. This state is helpful when you are creating multi-button navigation bars. For a moment, recollect the same example that I discussed in the previous section. After clicking on the Company button, if you move the mouse pointer over the button, the Over While Down state occurs.

You can create the Over While Down state by using the Over While Down tab of the Button Editor. To create the Over While Down state of a button, follow these steps:

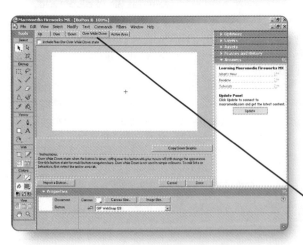

1. Click on Over While Down in the Button Editor. The Over While Down tab will be activated.

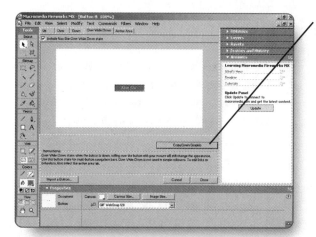

2. Click on Copy Down Graphic. A copy of the button in the Down state will appear in the Over While Down tab.

> **TIP**
>
> Also, a check will be placed next to Include Nav Bar Over While Down State. This is necessary if a button is a part of a navigation bar.

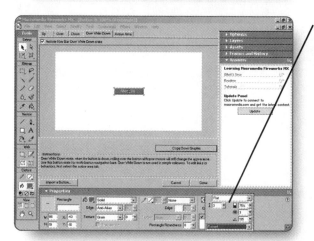

3. Make suitable changes to the appearance of the button to make it appear different from the other states. For example, I added the Inner Bevel effect to the button.

After you have created all the states of a button, you need to specify the active area for the button. The following section provides instructions to do so.

Creating the Active Area of a Button

The active area of a button makes a button interactive. It triggers the response when a user points to or clicks the button. You create the active area of a button in the Active Area tab of the Button Editor. When you activate this tab, Fireworks MX automatically inserts a slice on top of the button. You can then specify a URL for the button by using this slice.

CHAPTER 14: ADDING BUTTONS TO A GRAPHIC

To create the Active Area of a button, follow these steps:

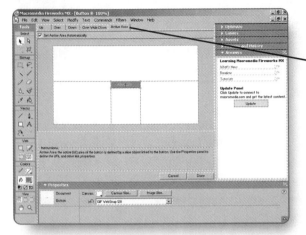

1. Click on Active Area in the Button Editor. The Active Area tab will be activated. The tab contains a copy of the button, which is covered by a slice.

> **TIP**
>
> See "Cutting and Optimizing Images using Slices" in Chapter 12, "Creating Hotspots and Slices," for more information on slices.

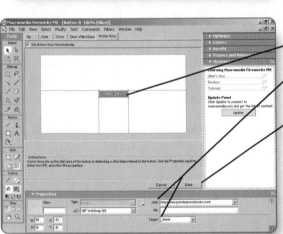

2. Optionally, select the slice.

3. Specify Link and Target for the slice in the Property Inspector.

4. Click on Done.

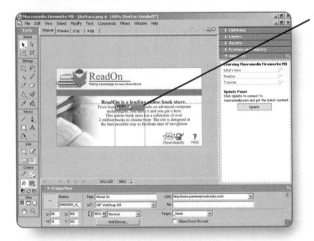

The button will appear in the document.

CREATING A BUTTON 217

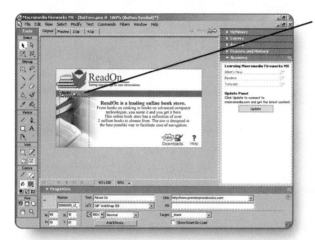

5. Move the button to an appropriate location.

> **TIP**
>
> To move a button, select it. Now, press and hold the mouse button and drag the mouse pointer to move it to an appropriate location.

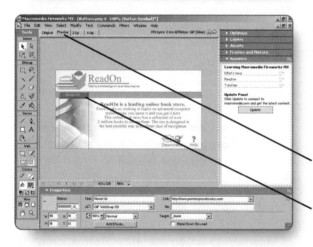

After you have created a button, you need to test it. The following section details the test procedure.

Testing a Button

To test a button, follow these steps:

1. Switch to the Preview tab in the Document window.

The button you created will be in the Up state.

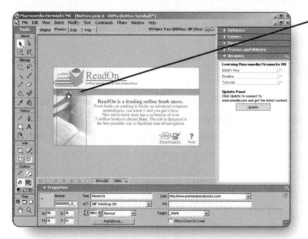

2. Point to the button. The button will move to the Over state.

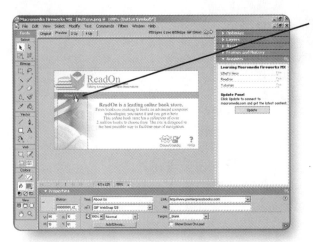

3. Click on the button. The button will move to the Down state.

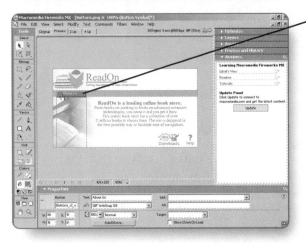

4. Move the mouse pointer on the button. The button will move to the Over While Down state.

> **TIP**
>
> To test the URL of a button, preview the document in the Web browser and click on the button.

At this point, you might be interested to know more about navigation bars. The following section presents information on creating a navigation bar.

Creating a Navigation Bar

A *navigation bar* is a group of buttons present on every Web page of a Web site. It helps you navigate between different pages of the Web site. Ideally, a button used on the navigation bar should have all four states. However, you may use two-state buttons for the navigation bar.

To create a navigation bar, create a button by using the Button Editor. Then, create instances of this button and edit them as per the requirements. In the following section, you will learn to create instances of a button and edit them.

Creating Button Instances

Your document may contain a number of buttons, and all of them will differ slightly in appearance. For example, all the buttons have similar colors and effects, but the text on each button is different. In such situations, what will you do? You can create all the buttons separately, which is a time-consuming task. Or, you can create one button, copy it, and then make the required changes in each button. Each copy of a button is called an *instance*. In Fireworks MX, you can create a button instance by any of the following methods:

- Using the Library panel
- Using the Clone command

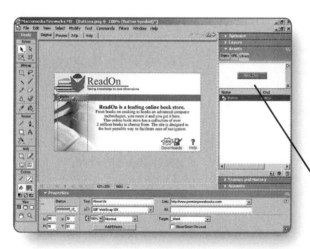

Using the Library Panel

When you create a button by using the Button Editor, it is added to the Library panel. See Chapter 17, "Automating Tasks," for more information on the Library panel. You can use this panel to create copies of a button. To do so, follow these steps:

1. Choose Library from the Window menu. The Library panel will open.

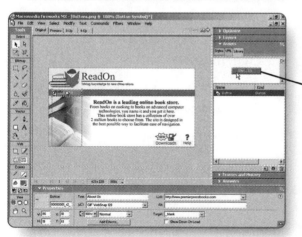

2. Select the appropriate button in the Library panel. The preview of the button will appear in the top portion of the panel.

3. Point to the button preview in the Library panel.

220 CHAPTER 14: ADDING BUTTONS TO A GRAPHIC

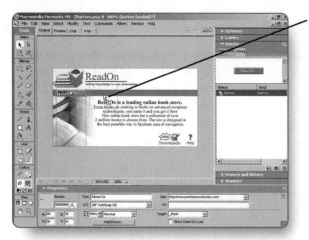

4. Press and hold the mouse button and drag the mouse pointer to an appropriate location.

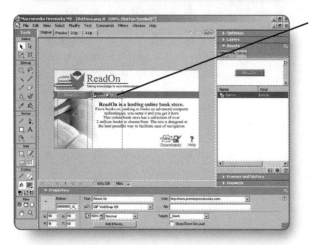

5. Release the mouse button. A copy of the button will appear in the document.

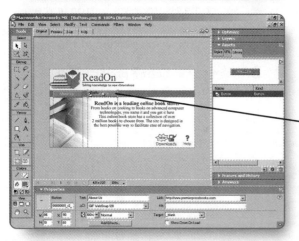

Using the Clone Command

To create copies of a button by using the Clone command, follow these steps:

1. Select the button.

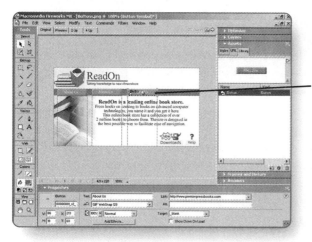

2. Choose Clone from the Edit menu. A copy of the button will be placed on top of the existing button.

3. Drag the new button to an appropriate location.

The button instances that you create are identical. You may need to edit these instances to make them appear different. The following section provides detail on editing a button.

Editing a Button

Your document contains a number of buttons, which you created by copying an existing button. Hence, all the buttons are identical. You may need to change the color of all the buttons in your document, or you may need to change the text of one single button. To help you do so, Fireworks MX allows you to edit the properties of a button at symbol or instance level. A property at *symbol-level* is applicable to all the instances of the button. A property at *instance-level* is applicable only to a particular instance.

In this section, you will learn to edit properties at the symbol and instance levels.

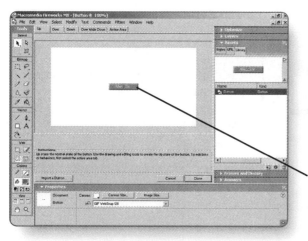

Editing Properties at Symbol-level

At symbol-level, you can modify various properties, such as stroke color, fill color, shape, images, effects, and URL. To modify a property at symbol-level, follow these steps:

1. Double-click on a button. The Button Editor will open.

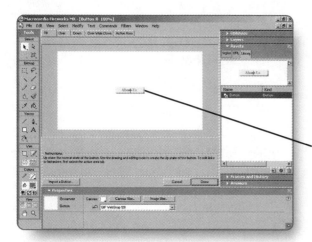

TIP

You can also double-click on the button preview in the Library panel to edit the button.

2. Make appropriate changes. For example, I changed the colors.

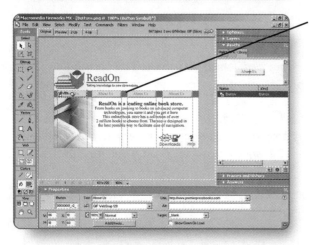

3. Click on Done. The change will be applied to all the buttons.

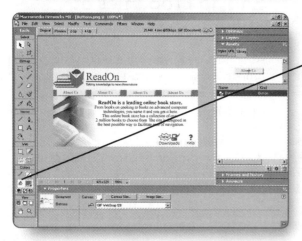

TIP

The slices may stop you from seeing the original color of the buttons. In such situations, click on the Hide slices and hotspots button in the Tools panel.

Editing Properties at Instance-level

You can make changes to the properties at instance-level by using the Property Inspector. When you select a button, the Property Inspector displays a number of options that allow you to edit text, effects, and the URL of a button. Some of these options are discussed in the following list:

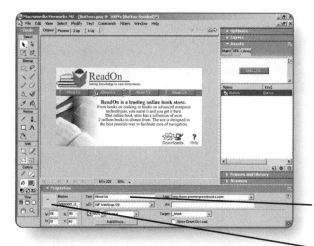

- **Text box**. Use this box to edit the text contained in the button.

- **Button export options list**. Use this list to specify export options for a button.

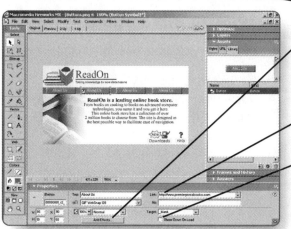

- **Add Effects button**. Use this button to add effects to a button. When you add effects to a button, it changes to Edit Effects button.

- **Link list**. Use this list to specify a URL for the button.

- **Show Down on Load check box**. Check this option to show the button in the Down state when the document is loaded in a Web browser. This option is used with the buttons present in a navigation bar and helps in identifying the currently active Web page.

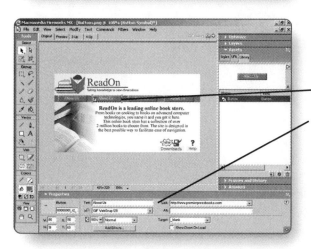

To edit properties at instance-level:

1. Select a button.

The corresponding properties will appear in the Property Inspector.

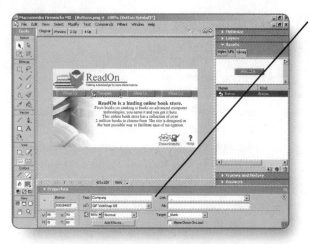

2. Specify the text for the new button in the Property Inspector.

The last step in creating a navigation bar is testing it. The following section provides instructions on testing a navigation bar.

Testing a Navigation Bar

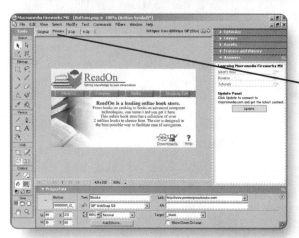

To test a navigation bar, follow these steps:

1. Switch to the Preview tab in the Document window. All the buttons will appear in the Up state.

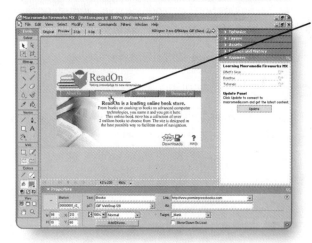

2. Point to a button. The button will move to the Over state.

EDITING A BUTTON 225

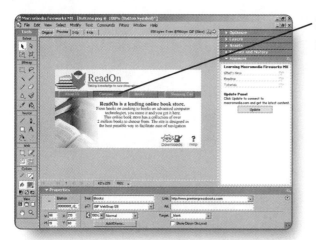

3. Click on the button. The button will move to the Down state.

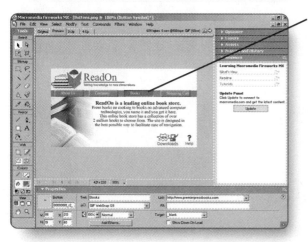

4. Click on some other button. The button in Step 3 will move to the Up state and the current button will move to the Down state.

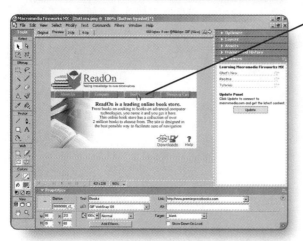

5. Move the mouse pointer on the button. The button will move to the Over While Down state.

With that, you have learned the basics of creating buttons. You can now add navigation bars to your Web sites. In the next chapter, you will learn to create pop-up menus.

15

Displaying Options Using Pop-up Menus

You use a number of pop-up menus while working in the Windows environment. These pop-up menus appear when you need them and display a number of useful options. Fireworks MX lets you use pop-up menus in your graphics for Web pages. These pop-up menus contain a number of menu items that help you navigate different pages of a Web site. For example, a graphic for the home page of a company can contain a pop-up menu that displays various options related to the company, such as About Us and Careers.

In this chapter, you'll learn how to:

- Create pop-up menus
- Test pop-up menus

CHAPTER 15: DISPLAYING OPTIONS USING POP-UP MENUS

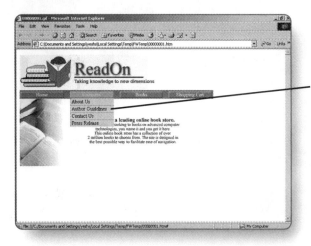

Creating a Pop-up Menu

You can use a pop-up menu on a Web page to display various options that help you navigate a Web site. A *pop-up menu* is like a rollover effect, which is displayed when you point or click on an object. For example, you can create a pop-up menu that displays various links related to the company, and this menu appears when you point at the Company button present on the Web page.

TIP
See Chapter 13, "Adding Rollovers to Graphics," for more information on rollovers.

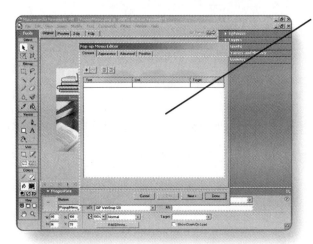

Fireworks MX provides the Pop-up Menu Editor that helps you create a pop-up menu in a flash. The Pop-up Menu Editor contains four tabs that help you add menu items (or options) to a pop-up menu and enhance its appearance. These tabs are listed here:

- **Content tab**. Lets you add menu items and specify links and targets for them. This tab also helps you create submenus within a pop-up menu.
- **Appearance tab**. Lets you design the appearance of a pop-up menu by specifying font, style, and size.

TIP
A pop-up menu has two stages, Up and Over, which are similar to those of a button. You can design both these stages in the Appearance tab. See "Creating a Button" in Chapter 14, "Adding Buttons to Graphics," to learn more about the various stages of a button.

- **Advanced tab**. Lets you specify cell dimensions, padding, spacing, cell border width and color, menu delay, and text indentation.
- **Position tab**. Lets you determine the position of the pop-up menu and submenu.

In the following sections, you will learn to use various tabs in the Pop-up Menu Editor.

Adding Content to a Pop-up Menu

You use the Content tab to actually create the structure of a pop-up menu. Using this tab, you can perform the following functions:

- Add menu items to a pop-up menu.
- Add links to various menu items.
- Indent menu items to create submenus.

To help you perform the aforementioned tasks, the Content tab contains a number of controls, such as button and list. The button controls help you perform tasks, such as adding and deleting menu items. The list control helps you provide link and target for a menu item, and is divided into three columns, Text, Link, and Target. The following list explains these controls:

- **Add Menu button**. Adds a new menu item.
- **Delete Menu button**. Deletes the selected menu item.
- **Indent Menu button**. Indents a menu item to make it a submenu.
- **Outdent Menu button**. Outdents the indented menu item.

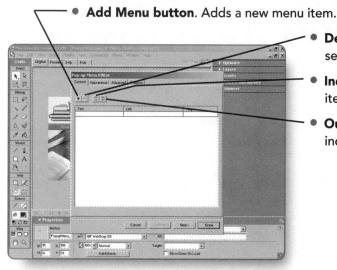

230 CHAPTER 15: DISPLAYING OPTIONS USING POP-UP MENUS

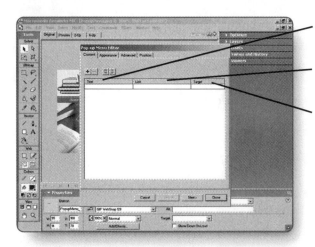

- **Text column**. Contains the text of the menu item.
- **Link column**. Contains the URL of the menu item.
- **Target column**. Contains the target for the URL of the menu item.

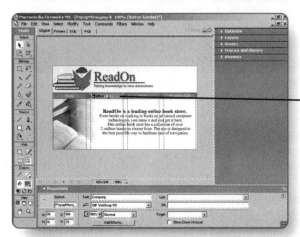

Adding Menu Items

To add menu items to a pop-up menu, follow these steps:

1. Select a slice or hotspot on which you need to create a pop-up menu.

> **CAUTION**
>
> You need to create a slice or hotspot on the object on which you need to create a pop-up menu. See Chapter 12, "Creating Hotspots and Slices," for more information on creating hotspots and slices.

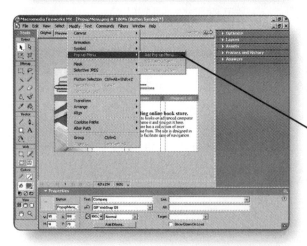

2. Click on Modify. The Modify menu will appear.

3. Point to Pop-up Menu and click on Add Pop-up Menu.

CREATING A POP-UP MENU   231

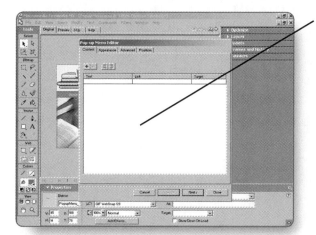

The Pop-up Menu Editor will appear and the Content tab will be activated.

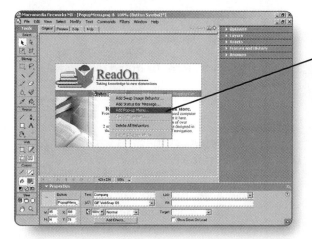

TIP
Alternatively, click on the Behavior handle present in the slice. Click on Add Pop-up Menu in the pop-up menu that appears.

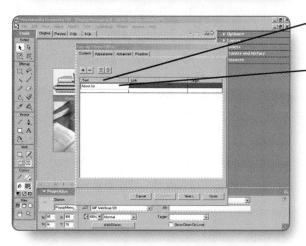

4. Double-click on the Text column. A text box will appear.

5. Type a value in the text box. This will be the first menu item.

TIP
The text box that appears also contains a drop-down list, which contains any previously used URLs.

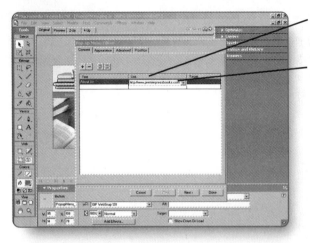

6. Double-click on the Link column. A text box will appear.

7. Type or select a URL.

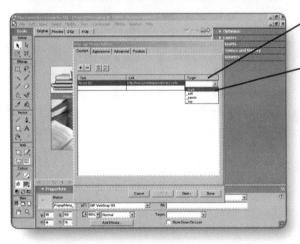

8. Double-click on the Target column. A drop-down list will appear.

9. Select a target from the drop-down list.

TIP

The target list specifies where the linked page will appear. For example, the _blank option makes the target page appear in a new browser window, and the _self option makes it appear in the same browser window. In addition, the target list contains two more options, _parent and _top, which are useful for documents containing frames. The _parent option makes the target page appear in the parent frameset or window of the frame that contains the link. The _top option makes the target page appear in the full browser window, thus removing all the frames.

CREATING A POP-UP MENU 233

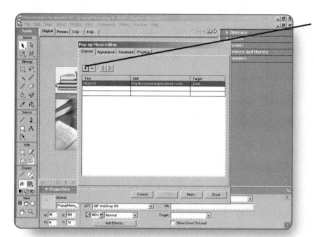

10. Click on the Add Menu button. A blank menu item is added to the pop-up menu.

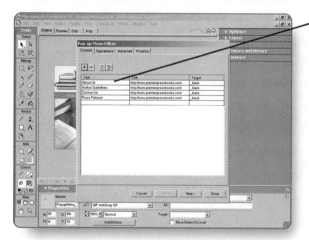

11. Repeat Steps 4-10 to add more menu items.

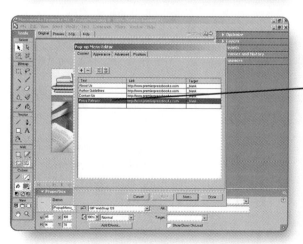

Deleting Menu Items

To delete a menu item, follow these steps:

1. Click on a menu item. The menu item will be selected.

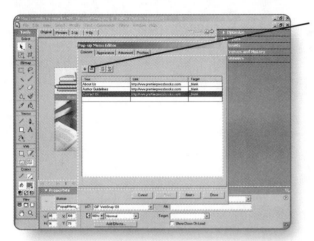

2. Click on the Delete Menu button. The selected menu item will be deleted.

Creating Submenus

To create a submenu, follow these steps:

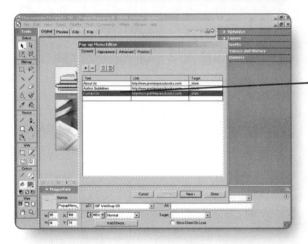

1. Select a menu item.

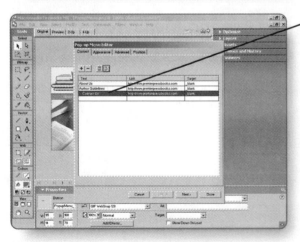

2. Click on the Indent Menu button. The selected menu item will be indented and will appear as a submenu for the menu item above it.

> **TIP**
>
> If you indent an incorrect menu item, select the menu item and click on the Outdent Menu button to outdent the menu item.

After you have created a menu, you need to make it presentable. The following section explains how to enhance the appearance of your pop-up menus.

Enhancing the Appearance of a Pop-up Menu

You enhance the appearance of a pop-up menu in the Appearance tab of the Pop-up Menu Editor. To activate this tab, click on Appearance in the Pop-up Menu Editor. Alternatively, you can click on Next. The Appearance tab allows you to perform the following tasks:

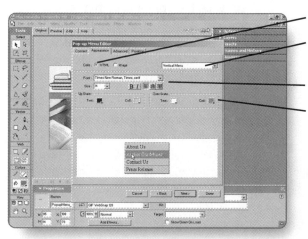

- Specify cell style of the pop-up menu.
- Specify the orientation of the pop-up menu.
- Format the text in the pop-up menu.
- Specify the Up and Over states of the pop-up menu.

In addition, the Appearance tab displays the effect of changes that you make. In the following sections, you will learn to perform all the aforementioned tasks.

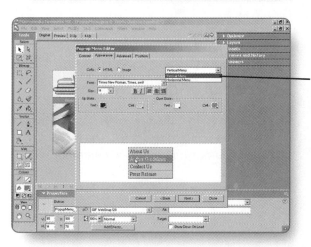

Specifying the Orientation of the Pop-up Menu

You can adjust a pop-up menu to appear either horizontally or vertically. To specify the orientation of a pop-up menu, choose the appropriate option from the list provided at the top of the Appearance tab.

CHAPTER 15: DISPLAYING OPTIONS USING POP-UP MENUS

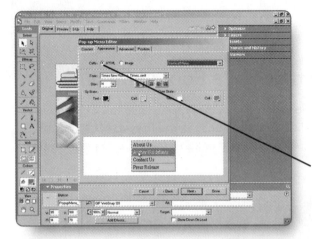

Specifying the Cell Style

You can add upon the appearance of your pop-up menu by specifying cell styles. A cell is the area that contains a menu item. Your pop-up menus can either contain HTML-based or image-based cells. The following list explains these two types of cells:

- **HTML-based cell**. Uses HTML code to enhance the appearance of the menu. Images using pop-up menus containing HTML-based cells are small in size. Select the HTML option to create HTML-based pop-up menus.

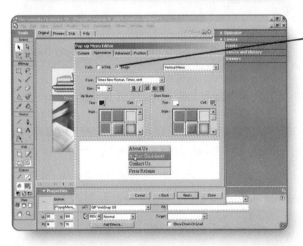

- **Image-based cell**. Allows you to specify selected image styles as the cell background. Images using pop-up menus containing image-based cells are larger in size. Select the Image option to create image-based pop-up menus.

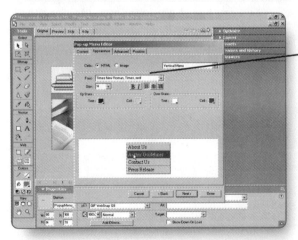

Formatting the Text

You can format the text of various menu items by using the Font list, the Size list, the Style buttons, and the Alignment buttons.

CREATING A POP-UP MENU 237

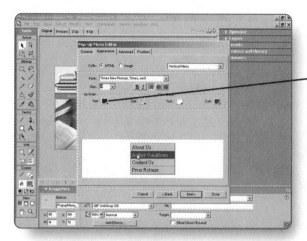

Specifying the Up and Over States

The Up state is the default state of a menu item and when you point at it, the state of the menu item changes to Over. Using Fireworks MX, you can easily design both the states by specifying different text and cell colors.

Specifying Advanced Pop-up Menu Settings

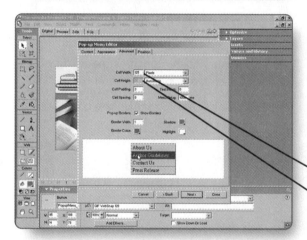

The advanced settings for a pop-up menu include specifying the dimensions of a cell, menu delay, and border dimensions and color. You make these settings in the Advanced tab of the Pop-up Menu Editor. This tab contains a number of options that help you specify these settings. These options are listed here:

- **Cell Width**. Specifies the width of a cell.
- **Cell Height**. Specifies the height of a cell.

> **TIP**
> You can specify the width and height of a cell in pixels, manually. Or, let Fireworks MX do it for you automatically. To do so, select Pixels or Automatic from the list corresponding to the Cell Width or Cell Height text box.

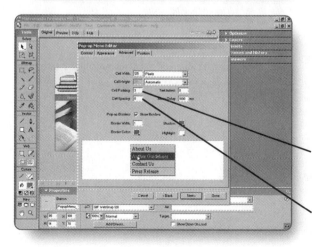

- **Cell Padding**. Specifies the distance between the menu item text and the edge of the cell.
- **Cell Spacing**. Specifies the amount of space between the cells of a pop-up menu.

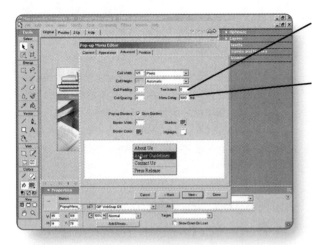

- **Text Indent**. Specifies the amount of indentation for the text contained in the pop-up menu.
- **Menu Delay**. Specifies the time (in seconds) for which the menu remains visible after you move the pointer away from it.

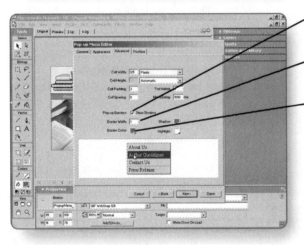

- **Show Borders**. Allows you to show or hide the borders of a pop-up menu.
- **Border Width**. Specifies the width of the border of the pop-up menu.
- **Border Color**. Specifies the color of the pop-up menu border.

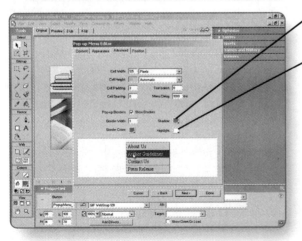

- **Shadow**. Specifies the shadow color of the pop-up menu border.
- **Highlight**. Specifies the highlight color of the pop-up menu border.

CREATING A POP-UP MENU 239

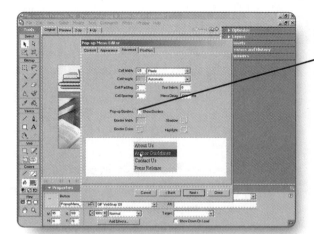

TIP
If you uncheck the Show Borders option, the Border Width, Border Color, Shadow, and Highlight options are disabled.

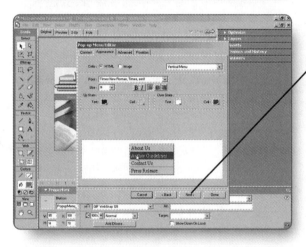

To specify advanced settings for a pop-up menu, follow these steps:

1. Click on Next in the Pop-up Menu Editor. The Advanced tab will be activated.

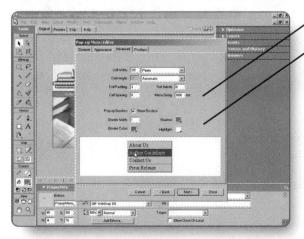

2. Make changes to the cell settings.

3. Make changes to the border settings.

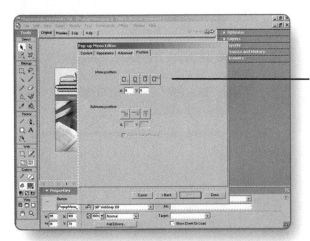

Specifying the Position of a Pop-up Menu

You can specify the display position of a pop-up menu by using the Position tab in the Pop-up Menu Editor. You can specify the position of a pop-up menu in either of the following two ways:

- By using the Menu Position buttons.
- By using the X and Y boxes that specify the X and Y coordinates of the pop-up menu position. For example, if you specify 0,0 as the position coordinates, the upper-left corner of the pop-up menu is aligned with the upper-left corner of the slice that contains it.

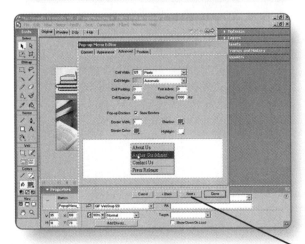

The Position tab also allows you to position any submenus contained in the pop-up menu. For doing so, the Position tab contains Submenu Position buttons and the X and Y boxes. However, these controls are activated only if your pop-up menu contains a submenu.

To specify the position of a pop-up menu, follow these steps:

1. Click on Next. The Position tab will be activated.

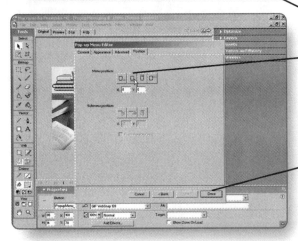

2. Click on the appropriate position button or specify the position in the X and Y boxes.

3. Specify the position of the submenu, if there is one.

4. Click on Done.

CREATING A POP-UP MENU   241

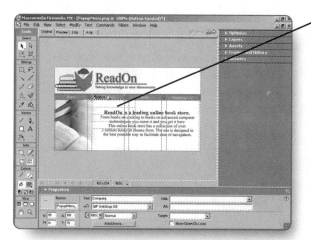

The Pop-up Menu Editor will close and the structure of the pop-up menu will appear.

You may need to make some changes to the pop-up menu. The following section provides details about modifying a pop-up menu.

Modifying a Pop-up Menu

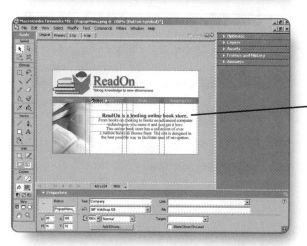

To modify a pop-up menu, follow these steps:

1. Select the slice containing the pop-up menu. The outline of the pop-up menu will appear.

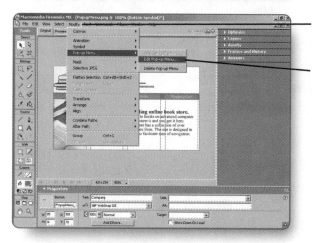

2. Click on Modify. The Modify menu will appear.

3. Point to Pop-up Menu and click on Edit Pop-up Menu. The Pop-up Menu Editor will open.

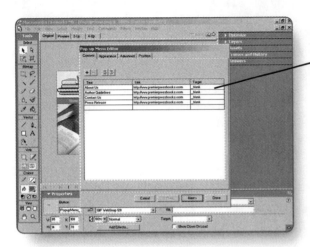

TIP

Alternatively, you can double-click on the pop-up menu outline. However, to perform this step you need to click the Show slices and hotspots button in the Tools panel.

4. Make the required modifications to the pop-up menu.

Testing a Pop-up Menu

Fireworks MX doesn't allow you to test a pop-up menu in the Preview tab. Therefore, to test a pop-up menu, you need to view it in a Web browser. To test a pop-up menu, follow these steps:

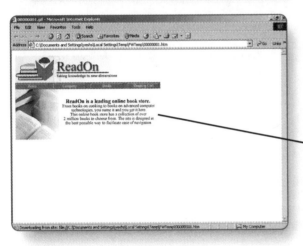

1. Press F12. The document will appear in the browser window.

TIP

You can test a pop-up menu in other browsers also by specifying a secondary browser. See "Specifying a Web Browser" in Chapter 12 to learn more on specifying Web browsers.

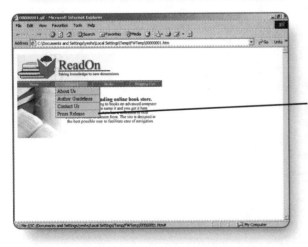

2. Point to the area that contains the pop-up menu. The pop-up menu will appear.

In this chapter, you learned to create pop-up menus by using the Pop-up Menu Editor. You can now further add to the interactivity of your Web graphics by using pop-up menus.

16

Adding Animations to Graphics

Animations have played an important role in increasing the popularity of the Web. Whether it is the scrolling images and text or flashing new attractions, animations add to the visual appeal of the Web page, which helps you attract new customers. Using Fireworks MX, you can also create animations for Web pages. Moreover, you can export these animations as animated GIFs, which are smaller in size, thus reducing the size of your Web page. In this chapter, you'll learn how to:

- Get started with animations
- Work with animations
- Export animations

Getting Started with Animations

An *animation* is a series of images that are displayed in quick succession to produce the effect of motion. For example, to make an animation that displays a moving arrow, you need to create an image with an arrow. Then, you make the required number of copies of this image and change the position of the arrow in each image. When you view all the images in quick succession, the arrow will appear as if it's moving.

Now, you will be thinking about combining all the images and viewing them as animation. To help you create animations, Fireworks MX uses *frames*. The following section provides more information about frames.

Looking at Frames

A *frame* is a placeholder that contains an image representing a specific stage of an animation. For example, if the animation that I talked about earlier contained 10 images, you need to place each of these images in a separate frame. To help you in adding and managing frames, Fireworks MX provides the Frames panel.

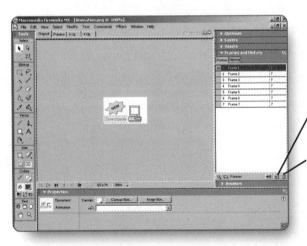

The Frames panel lists all the frames contained in an image. The panel also contains a number of controls that help you in working with frames. The following list describes some of these controls:

- **New / Duplicate Frame button**. Creates a new or duplicate frame.
- **Delete Frame button**. Deletes the selected frame.

> **NOTE**
> I'll discuss the other controls present in the Frames panel as they are required.

After getting a brief idea of working with frames, you will now learn to create animations.

Creating an Animation

In Fireworks MX, you can create images by using the following two methods:

- Opening multiple files as frames of an animation
- Creating an animation from scratch

The following subsections discuss the details of these methods.

Opening Multiple Files as Frames of an Animation

Assume, for example, you need to include an animation on your Web site that showcases all your books with a brief description. Now, you may have images of all the books, but they are stored as separate files. In such situations, you can open all these images in Fireworks MX as frames of an animation and then make the required changes. To open multiple images, follow these steps:

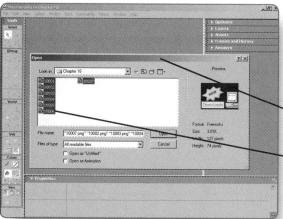

1. Display the File menu and choose Open. The Open dialog box will appear.

2. Select all the required files by using the Ctrl-click method.

> **TIP**
> Press and hold Ctrl and click on all the required files to select multiple files.

3. Click on Open as Animation. A check mark will be placed next to it.

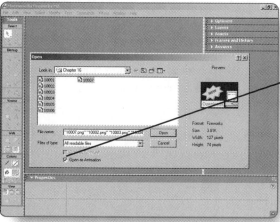

246 CHAPTER 16: ADDING ANIMATIONS TO GRAPHICS

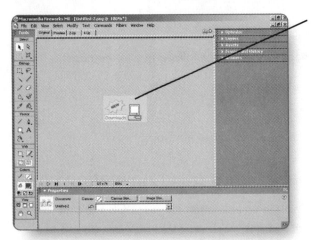

4. Click on Open. A single document will appear in the Document window.

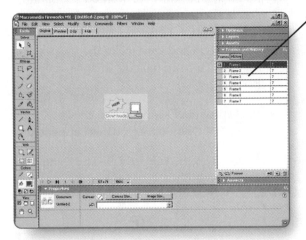

5. Display the Window menu and choose Frames. The Frames panel will open and display all the frames in your animation.

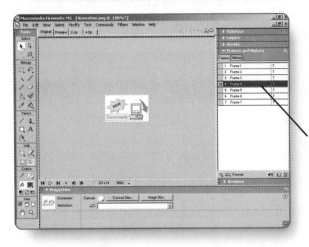

TIP
By default, the Frames panel displays the contents of the first frame, Frame 1, in the Document window.

6. Click on a frame to view its content. The contents of the selected frame will be displayed in the Document window and you can make the required changes.

GETTING STARTED WITH ANIMATIONS 247

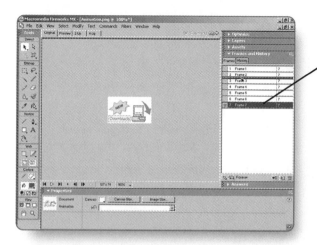

TIP

The Frames panel lists the Frames in an image starting from the topmost frame and moving down. However, you can change the order of the frames by dragging a frame to the appropriate position in the Frames panel.

Creating an Animation from Scratch

Fireworks MX provides the animation symbols to help you create your own animations. A *symbol* is any object that you can use over and again. See "Creating a Symbol" in Chapter 17, "Automating Tasks," to learn more about symbols. To create your own animation, follow these steps:

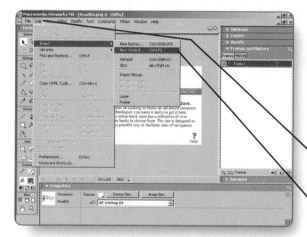

1. Display the Edit menu and point to Insert.

2. Click on New Symbol. The Symbol Properties dialog box will open.

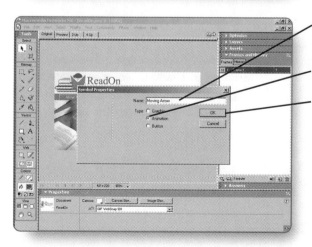

3. Type a name for the animation in the Name box.

4. Select Animation.

5. Click on OK. The Symbol Editor will open.

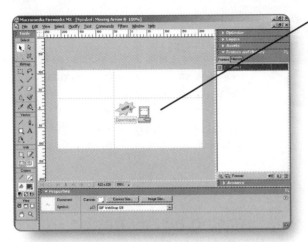

6. Create or import the required object. This will represent the first stage of animation.

TIP
You can use rulers and guides for accurate positioning of the object.

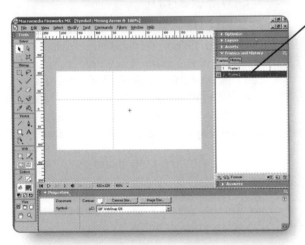

7. Click on the New/Duplicate Frame button in the Frames panel. A blank new frame, named Frame 2, will be added to the Frames panel.

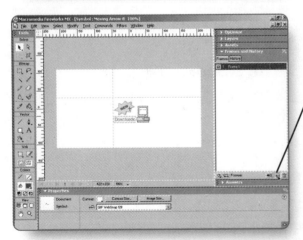

TIP
If the new frame needs only a small amount of changes, you can create a copy of the existing frame. To create a copy of a frame, drag the appropriate frame to the New/Duplicate Frame button.

GETTING STARTED WITH ANIMATIONS 249

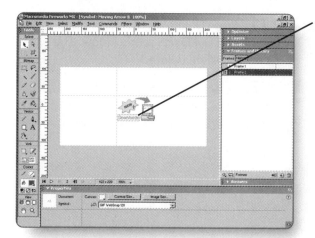

8. Create the object representing the next stage of the animation.

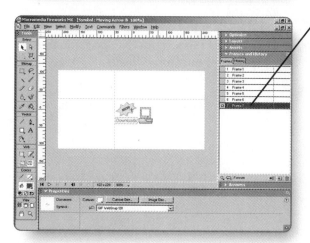

9. Repeat steps 7 and 8 to create the remaining stages of the animation.

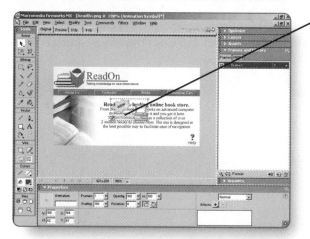

10. Close the Symbol Editor. A copy of the symbol will appear in the document.

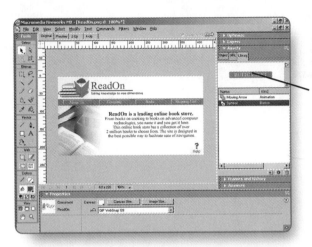

11. Press Delete after selecting the symbol in the Document window. The symbol will be deleted.

12. Select Library from the Window menu. The Library panel will open and display all the symbols that you created.

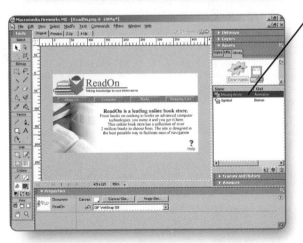

13. Select the symbol that you created. A preview of the symbol will appear in the top part of the Library panel.

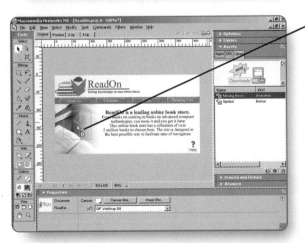

14. Press and hold the mouse button on the symbol and drag the mouse button to the document.

GETTING STARTED WITH ANIMATIONS   251

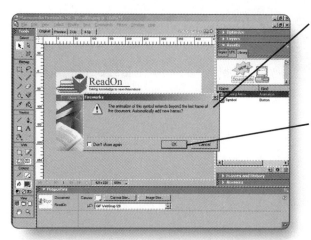

15. Release the mouse button. An instance of the symbol will be created and a message box will appear indicating that the document doesn't contain enough frames.

16. Click on OK.

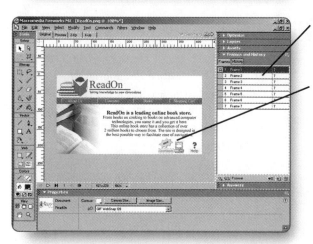

The number of frames in the document will become equal to that of the animation symbol.

17. Place the animation symbol at the appropriate location.

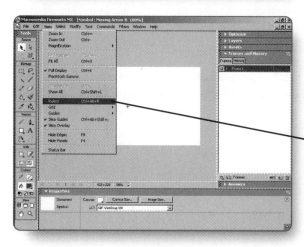

Placing Guides

Guides are lines that you can use for placing and positioning objects with precision. To create guides, follow these steps:

1. Select Rulers from the View menu.

252 CHAPTER 16: ADDING ANIMATIONS TO GRAPHICS

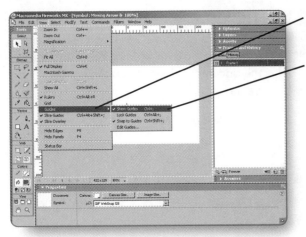

2. Display the View menu and point to Guides.

3. Check the Show Guides option, if not checked.

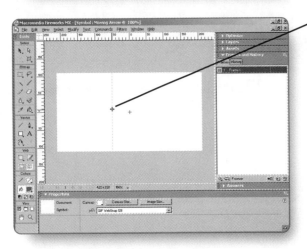

4. Drag the guide from the ruler to the canvas at an appropriate position.

After you've created the animation, you need to determine whether it works as expected. The following section provides instructions on testing and modifying an animation.

Working with Animations

Creating an animation also involves testing the animation and making any changes, if required. The following subsections provide details to perform these tasks.

WORKING WITH ANIMATIONS 253

Testing an Animation

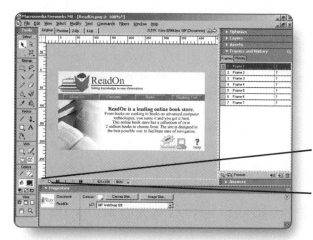

Fireworks MX provides the frame controls to test an animation. These controls help you scroll through the frames of an animation. The following list explains these controls:

- **First Frame button**. Moves you to the first frame of the animation.
- **Play/Stop button**. Plays or stops the animation.

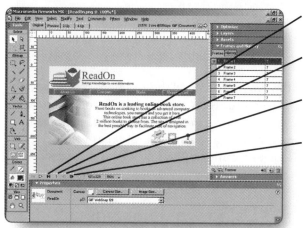

- **Last Frame button**. Moves you to the last frame of the animation.
- **Current Frame control**. Displays the number of the current frame.
- **Previous Frame button**. Moves you to the previous frame of the animation.
- **Next Frame button**. Moves you to the next frame of the animation.

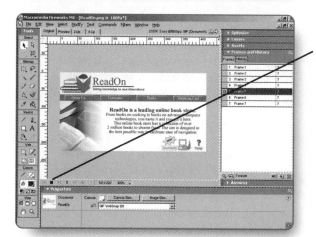

To test an animation, follow these steps:

1. Click on the Play/Stop button. The contents of each frame will be displayed in quick succession.

254 CHAPTER 16: ADDING ANIMATIONS TO GRAPHICS

TIP

The icon on the Play/Stop button will change to a solid black square when the animation is playing to indicate it is now a Stop button. When your animation is not playing, it appears as a white arrow to indicate a Play button.

2. Click on the Play/Stop button. The animation will stop playing.

If the animation doesn't play smoothly or is too fast, you can make modifications to it.

Modifying an Animation

If your animation doesn't play smoothly, you can view all the positions of the moving object, simultaneously, by using *onion skinning*. Then, you can rectify the inaccurate position. Using Fireworks MX, you can also control the movement of each frame by setting the time delay. Moreover, you can specify the number of times your animation should play by setting the looping options. The following subsections provide more information on using these techniques.

Using Onion Skinning

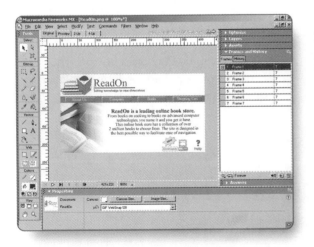

Onion skinning is a technique that allows you to see the contents of multiple frames, simultaneously, while designing an animation. The Frames panel contains the Onion Skinning button, which displays various options related to onion skinning.

The following list explains these options:

- **No Onion Skinning.** Displays the contents of the current frame only.

- **Show Next Frame.** Displays the contents of the current and the next frame.

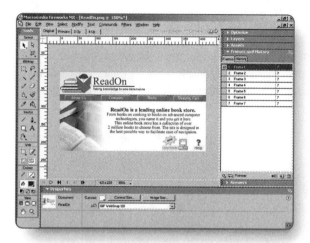

- **Before and After.** Displays the contents of the current, next, and previous frames.
- **Show All Frames.** Displays the contents of all the frames.
- **Custom.** Allows you to specify the number of frames visible.
- **Multi-Frame Editing.** Allows you to select and edit objects in any frame.

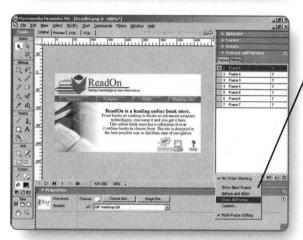

To set onion skinning options, follow these steps:

1. Click on the Onion Skinning button at the bottom of the Frames panel. A list containing various options will be displayed.

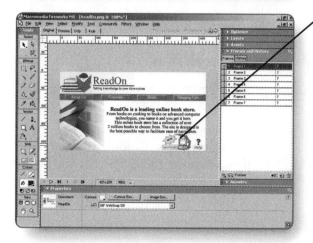

2. Select an option. The corresponding frames will be visible.

Setting Frame Delay

The amount of time for which each frame is displayed in animation is called the *frame delay*. To set the frame delay, follow these steps:

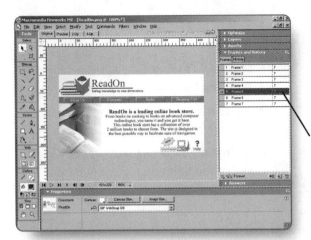

1. Click on a frame in the Frames panel. The frame will be selected.

TIP

You can also select multiple frames. To do so, press and hold Shift and select the required frames.

2. Click on the icon in the top-right corner of the Frames panel. The Frames panel menu appears.

3. Click on Properties. A pop-up window will open.

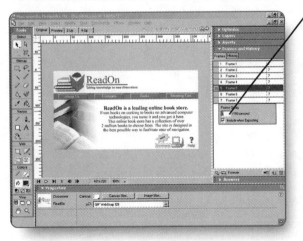

4. Type the appropriate value in the Frame Delay box and press Enter. The pop-up window will close.

TIP

The pop-up window also contains the Include when Exporting option. If you deselect this option, the frame will not be displayed in the animation and will not be exported.

Setting Looping Options

Another important task that you need to perform while creating animations is to specify the number of times the animation will play. The Frames panel contains the Looping button that helps you do so.

To specify the number of times an animation should play, follow these steps:

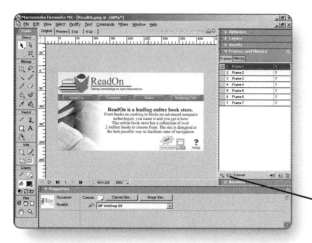

1. Click on the Looping button at the bottom of the Frames panel. A list will be displayed.

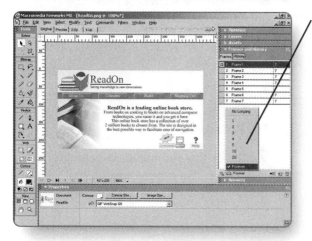

2. Select an appropriate value.

You can now test your animation by using the frame controls. See "Testing an Animation" for more information. After you have created the animation, the last task is to export it as an animated GIF. The following section provides instructions on exporting an animation.

Exporting an Animation

To export an animation, follow these steps:

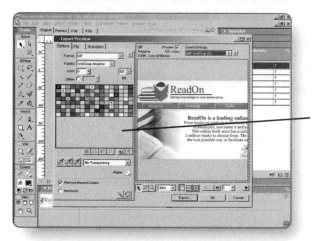

1. Select Export Preview from the File menu. The Export Preview dialog box will open.

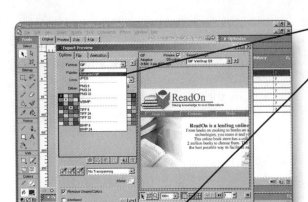

2. Select Animated GIF from the Format list.

3. Click on Export. The Export dialog box will open.

4. Specify the location to save the animation by using the Save In list.

5. Type a name for the animation in the File Name box.

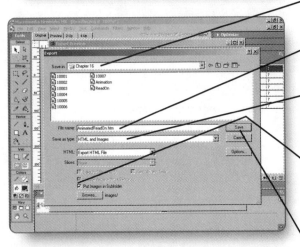

6. Select HTML and Images from the Save As Type list. The image will be saved as an HTML document.

7. Check the Put Images in Subfolder check box. The images used in the document will be saved in a separate folder.

8. Click on Save. The animation will be exported to the GIF format.

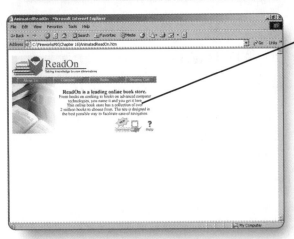

9. Open the GIF file that you created in Step 7, in the Web browser. The animation plays for the specified number of times.

You can now go ahead and start working on animations. In the next chapter, you will learn to automate tasks.

17

Automating Tasks

Fireworks MX further eases the process of working with graphics by allowing you to automate a number of tasks. You can find and replace text, colors, and URLs in your documents in a flash. You can create an object once and use it over and over again by storing it as a symbol. You can store some frequently performed tasks, such as applying effects to an object, as commands. To top it all, you can generate multiple data files by using a single Fireworks MX source file and an XML file. To help you do all this, Fireworks MX provides you with a number of panels and a wizard. In this chapter, you'll learn how to:

- Use the Find and Replace panel
- Use the Library panel
- Use the History panel
- Use the Data-Driven Graphics Wizard

Using the Find and Replace Panel

Your company decides to change the color of the buttons used on the Web site. The Web site contains a number of pages and each page contains a number of buttons. Performing this task manually would be time-consuming and may not be accurate. For example, you may choose an incorrect color, which leads to inconsistency across the site. To help you in such situations, Fireworks MX provides the Find and Replace panel. The Find and Replace panel will search all the occurrences of a particular color and replace them with the color you specify.

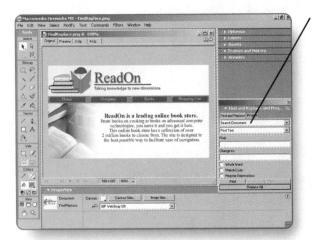

The Find and Replace panel helps you find and replace text, colors, fonts, and URLs. In addition, you can perform this operation in a document, selection, frame, and multiple files.

The Find and Replace panel contains two lists, which help you specify the object on which the search is to be performed and the object that is to be searched.

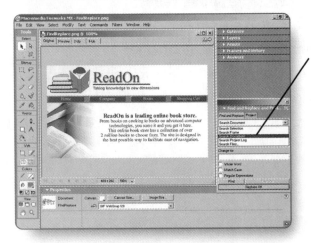

The following bullet points explain these lists:

- **Search list**. Specifies the object to be searched, such as the document, selection, frame, or multiple files.

USING THE FIND AND REPLACE PANEL   261

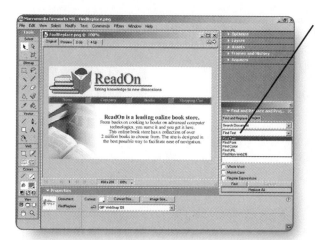

- **Find list**. Specifies the search type, such as text, font, color, or URL.

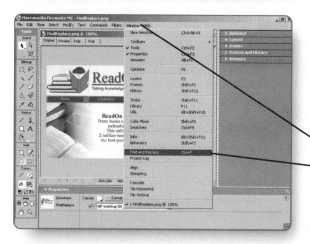

In addition to the aforementioned lists, the Find and Replace panel displays a number of controls depending on the values selected in the two lists. To find and replace a color by using the Find and Replace panel, follow these steps:

1. Display the Window menu.

2. Click on Find and Replace.

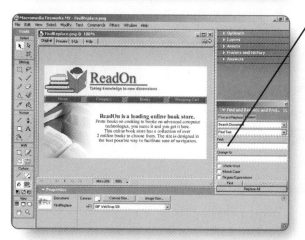

The Find and Replace panel will open.

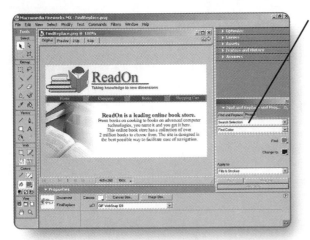

3. Choose an appropriate option from the Search list. For example, I selected Search Selection.

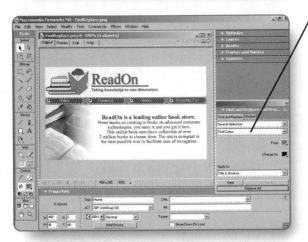

4. Choose Find Color from the Find list. The Find and Change To color boxes will open.

> **TIP**
> If you select Search Selection, you need to select the objects to be searched before proceeding with your search.

5. Specify the color to be found in the Find Color box.

USING THE FIND AND REPLACE PANEL   263

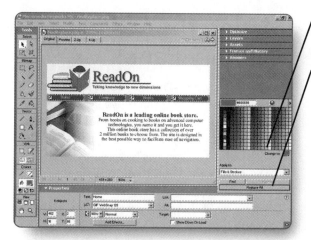

6. Specify the color that will replace the color found in Step 5.

7. Click on Replace All.

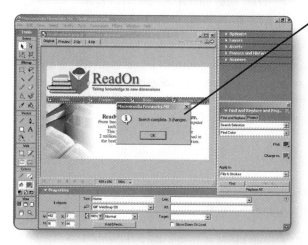

A message box will open indicating the number of changes made.

TIP

Alternatively, you can click on Find to find the color, and then click on Replace to replace the found color. You need to repeat the process until all the changes have been made.

CAUTION

Fireworks MX displays one less than the actual number of changes made. I suppose this is because it starts counting from zero.

Using the Library Panel

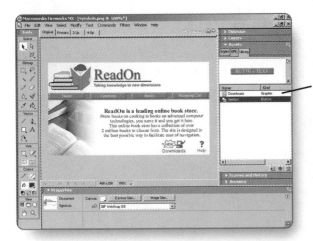

The Library panel helps you to store objects, which you can reuse later. For example, your company decides to include a Downloads object on all the pages of the Web site. You can easily do so by creating the object once and then copying the image and pasting it on all the Web pages. However, if there is a small change in the image, you will need to make it across the Web site, which is a tedious task.

In such situations, you can create a symbol, which is nothing but the desired object, and store it in the Library panel. You can now reuse this symbol by creating its instances whenever required. The advantage of using symbols and instances is that if there is any change required, you can change it in one place and the change can be easily replicated across all the instances. In this section, you will learn to create symbols and instances and export and import symbols.

Creating a Symbol

A *symbol* is any object that you can use over again. In Fireworks MX, you can create three types of symbols: graphic, button, and animation.

- **Graphic symbol**. Used to create any object that is to be used repeatedly.
- **Button symbol**. Used to create a button. See Chapter 14, "Adding Buttons to a Graphic," for more information on creating button symbols.
- **Animation symbol**. Used to create animations. See Chapter 16, "Adding Animations to Graphics," for more information on creating animation symbols.

USING THE LIBRARY PANEL 265

To create a symbol, follow these steps:

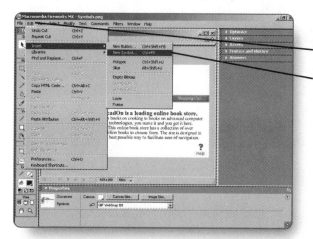

1. Display the Edit menu.

2. Point to Insert and click on New Symbol. The Symbol Properties dialog box will open.

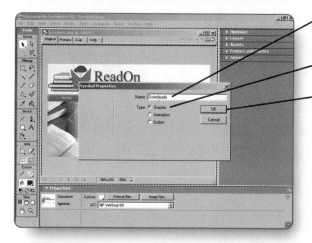

3. Type a name for the symbol in the Name box.

4. Select the Graphic option.

5. Click on OK. The Symbol Properties dialog box will close and the Symbol Editor will open.

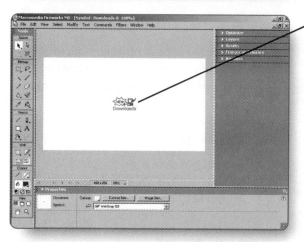

6. Create the required object in the Symbol Editor.

> ### TIP
> Alternatively, you can create the object and then choose the Convert to Symbol command from the Modify, Symbol menu to create a symbol.

266 CHAPTER 17: AUTOMATING TASKS

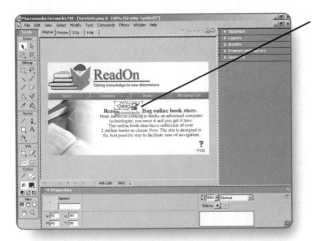

7. Close the Symbol Editor. The symbol will appear in the center of the document.

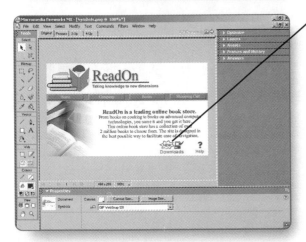

8. Move the symbol to the appropriate location.

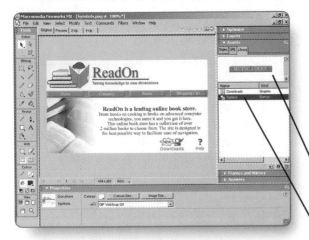

Creating an Instance

An *instance* is a copy of a symbol. You use the Library panel to create instances of a symbol, which stores all the symbols that you create in a document. The Library panel is divided into two parts, the symbol list and the symbol preview area.

- **Symbol preview area.** Displays the preview of the symbol selected in the symbol list.

- **Symbol list.** Lists all the symbols created in the document.

USING THE LIBRARY PANEL 267

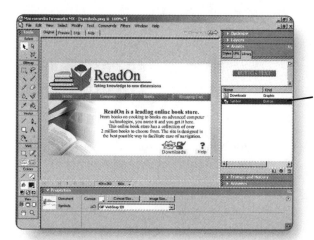

To create an instance of a symbol, follow these steps:

1. Display the Window menu.

2. Click on Library. The Library panel will open.

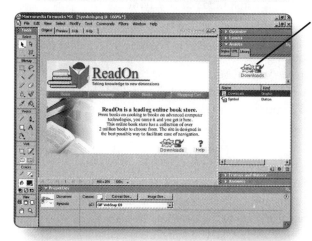

3. Click on the required symbol in the symbol list. The preview area will show the preview of the symbol.

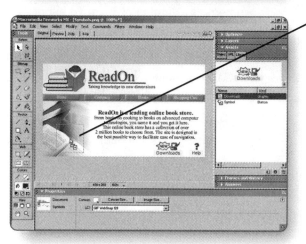

4. Press and hold the mouse button in the preview area and drag the mouse pointer to the Document window.

CHAPTER 17: AUTOMATING TASKS

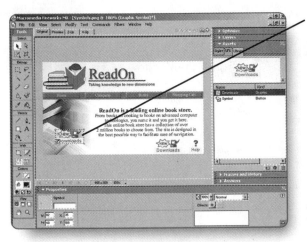

5. Release the mouse button at an appropriate location. An instance of the symbol will appear in the document.

> **TIP**
>
> You may need to make changes to the symbol you created. In order to do so, double-click on the symbol. The Symbol Editor, containing the symbol, will open. Make any changes to the symbol. However, doing so will make the change in all the instances of the symbol.

After you have created a symbol, you might be interested in using it in other documents. To use symbols in different documents, you need to export them. Once you export a symbol, you can use it in any other document. The following section provides instructions on exporting a symbol.

Exporting a Symbol

The symbols that you create are stored in the Library panel. This panel is document-specific, which means that it displays the symbols created in the current document only. For reusing the symbols in other documents, Fireworks MX allows you to export all the symbols you created in a document as a single PNG file. To export a symbol, follow these steps:

1. Click on the icon in the top-right corner of the Library panel. The Library panel Options pop-up menu will appear.

2. Click on Export Symbols. The Export Symbols dialog box will open.

USING THE LIBRARY PANEL   269

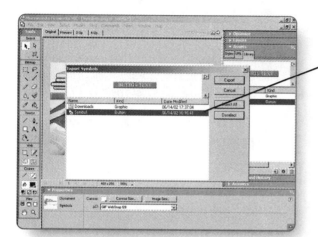

TIP
The Export Symbols dialog box lists all the symbols that you created in the current document.

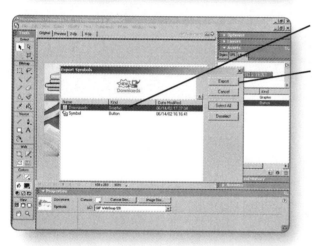

3. Click on the symbol that you need to export. The symbol will be selected.

4. Click on the Export button. The Save As dialog box will open.

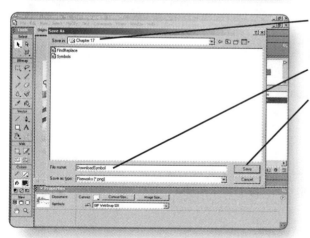

5. Select an appropriate location from the Save In list.

6. Type a name in the File Name box.

7. Click on Save. The symbol will be saved and the Save As dialog box will close.

CHAPTER 17: AUTOMATING TASKS

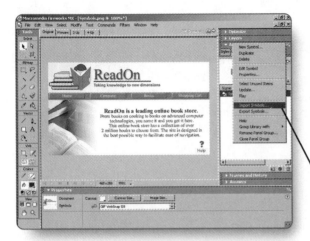

Importing a Symbol

You can import symbols that you exported earlier by using the Library panel. To import a symbol, follow these steps:

1. Display the Library panel Options pop-up menu.

2. Click on Import Symbols.

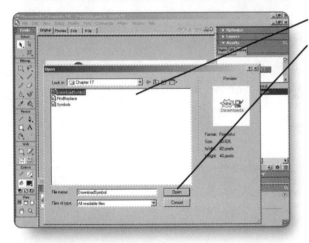

The Open dialog box will open.

3. Select the appropriate file and click on Open.

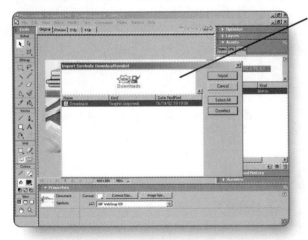

The Import Symbols dialog box will open.

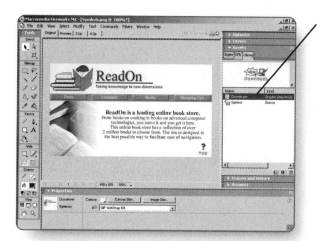

4. Select the symbol that you need and click on Import. The symbol will be added to the Library panel.

You can now use this symbol in your documents.

Using the History Panel

Each Web page on the Web site of your company contains five buttons, and there are hundreds of pages in the Web site. You need to apply an effect, such as Inner Bevel, to all the buttons. To help you in such situations, Fireworks MX provides the History panel.

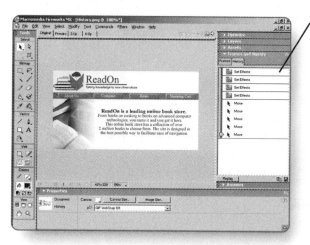

The History panel records all the steps that you perform while working on a graphic. You can replay all or some of these steps to reproduce the same effect. For example, the steps to apply Inner Bevel to a button will be recorded in the History panel. Now, to apply the same effect to another button, select the button and replay the steps in the History panel. The same effect will be applied to the second button. Moreover, the History panel allows you to save these steps as a command, which can then be used over again.

In the following sections, you will learn to replay steps and save steps as a command.

Replaying Steps

Replaying steps help you perform the same task again. To replay steps, follow these steps:

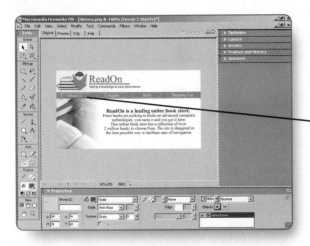

1. Perform the steps required for a task. For example, I applied the Inner Bevel effect to the About Us button.

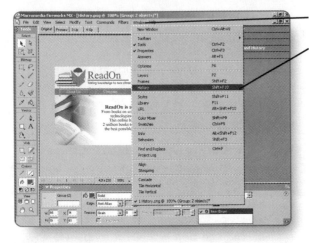

2. Display the Window menu.

3. Click on History. The History panel will open.

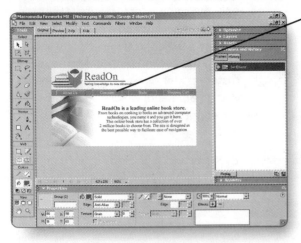

4. Select the object (in the Document window) on which you need to perform the same task.

USING THE HISTORY PANEL 273

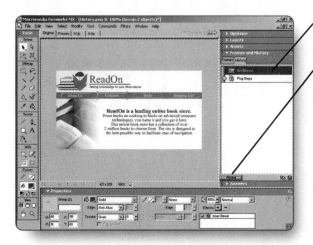

5. Select the steps that you need to replay.

6. Click on Replay at the bottom of the History panel. The same task will be performed on the selected object and another step named Play Steps will be added to the History panel.

> **TIP**
> You can select the Play Steps step to further perform the same task. This step is useful when you need to select a number of steps for replaying. Instead of selecting all the steps, you can select Play Steps and click on Replay.

Creating Commands

You can save the steps stored in the History panel as commands. To create commands, follow these steps:

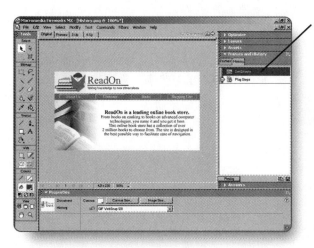

1. Select the step that you need to save as a command.

> **TIP**
> Click on a step to select it. If you need to select a set of continuous steps, press and hold Shift and click on the first and the last step. However, if you need to select a set of non-continuous steps, press and hold Ctrl and click on all the required steps.

274 CHAPTER 17: AUTOMATING TASKS

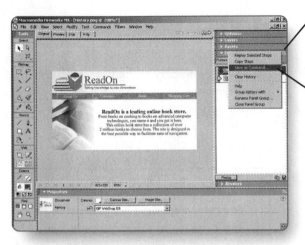

2. Click on the icon in the top-right corner of the History panel. The History panel Options pop-up menu will appear.

3. Click on Save as Command. The Save Command dialog box will open.

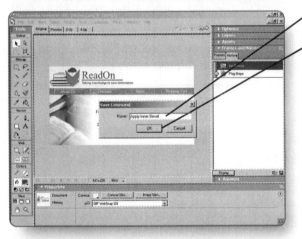

4. Type a name in the Name box.

5. Click on OK. The step will be saved as a command.

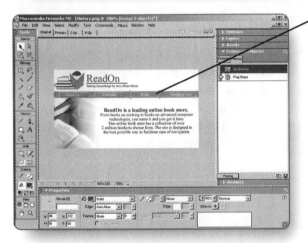

6. Select any object.

USING THE DATA-DRIVEN GRAPHICS WIZARD   275

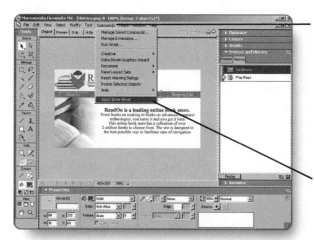

7. Click on Commands. The Commands menu will appear.

> **TIP**
> The Commands menu contains the command that you created.

8. Click on the command that you created.

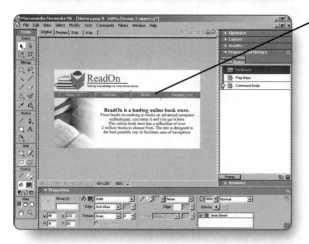

The effect of the command will be applied to the selected object.

Using the Data-Driven Graphics Wizard

Suppose you need to create a product catalog, which displays different products of your company. The catalog uses the same background for all the products. In such situations, you use the Data-Driven Graphics Wizard (DDGW). The DDGW generates multiple data files by using a single Fireworks MX source file and an XML file. The Fireworks MX source file used with the DDGW is referred to as the template file.

A *template file* is a Fireworks MX file containing variables. A *variable* is any text enclosed within the curly braces. For example, {Book} is a variable. You can create three types of variables: text, image, and URLs.

The following list explains these variables in detail:

- **Text**. Variables used for text.
- **Image**. Variables used for images. You can create an image variable by typing a name, such as {Image1}, for the image in the Name box of the Property Inspector.
- **URL**. Variables used for hotspots and slices. You can create a URL variable by typing a variable, such as {URL1}, in the Link text box of the Property Inspector.

CAUTION
There is a bug in Fireworks MX that doesn't allow the use of symbols in template files.

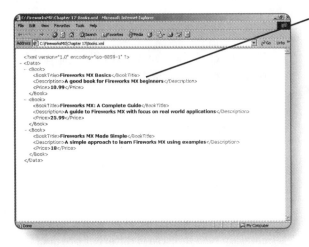

The XML file contains the data, which replaces the variables used in the template file.

TIP
See Appendix B, "Creating an XML Document," for more information about creating XML documents.

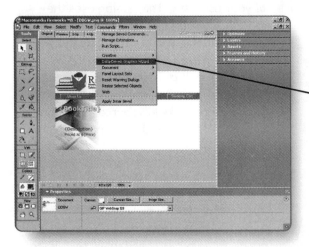

To generate multiple files by using the DDGW, follow these steps:

1. Open the template file.

2. Select Data-Driven Graphics Wizard from the Commands menu. Screen 1 of the Data-Driven Graphics Wizard will open.

USING THE DATA-DRIVEN GRAPHICS WIZARD 277

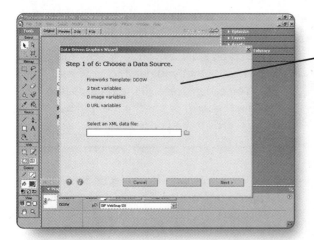

TIP
Screen 1 displays the total variables used in your document. It also allows you to specify the XML file to be used.

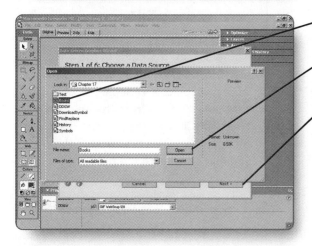

3. Click on the Folder icon. The Open dialog box will open.

4. Click on Open after selecting the appropriate XML file.

5. Click on Next. Screen 2 of the DDGW will open.

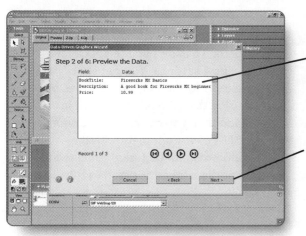

TIP
Screen 2 displays all the records stored in the XML file. You can browse through these records by using the VCR-like controls.

6. Click on Next. Screen 3 of the DDGW will open.

278 CHAPTER 17: AUTOMATING TASKS

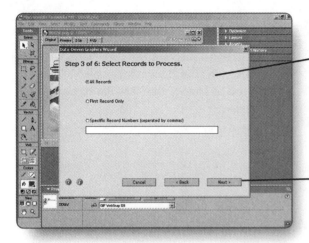

TIP

Screen 3 allows you to specify the records that you need to process. You can process all the records, the first record, or specify the number of records to be processed.

7. Click on Next after selecting an appropriate option. Screen 4 of the DDGW will open.

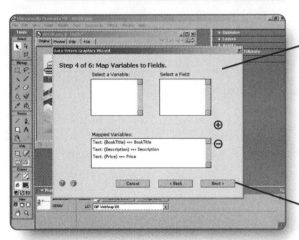

TIP

Screen 4 allows you to map the variables with the fields in the XML file. To do so, select a variable name from the Select a Variable list, and then select a field from the Select a Field list. Click on the + icon. The Mapped Variables list displays the variable along with the field.

8. Click on Next. Screen 5 of the DDGW will open.

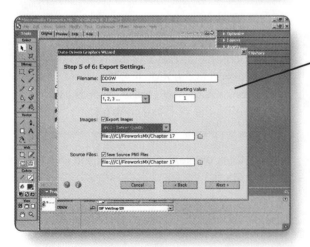

TIP

Screen 5 allows you to specify the export settings. You can specify the export format for the data files by using the list next to Images. In addition, you can create the source PNG files. For doing both the aforementioned tasks, you need to specify a folder for storing the files.

USING THE DATA-DRIVEN GRAPHICS WIZARD 279

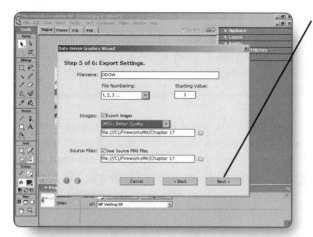

9. Click on Next after making appropriate settings. Screen 6 of the DDGW will open.

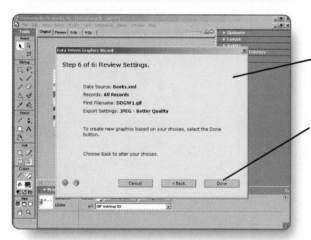

TIP
Screen 6 displays all the settings that you made.

10a. Click on Done to close the wizard. The data files will be generated.

OR

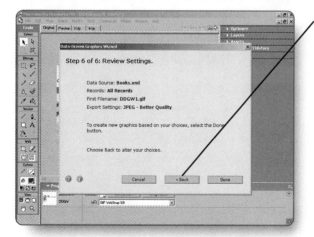

10b. Click on Back to make any other changes.

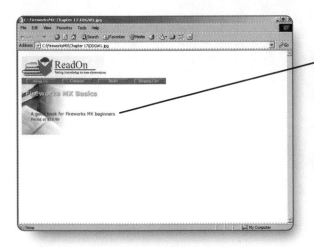

> **TIP**
> Open the exported files to check them.

With this, you have learned to reduce the time taken to perform various tasks by automating them. In the next chapter, you will learn to integrate Fireworks MX with other applications, such as Dreamweaver MX.

18

Integrating Fireworks MX with Macromedia Dreamweaver MX

You can enhance the Web development capabilities of Fireworks MX by integrating it with various Macromedia and non-Macromedia applications, such as Dreamweaver MX, Adobe Photoshop, and Microsoft FrontPage. In this chapter, you'll learn to integrate Fireworks MX and Dreamweaver MX. Dreamweaver MX allows you to perform professional-level HTML editing for designing and developing Web sites. You can easily design Web pages in its user-friendly editing environment. In addition, you can precisely control Web pages by hand-coding HTML into Web pages.

In this chapter, you'll learn how to:

- Use the Roundtrip HTML feature
- Work with Fireworks MX images in Dreamweaver MX
- Work with Fireworks MX HTML in Dreamweaver MX
- Export Fireworks documents with the Quick Export Button

Fireworks MX and Dreamweaver MX together provide an effectively organized and user-friendly workflow for designing and developing Web-based applications. Fireworks MX makes use of the Roundtrip HTML feature for integrating with Dreamweaver MX. In addition, Fireworks MX provides the Quick Export feature that lets you move your Fireworks MX documents between various Macromedia and non-Macromedia applications, quickly and easily.

Understanding the Roundtrip HTML Feature

Roundtrip HTML refers to the integration between Fireworks MX and Dreamweaver MX. This feature causes modifications made in one application to be reflected in the other. You can launch Fireworks MX from within Dreamweaver MX to edit images and HTML tables created in Fireworks MX. When you do so, the Fireworks MX source files are opened automatically. After you have performed the required modifications in Fireworks MX, you can return to Dreamweaver MX and the changes are reflected in the placed image or HTML table.

Before you can start using the Roundtrip HTML feature, you need to make the following settings in Dreamweaver MX:

- Make Fireworks MX the External Image Editor for Dreamweaver MX
- Set the launch-and-edit preferences in Fireworks MX

The following sections discuss these settings in detail.

Making Fireworks MX the External Image Editor for Dreamweaver MX

Dreamweaver MX allows you to specify Fireworks MX as the external image editor for the Web graphic file formats, which include the GIF, PNG, and JPEG file formats. To do so, follow these steps:

1. Launch the Dreamweaver MX application.

UNDERSTANDING THE ROUNDTRIP HTML FEATURE 283

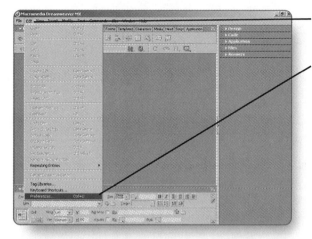

2. Click on Edit. The Edit menu will appear.

3. Click on Preferences. The Preferences dialog box will open.

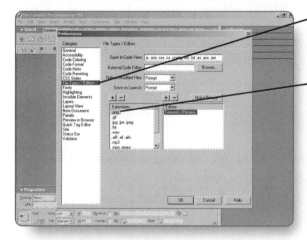

4. Select File Types/Editors from the Category list. The related options will become available.

5. Select a Web graphic file extension from the Extensions list. The default editors for the selected file extension will appear in the Editors list.

NOTE
The files saved in GIF, PNG, and JPEG formats have .GIF, .PNG, and .JPG extensions, respectively.

6. Select Fireworks from the Editors list.

7. Click on Make Primary. Fireworks MX will become the primary image editor for the selected file extension.

Setting Launch-and-Edit Preferences in Fireworks MX

You can set launch-and-edit preferences in Fireworks MX to control the way Fireworks MX source files are managed while launching them from other applications.

> **NOTE**
>
> Fireworks MX creates a Design Note for each source PNG file that you place in Dreamweaver MX. This Design Note contains a reference to the source PNG file. When you launch and edit a Fireworks MX file from Dreamweaver MX, this Design Note is used to locate the respective Fireworks MX source file. However, if the Design Note of the image that you are launching does not contain the correct path to the source PNG file, then Dreamweaver MX uses the launch-and-edit preferences specified in Fireworks MX.

You can specify any of the following settings for the source PNG files in Fireworks MX's launch-and-edit preferences:

- **Always Use Source PNG**. Launches the Fireworks MX source PNG file. In this case, both the source and the placed files are updated.

- **Never Use Source PNG**. Launches the placed Fireworks MX image. In this case, only the placed file is updated.

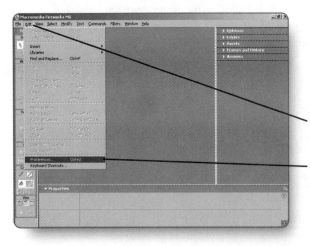

- **Ask When Launching**. Prompts you whether to launch the Fireworks MX source PNG file.

To set launch-and-edit preferences, follow these steps:

1. Click on Edit. The Edit menu will appear.

2. Click on Preferences. The Preferences dialog box will open.

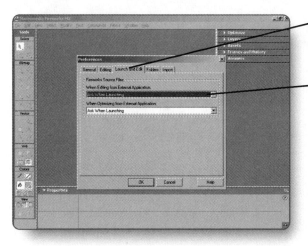

3. Click on the Launch and Edit tab. The launch-and-edit options will become available.

4. Specify the desired preference for editing or optimizing Fireworks MX source files placed in Dreamweaver MX.

After making the required settings, you can then work with Fireworks MX images or HTML in Dreamweaver MX. In the following section, you will learn how to work with Fireworks MX images in Dreamweaver MX.

Working with Fireworks MX Images in Dreamweaver MX

Dreamweaver MX allows you to create images by using Fireworks MX from within the Dreamweaver environment. To do so, it allows you to create image placeholders that can be used to launch Fireworks MX for creating images. You can edit these images by using Fireworks MX anytime from within Dreamweaver MX. The changes that you make to these images in Fireworks MX are reflected in Dreamweaver MX.

In this section, you will learn to create and edit Fireworks MX images from within the Dreamweaver MX environment.

Creating Fireworks MX Images from Dreamweaver MX Placeholders

To create Fireworks images from Dreamweaver MX, you need to perform the following two steps:

- Create image placeholders
- Create the images by using the image placeholders

The following subsections provide instructions to perform these steps.

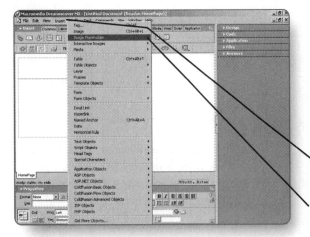

Creating Image Placeholders

To create an image placeholder in Dreamweaver MX, follow these steps:

1. Click at the appropriate location in the Dreamweaver MX document. The placeholder will be created at this location.

2. Click on Insert. The Insert menu will appear.

3. Click on Image Placeholder. The Image Placeholder dialog box will open.

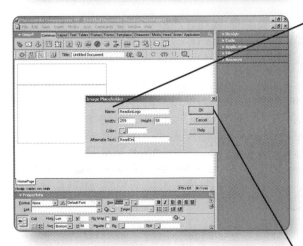

4. Enter Name, Width, Height, Color, and Alternate Text values for the image placeholder.

> **TIP**
>
> You can check the dimensions of an image in Fireworks MX by using the Page Preview box in the Document window. See "Working with Fireworks MX Documents" in Chapter 2, "Getting Started with Fireworks MX," to learn more about the Document window.

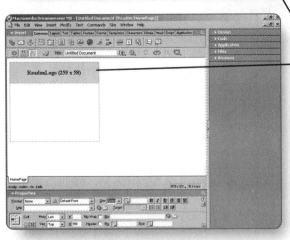

5. Click on OK.

The image placeholder will be inserted in the Dreamweaver document.

WORKING WITH FIREWORKS MX IMAGES IN DREAMWEAVER MX   287

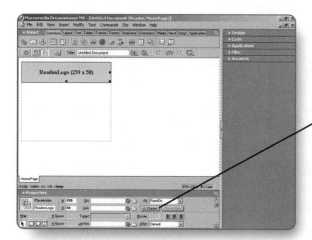

Creating Images by Using the Image Placeholders

To create an image by using an image placeholder, follow these steps:

1. Click on the Create button in the Dreamweaver MX Property Inspector. Fireworks MX will launch and the Document window will open for the new image file.

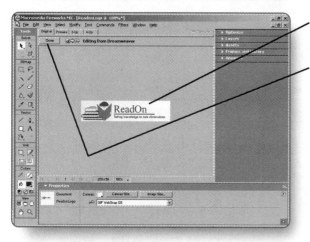

2. Create an image in the Fireworks MX document.

3. Click on Done. The Save As dialog box for saving the source PNG file will open.

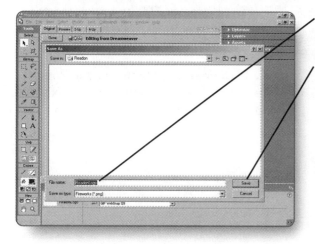

4. Enter a name and location for the source PNG file.

5. Click on Save. The Export dialog box for exporting the image file will open.

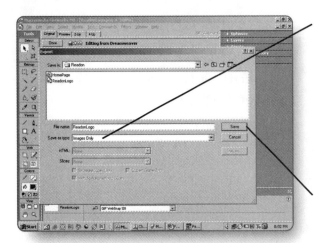

6. Enter the name, location, and other export settings for the image file.

> **NOTE**
> See "Optimizing and Exporting Graphics" in Chapter 11 to learn more about optimizing graphics.

7. Click on Save.

The file will be exported and the image placeholder will be replaced with the new image.

Editing Fireworks MX Images from Dreamweaver MX

To edit Fireworks MX generated images from Dreamweaver MX, follow these steps:

1. Select the image in Dreamweaver MX. The Dreamweaver MX Property Inspector will display the options related to the selected image.

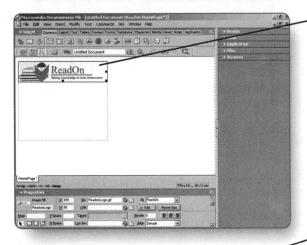

2. Click on the Edit button in the Property Inspector. The Find Source dialog box will open.

> **TIP**
> The Find Source dialog box can be used to locate an existing Fireworks MX source PNG file.

WORKING WITH FIREWORKS MX IMAGES IN DREAMWEAVER MX 289

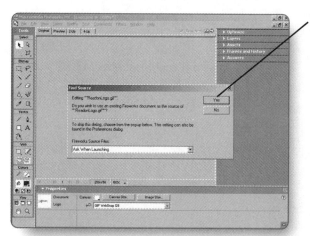

3. Click on Yes. The Open dialog box will open.

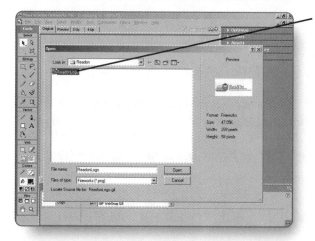

4. Select the source PNG file and click on Open. The source Fireworks MX document will open.

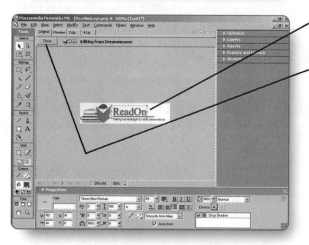

5. Make the required changes to the image.

6. Click on Done.

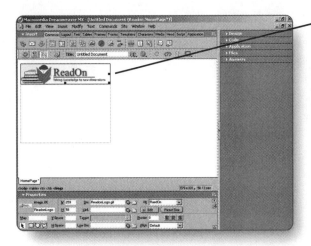

The image placed in Dreamweaver MX is updated.

You can also place Fireworks MX HTML in Dreamweaver MX and work with it. The following section provides the details to do so.

Working with Fireworks MX HTML in Dreamweaver MX

You can utilize the Roundtrip HTML feature for exporting Fireworks MX HTML to Dreamweaver MX HTML and updating the Fireworks MX HTML from Dreamweaver MX. Otherwise, you can use the Update HTML command for updating an HTML document that you've previously exported to Dreamweaver MX, with changes that you've made in Fireworks MX.

Exporting Fireworks MX HTML to Dreamweaver MX

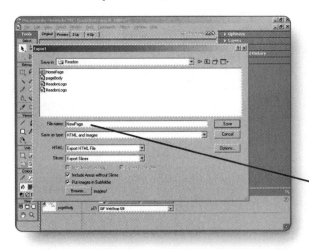

You can export HTML from a Fireworks MX document to a Dreamweaver MX compatible format, which can then be inserted into a Dreamweaver MX document. To do so, follow these steps:

1. Select Export from the File menu in Fireworks MX. The Export dialog box will open.

2. Enter a name and location for the exported HTML code.

WORKING WITH FIREWORKS MX HTML IN DREAMWEAVER MX 291

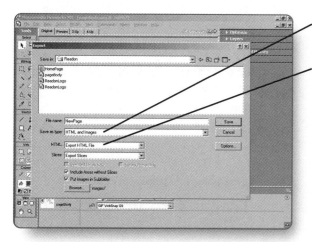

3. Select HTML and Images from the Save as Type pop-up list.

4. Select Export HTML File from the HTML pop-up list.

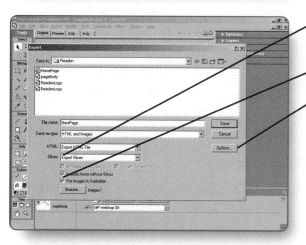

5. Select Export Slices from the Slices pop-up list.

6. Check the Put Images in Subfolder box.

7. Click on the Options button. The HTML Setup dialog box will open.

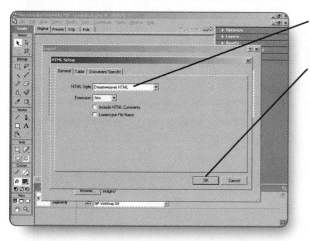

8. Select Dreamweaver HTML from the HTML pop-up menu.

9. Click on the OK button. The HTML Setup dialog box will close.

CHAPTER 18: INTEGRATING FIREWORKS MX WITH DREAMWEAVER MX

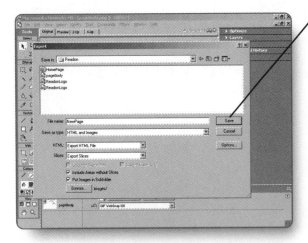

10. Click on the Save button. The HTML files are exported.

After exporting a Fireworks MX document to a Dreamweaver compatible HTML format, you need to insert it in Dreamweaver MX.

Inserting Fireworks MX HTML in Dreamweaver MX

To insert Fireworks MX HTML into a Dreamweaver MX document, follow these steps:

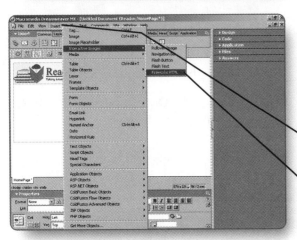

1. Click on an appropriate location in the Dreamweaver MX document. The Fireworks MX HTML code will be inserted at this location.

2. Click on Insert. The Insert menu will appear.

3. Point to Interactive Images and click on Fireworks HTML. The Insert Fireworks HTML dialog box will open.

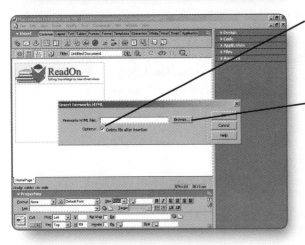

4. Check the Delete File After Insertion option. The HTML file will be deleted from the hard disk after it is inserted in the Dreamweaver MX document.

5. Click on the Browse button. A dialog box for choosing the Fireworks MX HTML file will open.

WORKING WITH FIREWORKS MX HTML IN DREAMWEAVER MX   293

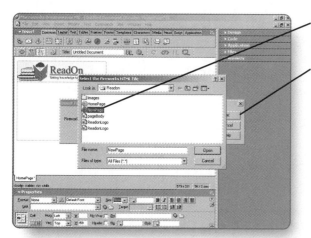

6. Click on Open after selecting the required file.

7. Click on OK.

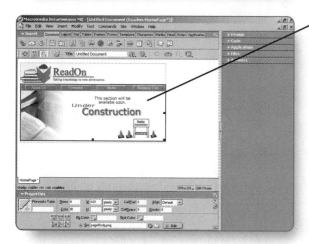

The Fireworks MX HTML file will be inserted in the Dreamweaver MX document as a table.

Editing Fireworks MX HTML from Dreamweaver MX

To edit Fireworks MX HTML inserted in a Dreamweaver MX document, follow these steps:

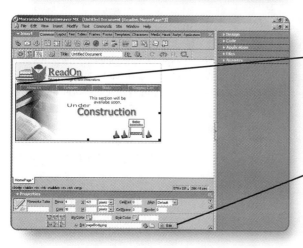

1. Click in the upper-left corner of the Fireworks MX table in Dreamweaver MX. The entire table will be selected and the Dreamweaver MX's Property Inspector will display the name of the Fireworks MX source file.

2. Click on Edit in the Property Inspector. The source Fireworks MX PNG file will open in Fireworks MX.

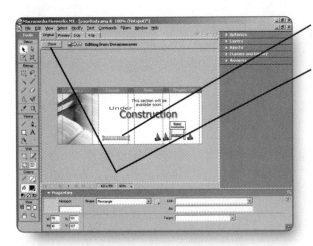

3. Make the required changes in the source Fireworks MX PNG file.

4. Click on Done.

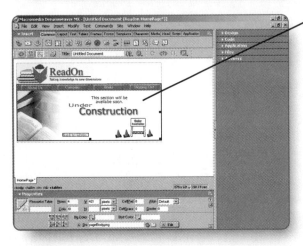

The changes made in Fireworks MX will be reflected in the Dreamweaver MX document.

You can also update Fireworks MX HTML exported to Dreamweaver MX by using the Update HTML command.

Updating Fireworks MX HTML Exported to Dreamweaver MX

You can modify Fireworks MX source PNG files, exported to Dreamweaver MX, in Fireworks MX and then use the Update HTML command to update the Dreamweaver MX file that contains a previously exported HTML code. To do so, follow these steps:

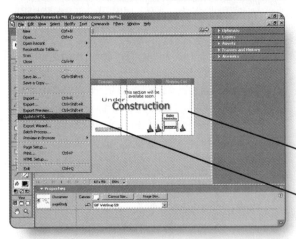

1. Make required changes in the Fireworks MX document.

2. Select Update HTML from the File menu. The Locate HTML File dialog box will open.

WORKING WITH FIREWORKS MX HTML IN DREAMWEAVER MX   295

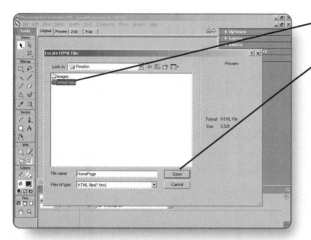

3. Select the Dreamweaver MX file that you want to update.

4. Click on Open. The Update HTML dialog box will open.

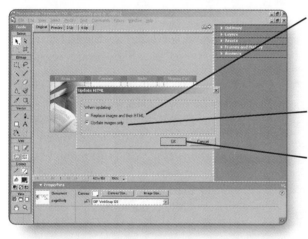

5a. Select Replace Images and their HTML. Images as well as the HTML code will be updated.

OR

5b. Select Update Images only. Only the images will be updated.

6. Click on OK.

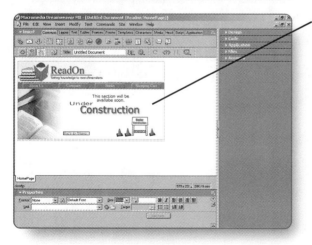

The Dreamweaver MX document will be updated.

In addition to Dreamweaver MX, you can integrate Fireworks MX with various other applications, such as Photoshop and FrontPage. The Quick Export feature in Fireworks MX serves as a convenient and quick means to do so. Read the following section to learn how to use the Quick Export button.

Exporting Documents with the Quick Export Button

Fireworks MX provides you with the Quick Export button, which provide some commonly used options for exporting Fireworks MX documents to other applications. These options are available in the Quick Export pop-up menu. To view the Quick Export pop-up menu, click on the Quick Export button present in the Document window.

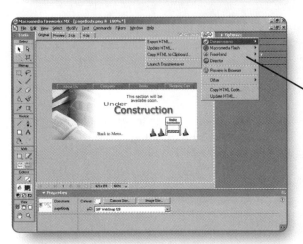

The following list describes the options available in the Quick Export pop-up menu:

- **Macromedia applications**. For working with Macromedia applications, such as Dreamweaver MX, Flash MX, FreeHand MX, and Director MX. Each of these applications contains a submenu. You can use a submenu for launching the respective application or exporting Fireworks MX documents to that application.

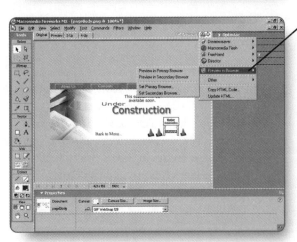

- **Preview in Browser**. For previewing Fireworks MX documents in specified browsers. You can also set a primary and a secondary browser by using this option.

EXPORTING DOCUMENTS WITH THE QUICK EXPORT BUTTON   297

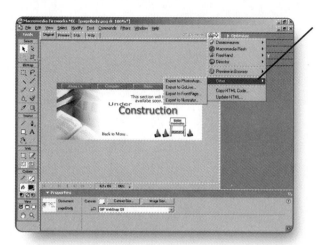

- **Other**. For exporting Fireworks MX documents to applications other than the Macromedia applications, such as Adobe Photoshop, Adobe GoLive, Microsoft FrontPage, and Adobe Illustrator.

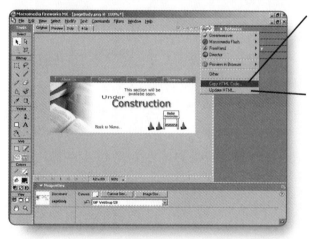

- **Copy HTML code**. For copying the HTML and JavaScript files, which are associated with a Fireworks MX document, to the Clipboard.

- **Update HTML**. For updating the existing HTML file with the HTML associated with a Fireworks MX document.

In this chapter, you have learned to integrate Fireworks MX with Dreamweaver MX. You can go ahead and use the Quick Export button to integrate Fireworks MX with other applications as well.

This ends our discussion on using of Fireworks MX for Web development. You've learned creating, editing, and modifying Web graphics. You've also learned about designing and developing Web pages. You can now go ahead and start experimenting with all the techniques taught in this book. This book contains two appendixes. Appendix A is a quick reference to various shortcut keys, which you can refer to while working with Fireworks MX. Appendix B teaches you the techniques to create an XML document for use with the Data-Driven Graphics wizard.

PART IV

Appendixes

Appendix A
Keyboard Shortcuts in
Fireworks MX 301

Appendix B
Creating an XML Document 307

A
Keyboard Shortcuts in Fireworks MX

Keyboard shortcuts help you perform tasks easily. For example, to view the Frames panel, instead of clicking the Window menu and then selecting Frames, you can press the Shift and F2 keys simultaneously. I will refer to these key combinations as Shift+F2.

In this appendix, I've provided a list of shortcut keys that help you perform a number of frequently performed tasks.

Keyboard Shortcuts for the Document Window

Keyboard shortcuts for the Document window are used to save, close, or create new documents. The Document window also includes shortcuts to work with the objects present in the document. The commonly used shortcut keys are listed in Table A-1.

Table A-1 Keyboard Shortcuts for the Document Window

Task	Shortcut Key(s)
Creating a new document	Ctrl+N
Opening a document	Ctrl+O
Saving a document	Ctrl+S
Importing an object	Ctrl+R
Exporting a document	Ctrl+Shift+R
Cutting an object	Ctrl+X
Copying an object	Ctrl+C
Pasting an object	Ctrl+V
Undoing steps	Ctrl+Z
Redoing steps	Ctrl+Y
Selecting all the objects	Ctrl+A
Deselecting all the objects	Ctrl+D

Keyboard Shortcuts for the Panels in the Fireworks MX Workspace

Keyboard shortcuts for the panels in the Fireworks MX workspace are used to display various panels. The commonly used shortcut keys are listed in Table A-2.

Table A-2 Keyboard Shortcuts for the Panels

Panel	Shortcut Key(s)
Tools panel	Ctrl+F2
Property Inspector	Ctrl+F3
Answers panel	Alt+F1
Optimize panel	F6
Layers panel	F2
Frames panel	Shift+F2
History panel	Shift+F10
Styles panel	Shift+F11
Library panel	F11
URL panel	Alt+Shift+F10
Color Mixer panel	Shift+F9
Swatches panel	Ctrl+F9
Info panel	Alt+Shift+F12
Behaviors panel	Shift+F3
Find and Replace panel	Ctrl+F

Keyboard Shortcuts for the Tools Panel

Keyboard shortcuts for the Tools panel are used for selecting a particular tool. The commonly used shortcut keys in the Tools panel are listed in Table A-3.

Table A-3 Keyboard Shortcuts for the Tools Panel

Tool	Shortcut Key(s)
Pointer tool	V or 0
Subselection tool	A or 1
Marquee tool	M
Lasso tool	L
Crop tool	C
Magic Wand tool	W
Line tool	N
Pen tool	P
Rectangle tool	U
Text tool	V
Pencil tool	B
Brush tool	B
Eyedropper tool	I
Paint Bucket tool	G
Knife tool	Y
Rectangle Hotspot tool	J
Slice tool	K
Hand tool	H
Zoom tool	Z

All the aforementioned tables include shortcut keys for very frequently used tools and panels. However, Fireworks MX provides you with an option to generate a comprehensive list of shortcut keys for your reference. In the following section, you'll learn to generate a list of shortcut keys.

Generating a List of Shortcut Keys

You can generate a list of shortcut keys used in Fireworks MX in the HTML format. To do so, follow these steps:

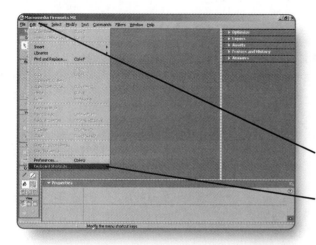

1. Click on Edit. The Edit menu will appear.

2. Click on Keyboard Shortcuts.

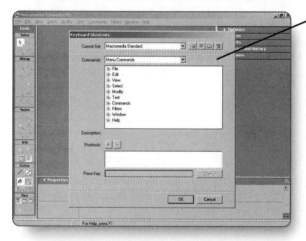

The Keyboard Shortcuts dialog box will open.

3. Click on the Export Set as HTML button. The Save As dialog box will open in front of the Keyboard Shortcuts dialog box.

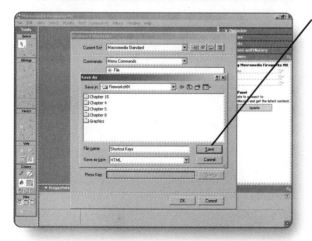

4. Click on Save after making appropriate settings. The Save As dialog box will close and the Keyboard Shortcuts dialog box becomes active.

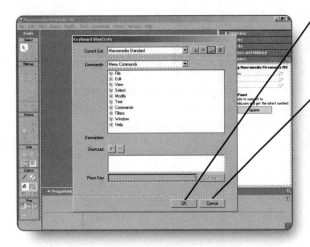

5a. Click on OK. The Keyboard Shortcuts dialog box will close.

OR

5b. Click on Cancel. The Keyboard Shortcuts dialog box will close.

You can open the HTML file generated by Fireworks MX and take its printout, which you can refer to as needed.

B

Creating an XML Document

The Data-Driven Graphics Wizard uses an XML file as a data store. XML (Extensible Markup Language) is a markup language that is used to store information that's presented on a Web browser. An XML file stores data in a hierarchical structure by using a number of components.

The following list explains these components:

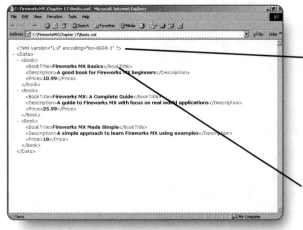

- **Processing Instruction**—An XML document usually begins with the XML declaration statement, also called the *Processing Instruction* (PI). The PI provides information regarding the way in which the XML file should be processed.

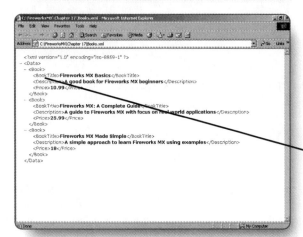

- **Tags**—Used to identify data. They specify a name for the given piece of information. A tag consists of opening and closing angular brackets (<>). These brackets enclose the name of the tag. Tags usually occur in pairs. Each pair consists of a start tag and an end tag. The start tag only contains the name of the tag, whereas the end tag includes a forward slash (/) before the name of the tag.

- **Elements**—Basic units used to identify and describe data in XML. They are the building blocks of an XML document. Elements are represented using tags. For example, if you need to represent data pertaining to books, you can create elements such as BookTitle, Description, and Price.

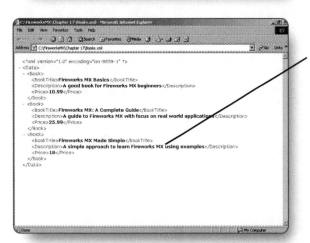

- **Content**—The information that is represented by the elements of an XML document is referred to as the content of that element. For example, Fireworks MX Basics can be the content of the BookTitle element.

CREATING AN XML DOCUMENT

To create an XML file, follow these steps:

1. Launch Notepad.

2. Type the appropriate Processing Instruction.

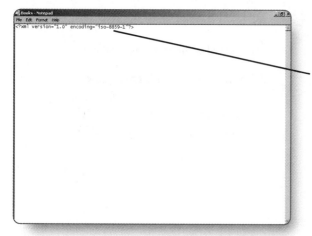

3. Create the elements to be used. For example, I created the elements to contain the details of books.

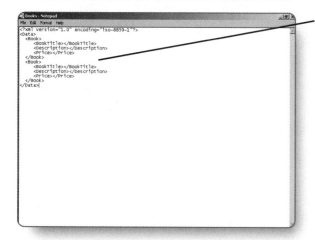

4. Enter the contents within the elements.

CAUTION
There should be no space between the element name and its contents.

5. Save the file with an .XML extension.

6. View the file in a Web browser.

With this, you have learned to create a simple XML document. You can now go ahead and create your own XML documents to use with the DDGW.

Index

A

active area, buttons, 215–217
Adaptive palette, 157
Align panel, 19
animations, 244
    creating
        from scratch, 247–251
        multiple files as frames of, 245–247
    exporting, 257–258
    frame delay, setting, 256
    Frames panel, 244
    guides, placing, 251–252
    looping options, 257
    onion skinning, 254–255
    testing, 253–254
Answers panel, 19
anti-alias option, Marquee tool, 78
Appearance tab (Pop-up Menu Editor), 228, 235–240
auto naming image slices, 189–190
auto-size text blocks, 117
automation
    Data-Driven Graphics Wizard, 275–280
    Find and Replace panel, 260–263
    History panel, 271
        commands, creating, 273–275
        replaying steps, 272–273
    Library panel
        instances, creating, 266–268
        symbols, creating, 264–266

B

Behavior handle, disjoint rollovers, 202–204
behaviors, rollovers, 202–206
Behaviors panel, 19
Bezier curves, drawing, 57–59
bitmap objects options, 30
Bitmap tools, 16
bitmaps, 69. *See also* images; vector graphics
    Brush tool, 73–74
    cloning, 89–91
    Eraser tool, 74–75
    importing, 70–71
    lightening and darkening, 86–87
    masks, creating, 150–151
    Pencil tool, 71–72
    retouching tools, 84–85
    smudging, 88–89
Black and White palette, 157
Blend Mode list, 135
Blur tool, 84
browsers
    documents, previewing, 181–182
    primary and secondary, specifying, 180–181
Brush tip size box, 85
Brush tool, 73–74
Burn tool, 86–87
buttons
    active area, 215–217
    Down state, creating, 213–214
    moving, 217

INDEX

buttons *(continued)*
    navigation bars, 218
        Clone command, 220–221
        creating button instances, 219–221
        testing, 224–225
    Over state, creating, 212–213
    Over while Down state, creating, 214–215
    properties, editing, 221–224
    states of, 210
    testing, 217–218
    types of, 210
    Up state, creating, 210–212
    URLs, testing, 218

C

canvas, 12
character spacing, 122
Circle Hotspot tool, 176
circles, drawing, 55
Clone command, button instances, 220–221
cloning. *See also* duplicating
    bitmap objects, 89–91
closing, documents, 15
CMY color model, 101
collapsing and expanding, panels, 22
color
    creating and applying to objects
        color bar, 103–104
        color models, 102–103
    Eyedropper tool, 93–94
    fills, 66–68
    gradient fills, 104–105
        editing, 105–107
        transforming, 108
    Magic Wand tool, 78–79
    Paint Bucket tool, 94–96
    strokes, 64–66
    Web Dither fills, 109–110
    Web-safe, 109
color bar, creating and applying color to objects, 103–104
color defaults (General preferences tab), 27–28
Color Mixer panel, 18, 101
color models, 101
color palettes
    compressing images, 160
    dithering images, 159
    interlacing, 161
    modifying, 157–158
    Optimize panel settings, 156–159
    restricting/removing colors, 159
    transparency, 160–161
color tolerance, 79
Colors panel group, 96
Colors tools, 16
compositing, layers, 135–136
compressing images, 160
Content tab (Pop-up Menu Editor), 228
Crop tool, 47
cropping images, 47–48
curves
    attaching text to, 125–127
    Bezier, 57–59
    drawing, 56
    freeform objects, 59–60
    Pencil tool, 72
Custom palette, 157

D

Data-Driven Graphics Wizard, 275–280
default, preferences, restoring, 33
deleting
    behaviors, rollovers, 206
    effects, 145–146
    keyboard shortcuts, 36
    layers, 139–140
    pop-up menu items, 233–234
disjoint rollovers, 200
    behaviors
        Behavior handle, 202–204
        drag-and-drop method, 204–206
    target areas, 202
    trigger areas, creating, 201
dithering images, 159
docking and undocking panels, 20
Document window, Preview tabs, 167–168

document window, 11
    components, 11–12
    keyboard shortcuts, 302
documents
    closing, 15
    creating, 12–14
    cropping, 47–48
    existing, opening, 15
    exporting, 296–297
    image slices, exporting, 190–192
    previewing, in browsers, 181–182
    saving, 14
    XML (extensible markup language), creating, 307–310
    zooming, 43–46
Dodge tool, 86–87
Down state, buttons, 213–214
drawing
    bitmaps
        Brush tool, 73–74
        Eraser tool, 74–75
        Pencil tool, 71–72
    circles, 55
    color, adding to objects, 64–68
    curves, 56
    ellipses, 54–55
    freeform objects, 59–60
    lines, 50–51
    modifying objects, 60–64
    polygons, 55–56
    rectangles, 51–54
    rounded rectangles, 53–54
    squares, 53
    stars, 56
Dreamweaver
    Fireworks MX, as external image editor, 282–283
    HTML (Hypertext Markup Language)
        importing Fireworks MX, 290–292
        inserting Fireworks MX, 292–293
        updating Fireworks MX, 294–295
    images, editing from, 288–290
    roundtrip HTML, 282
duplicating. *See also* cloning
    layers, 137–139

E

Edit Stroke dialog box, 110–111
    Options tab, 111–112
    Sensitivity tab, 113–114
    Shape tab, 112–113
editing. *See also* modifying
    button properties, 221–224
    effects, 144–145
    gradient fills, 104–105
    images, from Dreamweaver, 288–290
Editing preferences tab (Preferences dialog box), 29
    bitmap objects options, 30
    mouse pointer options, 29
    Pen tool options, 30
editors, image, Fireworks as (for Dreamweaver), 282–283
effects
    editing, 144–145
    objects, applying to, 142–144
    Property Inspector, 142
    removing, 145–146
    saving, 146–147
Ellipse tool, 55
ellipses, drawing, 54–55
Eraser tool, 74–75
Exact palette, 157
expanding and collapsing, panels, 22
Export Preview window, 170–172
Export Wizard, 169–172
exporting
    animations, 257–258
    documents, 296–297
    graphics, 155–156, 168
    image maps, creating, 181–182
    image slices, 190–192
    symbols, 268–269
external image editor, Fireworks as for Dreamweaver, 282–283
Eye Candy 4000 LE, 148–149

Eyedropper tool, 93–94

F

file formats, 154–156
files, importing, Photoshop, 31–32
fills
    color, 66–68
    gradient, 104–105
        editing, 105–107
        transforming, 108
    pattern, 108–109
    text, applying to, 124–125
    Web Dither fills, 109–110
Filter menu, 148
filters, Eye Candy 4000 LE, 148–149
Find and Replace panel, 19, 260–263
fixed-width text blocks, 117
Folders preferences tab (Preferences dialog box), 31
formatting, text, 120–121
    pop-up menus, 236
Frame controls, 12
frame delay (animations), setting, 256
frames, rollovers, 196–197
Frames panel, 18
    animations, 244
freeform objects, drawing, 59–60
Freeform tool, 60–62

G

General preferences tab (Preferences dialog box), 26–27
    color defaults, 27–28
    interpolation, 28
    Undo Steps, 27
    workspace options, 28
GIF (Graphics Interchange Format) file format, 154
    preset optimization settings, 165–167
    settings for, 156
gradient fills, 104–105
    editing, 105–107
    transforming, 108
graphics. *See also* animations; images
    adding Text, 116–118
    Export Wizard, 169–172
    exporting, 168
    optimizing, 154–156
        file formats, 154–156
    Web, resolution for, 13
grayscale color model, 101
Grayscale palette, 157
grouping panels, 20–21
guides (animations), 251–252

H

Hand tool, scrolling zoomed images, 46
help, 23–24
hexadecimal color model, 101
hiding, layers, 136–137
History panel, 19, 271
    commands, creating, 273–275
    replaying steps, 272–273
horizontal scale box, 122
hotspots, 176–177
    polygonal, 179–180
    rectangular, 178
    testing, 180–182
HSB color model, 101
HTML (Hypertext Markup Language), in Dreamweaver, 290–295
HTML slices, creating, 186–187
hyperlinks. *See* links; hotspots

I

image editor, Fireworks as for Dreamweaver, 282–283
image maps, 176–180
    creating, 182–182
image placeholders, creating, 286
images. *See also* animations; bitmaps; graphics; vector graphics
    compressing, 160
    creating from Dreamweaver placeholders, 285–288
    creating using placeholders, 287–288
    cropping, 47–48
    dithering, 159
    editing from Dreamweaver, 288–290
    exporting, 155–156
    interlacing, 161
    selecting

INDEX

Pointer tool, 40–41
Subselection tool, 41–42
slices, exporting, 190–192
slicing
    creating HTML slices, 186–187
    creating slices, 185–186
    naming slices, 187–190
    reasons for, 184
transparency, 155, 160–161
viewing, 42
    Zoom tool, 43–46
Import preferences tab (Preferences dialog box), 31
    layer options, 32
    text options, 32
importing
    bitmaps, 70–71
    Photoshop files, 31–32
    symbols, 270–271
    text, 118–119
Index Transparency, 161
Indexed Palette list, 156–157
Info panel, 18
installation
    system requirements, 4
    Windows computers, 5–8
instance-level button properties, editing, 223–224
interface
    Align panel, 19
    Answers panel, 19
    Behaviors panel, 19
    Color Mixer panel, 18
    Find and Replace panel, 19
    Frames panel, 18
    History panel, 19
    Info panel, 18
    Layers panel, 18
    Library panel, 19
    Optimize panel, 19
    Preferences dialog box, 26
    Project log, 19
    Property Inspector, 17-18
    Styles panel, 18
    Swatches panel, 18
    Tools panel, 16–17
    URL panel, 19
    workspace features, 11

interlacing, 161
interpolation (General preferences tab), 27–28

J

JavaScript code, rollovers, viewing, 199–200
JPEG (Joint Photographic Experts Group) file format, 154
    optimization settings, 162–164
    preset optimization settings, 165–167
    transparency issues, 160

K

kerning box, 122
keyboard shortcuts
    creating custom, 34–36
    deleting, 36
    document window, 302
    Freeform tool, 61–62
    Line tool, 50
    list, generating, 305–306
    panels, 303
    Pen tool, 57
    Pointer tool, 40
    Rectangle tool, 52
    Rectangle tools, selecting, 55
    sets, specifying, 33–34
    Subselection tool, 42
    Text tool, 116
    Tools panel, 304
Knife tool, 63–64

L

Lasso tool, 80–81
Launch and Edit preferences tab (Preferences dialog box), 30–31, 284–285
launching, 10
layer options, 32
layers
    compositing, 135–136
    creating, 131–133
    deleting, 139–140
    duplicating, 137–139
    hiding, 136–137
    locking, 134
    order, changing, 134–135

INDEX

Layers Options pop-up menu, 130–131
Layers panel, 18, 130
    bitmap masks, 150–151
layouts, panels, saving, 22–23
leading box, 122
Library panel, 19
    button instances, 219–220
    instances, creating, 266–268
    symbols, creating, 264–266
Line tool, 50–51
lines, drawing, 50–51
links. *See also* hotspots
    image maps, 176–180
locking, layers, 134
looping options (animations), 257

M

Macintosh, system requirements, 4
Macintosh palette, 157
Magic Wand tool, 78–79
Magnification list, 12
Marquee tool, 76–78
marquees, modifying, 82–84
masks
    bitmap, creating, 150–151
    vector, creating, 151–152
measurements, units of, text spacing, 123
menu bar, 11
menus. *See also* pop-up menus
    Filter, 148
    Options, rearranging panels, 20–21
    Set Magnification, 44
modifying
    animations
        frame delay, setting, 256
        onion skinning, 254–255
    bitmap objects
        Magic Wand tool, 78–79
        Marquee tool, 76–78
        Polygon Lasso tool, 81–82
    objects, 60–64
    pop-up menus, 241–242
    Swatches panel, 97–100
mouse. *See* rollovers
mouse pointer options, 29
moving, buttons, 217

N

naming
    panel layouts, 23
    slices, 187–190
navigation bars
    button instances
        Clone command, 220–221
        creating, 219–221
    buttons, 218
    testing, 224–225

O

onion skinning (animations), 254–255
Opacity slider, 135
opacity switches, 106
opening
    existing documents, 15
    Preferences dialog box, 26
Optimize panel, 19
    file format specific settings, 156
    graphics, exporting, 155–156
    preset optimization settings, 165–167
optimizing
    graphics, 154
        file formats, 154–156
        JPEG images
            progressive display, 163
            quality, 162
            selective compression, 164
            sharpness, 163
            smoothing, 162
        previewing, 167–168
Options menu, rearranging panels, 20–21
Options tab (Edit Stroke dialog box), 111–112
Original tab, 12
Over state
    buttons, 212–213
    pop-up menus, 237
Over while Down state, buttons, 214–215

P

Paint Bucket tool, 94–96
palettes. *See* color palettes

panels
   Align, 19
   Answers, 19
   Behaviors, 19
   Color Mixer, 18
   docking and undocking, 20
   expanding and collapsing, 22
   Find and Replace, 19, 260–263
   Frames, 18
      animations, 244
   History, 19, 271
      commands, creating, 273–275
      replaying steps, 271–272
   Info, 18
   keyboard shortcuts, 303
   Layers, 18, 130
      bitmap masks, 150–151
   layout, saving, 22–23
   Library, 19
      creating button instances, 219–220
      instances, creating, 266–268
      symbols, creating, 264–266
   Optimize, 19
   Project log, 19
   rearranging, 20–21
   Styles, 18, 147–148
   Swatches, 18
   Tools, 11, 16–17
   URL, 19
paragraph indent box, 122
Path Scrubber tool, 60
pattern fills, 108–109
Pen tool
   Bezier curves, 57–59
   options, 30
Pencil tool, bitmaps, 71–72
Photoshop files, importing, 31–32
PNG (Portable Network Graphic) file format, 155
   settings for, 156
Pointer tool, images, selecting, 40–41
Polygon Hotspot tool, 176
Polygon Lasso tool, 81–82
Polygon Slice tool, 184
Polygon tool, 55–56
polygonal hotspots, 179–180
polygons, drawing, 55–56

Pop-up Menu Editor, 228
pop-up menus. *See also* menus
   advanced settings, 237–239
   cell style, 236
   content, adding, 229–230
   creating, 228–229
   items
      adding, 230–233
      deleting, 233–234
   menu items, adding, 230–233
   modifying, 241–242
   orientation, 235
   positioning, 240–241
   submenus, 234–235
   testing, 242
   text formatting, 236
   text indent, 238
   Up and Over states, 237
positioning
   pop-up menus, 240–241
   rectangles, 53
   text, 122–123
preferences, restoring default, 33
Preferences dialog box
   Editing tab, 29–30
   Folders tab, 31
   General tab, 26–28
   Import tab, 31–32
   Launch and Edit tab, 30–31, 284–285
   opening, 26
Preview tabs, 12, 167–168
previewing
   documents, in browsers, 181–182
   optimization effects, 167–168
Project log, 19
properties. *See also* Property Inspector
   buttons, editing, 221–224
Property Inspector, 11, 17–18
   Blur tool options, 85
   Brush tool options, 73
   collapsing, 22
   color controls, 92
   Edit Stroke dialog box, 110–111
   effects, 142
   Eraser tool options, 74–75
   fill settings, 66–67

Property Inspector *(continued)*
    hotspot options, 177
    image slices, naming, 188–190
    Lasso tool options, 80
    Magic Wand tool options, 78–79
    Marquee tool options, 77
    mask objects, 150
    Paint Bucket tool options, 94–95
    pattern fills, 108–109
    Pencil tool options, 71–72
    polygons, 55–56
    rectangles, modifying, 52
    rounded rectangles, 53
    Rubber Stamp tool options, 89
    Sharpen tool options, 85
    Slice tools options, 185
    Smudge tool options, 88
    stroke settings, 64–65
    text, formatting options, 120
    text spacing options, 122
pulling objects, 62
pushing objects, 61–62

Q

Quick Export button, 12

R

rearranging panels, 20–21
Rectangle Hotspot tool, 176
Rectangle tool, 51–54
rectangles, drawing, 51–54
rectangular hotspots, 178
Reshape Area tool, 60
resolution, Web graphics, 13
resources, help, 23–24
retouching tools, bitmap objects, 84–85
RGB color model, 101
rollovers
    behaviors, assigning, 197–198
    disjoint, 200
        Behavior handle, 202–204
        creating trigger areas, 201
        drag-and-drop method, 204–206
        target areas, 202
    frames, 196–197
    JavaScript code, viewing, 199–200
    simple, 194
        creating source object, 194–195
        creating target object, 195–196
        testing, 198–199
    testing, 207
    triggering event, changing, 206
Rounded Rectangle tool, 54
rounded rectangles, drawing, 53–54
roundtrip HTML, 282
Rubber Stamp tool, 89–91

S

saving
    documents, 14
    effects, 146–147
    panel layouts, 22–23
scrolling, zoomed images, 46
searching. *See* Find and Replace panel
Select tools, 16
selecting
    images
        Pointer tool, 40–41
        Subselection tool, 41–42
    Lasso tool, 80–81
    Magic Wand tool, 78–79
    Marquee tool and, 76–78
    marquees, modifying, 82–84
    Polygon Lasso tool, 81–82
    Swatch groups, 98
Sensitivity tab (Edit Stroke dialog box), 113–114
Set Magnification pop-up menu, 44
Shape tab (Edit Stroke dialog box), 112–113
Sharpen tool, 84
shortcut keys. *See* keyboard shortcuts
simple rollovers, 194
    source object, creating, 194–195
    target object, creating, 195–196
    testing, 198–199
Slice tool, 184
slicing
    creating HTML slices, 186–187
    creating slices, 185–186
    images
        exporting, 190–192
        reasons for, 184

naming slices, 187–190
tools, 184
Smudge tool, 88–89
smudging, bitmaps, 88–89
source objects, simple rollovers, 194–195
space after paragraph box, 122
space preceding paragraph box, 122
spacing, text, 122–123
spell checking, 127–128
squares, drawing, 53
stars, drawing, 56
state, buttons, 210
    Down, 213–214
    Over, 212–213
    Over while Down, 214–215
    Up, 210–212
strokes
    color, 64–66
    options, 110–114
    text, applying to, 124–125
styles, creating, 147–148
Styles panel, 18, 147–148
submenus, pop-up menus, 234–235
Subselection tool, images, selecting, 41–42
swatches, groups
    adding to, 99
    removing from, 100
Swatches panel, 18, 96–97
    modifying, 97–100
symbol-level button properties, editing, 221–222
symbols
    creating, 264–166
    exporting, 268–269
    importing, 270–271
system requirements, 4

T

tabs
    Document window, Preview, 167–168
    document window
        Original, 12
        Preview, 12
    Edit Stroke dialog box
        Options, 111–112
        Sensitivity, 113–114
        Shape, 112–113

Pop-up Menu Editor
    Appearance, 228, 235–240
    Content, 228
Preferences dialog box
    Editing, 29–30
    Folders, 31
    General, 26–28
    Import, 32
    Launch and Edit, 30–31, 284–285
target areas, disjoint rollovers, 202
target objects, simple rollovers, 195–196
testing
    animations, 253–254
    buttons, 217–218
    hotspots, 180–182
    navigation bars, 224–225
    pop-up menus, 242
    rollovers, 207
    simple rollovers, 198–199
    URLs, buttons, 218
text
    curved, 125–127
    enhancing appearance, 119–120
    formatting, 120–121
        pop-up menus, 236
    importing, 118–119
    spacing, 122–123
    spell checking, 127–128
Text Editor, 125
text options, 32
Text tool, 116–118
    character spacing, 122
title bar, 11
tools
    Blur, 84
    Brush, 73–74
    Burn, 86–87
    Circle Hotspot, 176
    Crop, 47
    Dodge, 86–87
    Ellipse, 55
    Eraser, 74–75
    Eyedropper, 93–94
    Freeform, 60–62
    Hand, scrolling zoomed images, 46
    Knife, 63–64
    Lasso, 80–81

tools *(continued)*
  Line, 50–51
  Magic Wand, 78–79
  Marquee, 76–78
  marquees, modifying, 82–84
  modifying objects, 60
  Paint Bucket, 94–96
  Path Scrubber, 60
  Pen
    Bezier curves, 57–59
    options, 30
  Pencil, bitmaps, 71–72
  Pointer, selecting images, 40–41
  Polygon, 55–56
  Polygon Hotspot, 176
  Polygon Lasso, 81–82
  Polygon Slice, 184
  Rectangle, 51–54
  Rectangle Hotspot, 176
  Reshape Area, 60
  Rounded Rectangle, 54
  Rubber Stamp, 89–91
  Sharpen, 84
  Slice, 184
  Smudge, 88–89
  Subselection, selecting images, 41–42
  Text, 116–118
  Vector Path, 59–60
  Zoom, viewing images, 43–46
Tools panel, 11, 16–17
  Colors section, 92–93
  Edit Stroke dialog box, 110–111
  hotspot tools, 176–177
  keyboard shortcuts, 304
transparency, 160–161
  file formats supporting, 155
trigger areas, disjoint rollovers, 201

U

Undo Cropped Document command, 48
Undo Steps (General preferences tab), 27
undocking and docking panels, 20
undoing, cropped images, 48
Uniform palette, 157
Uniform Resource Locators (URLs), 177
units of measure, text spacing, 123

Up state
  buttons, 210–212
  pop-up menus, 237
URL panel, 19
URLs (Uniform Resource Locators), 177
  buttons, testing, 218

V

vector graphics, 49. *See also* bitmaps; images
vector masks, creating, 151–152
Vector Path tool, 59–60
Vector tools, 16
View tools, 16
viewing
  images, 42
    Zoom tool, 43–46
  JavaScript code, rollovers, 199–200

W

Web 216 palette, 157
Web browsers. *See* browsers
Web Dither fills, 109–110
Web graphics, resolution for, 13
Web sites, Macromedia, 3
Web tools, 16
Web-safe colors, 109
WebSnap Adaptive palette, 157
Windows
  installing Fireworks MX, 5–8
  system requirements, 4
windows. *See* panels; workspace
Windows palette, 157
wizards
  Data-Driven Graphics, 275–280
  Export, 169–172
workspace
  features, 11
  options (General preferences tab), 27–28

X

XML (extensible markup language), documents, creating, 307–310

Z

Zoom tool, images, viewing, 43–46